NEW AGE
BIBLE INTERPRETATION

VOLUME V

NEW AGE BOOKS
by
Corinne Heline

NEW TESTAMENT

An exposition of the inner significance of the Holy Scriptures in the light of the Ancient Wisdom,

NEW AGE BIBLE & PHILOSOPHY CENTER
1139 Lincoln Blvd.
Santa Monica, CA 90403

ISBN: 0-933963-05-X

NEW AGE BIBLE & PHILOSOPHY CENTER
1139 LINCOLN BLVD.
SANTA MONICA, CA 90403

IN
DEDICATION
TO THOSE WHO HAVE GLIMPSED
THAT CROSS OF LIGHT WHEREBY
THE BLOOD ESSENCE IS TRANS-
FORMED INTO A FRAGRANCE AS
OF FLOWERS
AND THE
VIA
DOLOROSA
BECOMES
THE
HIGHWAY
OF THE
KING
MY YOKE IS EASY AND MY BURDEN IS LIGHT

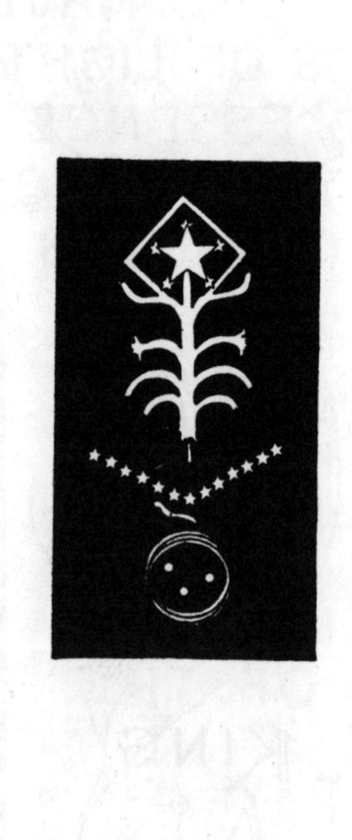

CONTENTS

THE CHRIST AND HIS MISSION

CHAPTER I

CHAPTER II

CHAPTER III

CHAPTER IV

CHAPTER V

CHAPTER VI

ILLUSTRATIONS

NEW AGE BIBLE INTERPRETATION

Louis Chavez

If we really understood *the rituals and creeds of Christianity and also the inner meaning of the story as told in the Gospels, we should know as much as we can know of the Mysteries short of being initiated therein. It is the importance of really understanding these rituals and ceremonies of Christianity that we here stress, for therein are preserved for us an archaic language and an archaic symbolism, the* full *meaning of which can come only by much study; in fact, the* full *meaning can come only at initiation.*

Such a study may now be undertaken, as some keys to its understanding have been given to us by our Teachers, and because the cyclic time has come again when the Ancient Wisdom may be publicly taught. In other words, the cyclical time has come again for a re-statement. All thinking people today realize the need for this re-statement.

— F. Chapman Clemeshaw
in *The Mysteries and Christianity*

PREFACE

An inner interpretation of the Bible along the lines followed in this work has been looked for by earnest occult students for a long time past. The aids hitherto available on the subject have not been commensurate with the progress that has been made in other branches of esoteric knowledge. Similar interpretations are mostly older works written in the terminology of another day, and are, moreover, for the most part, not easily accessible to the average student.

It is not the purpose of the present volume to provide an exhaustive occult commentary, but rather to furnish the student with keys by which he may himself unlock the treasures not only of the Holy Scriptures, but those of any other inspired work as well.

It is realized that the profundity of many of the truths touched upon in this volume are beyond adequate expression; yet, however fragmentary and incomplete the interpretations may be, they go forth imbued with the earnest prayer that some additional light may be cast upon the path of progress and hasten the Master's work of human regeneration and redemption.

This work is not representative of any one school or system of thought. The Bible, the supreme spiritual Textbook of Life, is above all creeds, dogmas and differences in religious beliefs. So also, this, a deeper and larger interpretation of its meaning, is offered as a manual of study for all groups, organizations, and individuals who seek to know the inner Christ and to develop increasingly the consciousness of the kingdom of heaven within.

Corinne Heline

PREFACE TO THE FIFTH EDITION

The first volume published in this series of Bible Interpretations was one covering the New Testament. This appeared in 1935. In 1938 Volume I of the Old Testament was issued, followed by Volume II in 1946 and Volume III in 1955. This completed a trilogy on the Old Testament.

In the years 1950, '51, '52, the New Testament volume of 1935 was enlarged to embrace three volumes. These were first issued as Volume IV, Part I, II, and III. This listing was later changed to Volume IV, V, and VI. Volume IV went into a new edition in 1969, Volume VI in 1970 and the present Volume V in 1971.

The reception given these interpretations from students and teachers of the Esoteric Tradition as this finds embodiment in the Sacred Scriptures of the West has been of such encouragement as to make of this a most joyous labor of love.

It is the soul hunger which so many have voiced in their expressed appreciation of these interpretations that is responsible, at least in part, for the new material that has been incorporated in this edition. Besides a general revision, several new chapters have been added. Among these are one on the Parables of Christ and another dealing with His Healing Miracles, both of which are included in this volume.

It is the hope and the prayer of the writer that the interpretations here offered will prove a helpful contribution toward meeting a present need in restoring the Bible to its rightful place as a guide to individual and communual life and living.

Corinne Heline

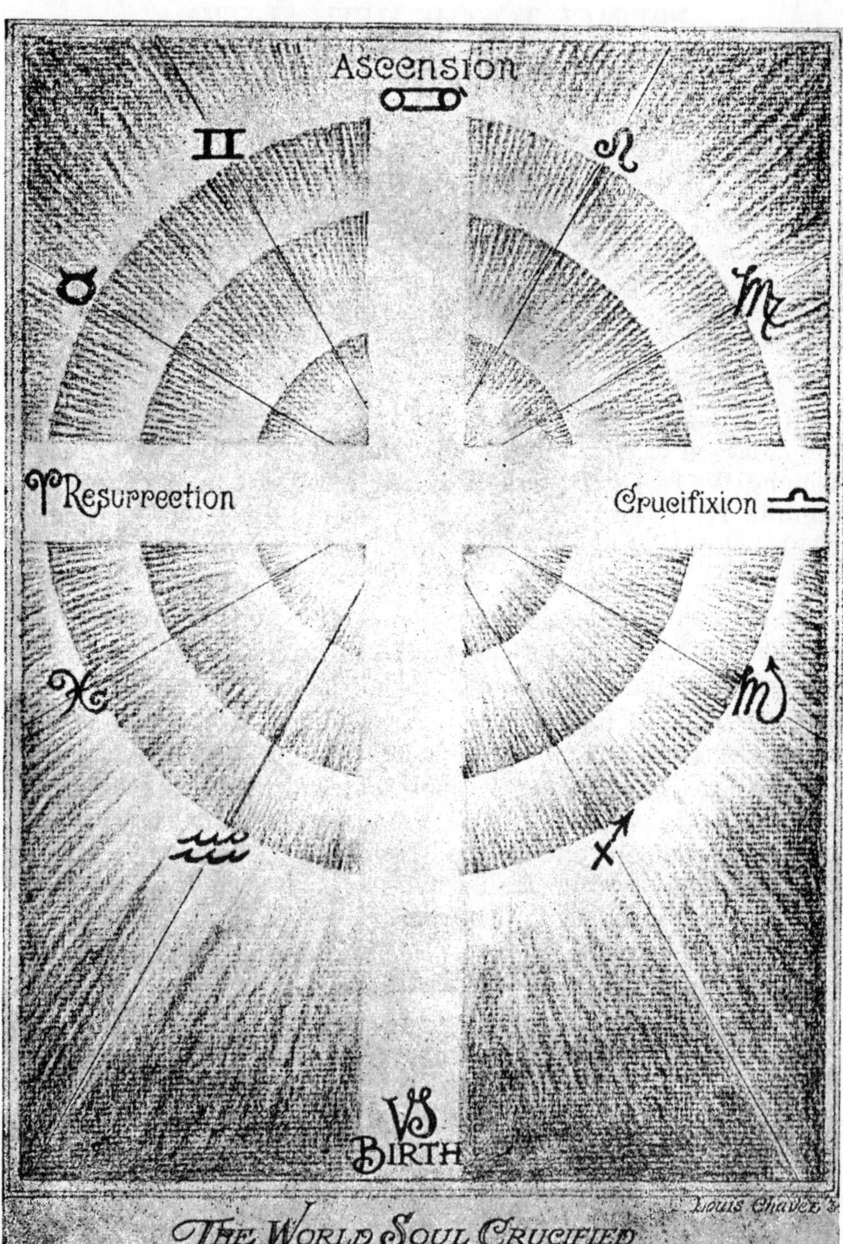

THE WORLD SOUL CRUCIFIED

NEW AGE BIBLE INTERPRETATION

The Christ and His Mission

CHAPTER I

The Healing Miracles of The Christ

Christ Jesus commanded: "Preach the gospel and heal the sick." Permanent healing demands that this twofold injunction be obeyed. By the "gospel" is meant an inner understanding of the laws of life and being. Early man knew himself, as Virgin Spirit, to be made in the image and likeness of God. He was the ward of Angels and lived in harmony with the music of the spheres. Parturition was painless, youth eternal and death unknown. Then came the Lucifer Spirits who impregnated the desire body of man with a new impulse—the lower destructive fire force, as a result of which man gradually lost conscious touch with Cosmic Law. He fell into "coats of skin" and his consciousness became focused in the personal life instead of in the universal as hitherto. This opened the way for sorrow through disease, poverty and death.

The Old Testament carries the story of the coming of Lucifer, the False Light. The New Testament tells the story of Christ, the True Light, the World Saviour who was born of an Immaculate Conception and who came with healing in His Wings.

The purpose of Christ's coming was to teach man how to save himself through regeneration, and this He taught by example as well as by precept, for not otherwise could it be successfully taught. By awakening the Christ within himself, man lifts himself above and beyond all personal limitations into a consciousness of peace, harmony and plenty. He then realizes a new life where there is "no more sorrow, no more tears, no more death, for the former things have passed away."

The Supeme healer was also the Master Occultist. His healing ministry held a twofold purpose—to heal the sick and to impart lessons of profound metaphysical import to His disciples at the same time. Every biblical healing contains a key to spiritual Illumination or Initiation.

If we study carefully the various methods and words which the Christ employed in His healing works, we shall discover that all of the most important phases of occult law were brought into operation. He was concerned not alone with the imperfections of the outer physical instrument but took into account also the invisible bodies, wherein lies the origin of all disease as well as the beginning of the healing process.

Illness of any kind is nature's endeavor to focus attention on a weak link in the chain of perfect becoming and being. If we learn the lesson aright, permanent cure is the inevitable result. Illness should never leave us where it found us. This truth is emphasized throughout the ministry of Christ Jesus. Those who refused to heed it went away unhealed "because of their unbelief." In the light of this understanding, remember there is no such thing as incurable disease.

The Blind Man of Bethsaida
Mark 8:22-25

Every organ of the body is a replica of a mental concept and is a projection of that concept into physical manifestation. The eyes represent the conscious knowing of Spirit. The ego in its many earthly pilgrimages ofttimes loses the perfect attunement with the Ideal World which it enjoyed prior to descending into rebirth, and the imperfect sight which usually accompanies the maturity of years attests to this fact. Deliberately shutting ourselves away from spiritual truth during one or more lives tends toward physical blindness in some future incarnation.

Christ Jesus prefaced each of his restorings of sight with a lesson stressing the importance of spiritual understanding. *Having eyes, see ye not? and having ears, hear ye not? and do ye not remember?* These were His words just preceding the healing of the blind man as recounted in Mark 8:22-25.

John refers to Christ as the bread of life. The Disciples lament that they do not understand Him better because they have no bread—which is symbolic of their lack of spiritual knowledge.

Bethsaida means a house or place of fishing, and fish is representative of the Initiate in the New Dispensation inaugurated by Christ Jesus and outlined in the New Testament. That the healing of the blind man of Bethsaida deals with initiatory processes is evident from the rite observed by the Master in its enactment. The blind man (or neophyte) was taken to a holy place away from the town, and there the Teacher focused His great life force upon him. His vision was opened to the evolutionary epochs of the past and he was enabled to trace the path of human development through the mists of the past until in the clear light of the present Aryan age he "saw every man very clearly."

Bartimaeus—The Blind Man of Jericho
Mark 10:46-52.

Of the four healings of blindness, one is given by Matthew as occurring at Capernaum, one by Mark at Bethsaida, one by John at Jerusalem, and the healing now under consideration is described in all three of the synoptic accounts as taking place at Jericho.

Jericho is the Moon City, a symbol of the sense life. Here is the story of one Bartimaeus, blinded by the intensity of emotional reactions: Observe that he cast off his garment before he could receive healing. Then, "he immediately received his sight and followed Jesus in the Way." Through purification he became one of the pupils of the Master and began to walk in the path of discipleship. The healing at Bethsaida and that at Jericho do not represent equal degrees of advancement. One deals with the preparation for the novitiate, the other with definite attainment of first-hand development.

The pledging of the neophyte by the Master was preceded then, as now and always, by the words: "Whosoever would be first among you shall be your servant."

Two Blind Men Healed
Matt. 9:27-30.

None are so blind as those who are unawakened to spiritual truth. Faith is emphasized in most New Testament healings because this attribute is one of the necessary essentials for true inner-plane illumination; not in the sense of a blind intellectual acceptance of certain statements supposed to be authoritative, but in the quiet, deep conviction that spiritual things do exist, and that they represent the Ultimate Good. Without that conviction, we have not sufficient incentive to put forth the effort necessary to attain liberation.

"According to your faith be it unto you." So said the Great Physician. In Nazareth He was not able to perform many works because of the people's unbelief.

Practitioners of all schools of healing realize the curative power of faith, and that permanent healing is effected to the degree that the consciousness of the patient becomes centered in the realization of the power of Spirit to heal. Will, Imagination and Faith are triune powers by means of which the wonders of magic are performed. By calling them into action disease can be cured. They must, however, be sufficiently developed to accomplish such a result, but we are reminded that if we have even the faith of a mustard seed we can perform miracles.

In the incident under discussion, the restoration of sight for the two blind men took place immediately after the raising of Jairus' daughter, and bears reference to the raising into equilibrium of the two poles of the Spirit in man by which means the darkness of material blindness and ignorance is dissipated for all time and the powers of eternal life made manifest here and now.

The Blind Man by the Pool of Siloam
John 9th Chapter

Disease is not a punishment but is the inevitable result of a violation of nature's laws. The suffering it brings will in time prove to be an enlightener restoring us to the ways of the highest law. When the ego awakens to a consciousness of its lack of proper adjustment to Cosmic Law, disease disappears and harmony or health is restored. This is the meaning of the Master's question related in John's Gospel 9:1-7.

"And as he passed by, he saw a man blind from his birth. And his disciples asked him, saying, Rabbi, who sinned, this man or his parents, that he should be born blind? Jesus answered, Neither did this man sin, nor his parents."

"But," continued the Master, "that the works of God should be made manifest in him, I must work the works of him that sent me, while it is day: the night cometh, when no man can work. As long as I am in the world, I am the light of the world. When he had thus spoken, he spat on the ground, and made clay of the spittle, and he anointed the eyes of the blind man with the clay, and said unto him, Go, wash in the pool of Siloam, (which is by interpretation, Sent). He went his way therefore, and washed, and came seeing."

"The body proclaims the shortcomings of the soul:" Blindness is also the result of a neglected effort in the past to think clearly. A warped and twisted mental viewpoint will eventually produce a similar condition in physical sight; as deafness in like manner results from turning away from spiritual instruction.

"The body always represents the past; but the personal past of Everyman is a microcosmic fragment of his macrocosmic past, and both are impressed in his body." The Supreme Healer never observed the apparent limitations of the physical body. He worked always with the inner man, demanding that the spirit exert its own God-given powers, for only in this manner can permanent healing be obtained. His first question to this man according to Tyndale's version was, "Wilt thou be whole?" Will is the positive, masculine pole of Spirit. Faith belongs to the feminine principle symbolized in clear, pure water. When these two conjoin "Whatsoever ye ask in My name, it shall be done unto you."

In all pre-Christian ceremonials of Initiation the neophyte was required in the preparatory purification exercises to wash in a lake or pool. Those sacred waters were near the Temple or holy place. The pool of Siloam is an old Egyptian Temple term familiar to all Temple aspirants.

Familiar also to the ancient novitiate was the anointing of the eyes with clay which is afterward washed away in the holy water. This ritual gesture has reference to the opening of the interior organs of vision by means of which the neophyte is able to see at will into the spiritual worlds, though as yet he may be unable to function therein. (That requires still further preparation.) The pineal gland is often called the third eye, but balanced vision requires the harmonious functioning of both the pineal gland and the pituitary body. Of these glands,

Uranus rules the pituitary body and Neptune the pineal; the pituitary is predominantly feminine, in potency, the pineal masculine. Their awakening and manner of development determine the nature of the inner sight which is achieved by the neophyte.

The work of transfiguration or regeneration of which these supernormal faculties are but the earliest tokens, must take place while the ego inhabits a physical body. All egos after putting off the fleshly sheath in the process of death become awake in the spiritual worlds, and therefore possess to some degree the power to see and experience the realities of that world. This, however, is not the same power as that of the Initiate in the Christ Mysteries who, *while yet in the body,* accomplishes a conscious severance of the soul from the body before this occurs in the normal process of death. To achieve this, the neophyte must cleanse his moral and mental nature by his own efforts as nature would otherwise cleanse it for him in the after-death state of Purgatory. Thus the Initiate lives both his Purgatory and his Heaven while still on earth in the body of clay. Hence the words of the Christ: "I must work while it is day; the night [death] cometh when no man can work."

His final triumphant proclamation will resound through all eternity, a clarion call to whosoever *wills* to follow in the Christed Way, the Way of Initiation, which was opened by the highest Initiator of them all, earth's Supreme Teacher when He declared I AM THE LIGHT OF THE WORLD.

The Leper Cleansed
Mark 1:40-44.

Leprosy, the causation of which was the unbridled misuse of the creative life forces in ancient Lemuria and Atlantis, is one of the most terrible of all diseases. "An intimate tie binds the generator to that which is generated. Past generations are utilized in the construction of the future body; they are woven into the body as a tendency to some ailment, affecting either disposition or the life forces. This poison of past lives must somewhere be changed into healthfulness. This struggle comes through infections. Epidemics of races are materialized evils of the past. The Plague of Black Death takes its heaviest toll in countries where the practice of black magic flourished in incantations and passion charms." (Paracelsus.)

There is perhaps no more interesting phase of rebirth than that which reveals the past causation of disease. All disease is the result of some previously existing cause. Again quoting the celebrated Swiss physician, Paracelsus, who has given so much light on the problem of disease in relation to reincarnation, we read: "No physician should presume to know the hour of recovery because it is not given man to judge the offense of another and the inner temple containing mysteries in which no uninitiated stranger is permitted to spy. If the trial is over, God will send the healer; if the patient recovers it is a sign the help was sent by God. If no recovery takes place, God did not send the physician."

Leprosy and cancer are "fire diseases" and have their matrix in the desire body. Both maladies are the consequence of an ungoverned desire nature in either present or past incarnations. Cancer takes the heavy toll in modern life that leprosy did in the past, and for like reasons.

Both the mind and the body of man are composed of rotating and revolving atoms. The stronger control the weaker. Mind is superior to matter, such is nature's law.

During health, the atoms of the body rotate positively from left to right. In a diseased matrix, as of cancer or leprosy for instance, they rotate negatively from right to left. In the latter case the rate of rotation is slower and the atoms also differ in color from those in a state of health. Negative mind atoms breed destruction, poverty, disease, anarchy and death. Positive mind atoms manifest peace, health, happiness, harmony and plenty. All things either evolve or "de-volve." Death is a dissolution of the body atoms. Life is evolution, and the goal of its interrelated cycles is spiritualized man.

During the Old Testament Dispensation leprosy was referred to as the "finger of God." People in general knew of its ancient origin and had become familiar with its terrible and inexorable expiation. An eye for an eye and a tooth for a tooth—the function you misuse becomes your enemy. Thus they understood the Jehovistic law which regulated man's relation to his own body.

The New Dispensation under Christ has brought grace to supersede Law, Love to overcome and replace fear. "And being moved with compassion, He stretched forth His hand and touched him. . . . saith unto him, *I will,* be thou made clean." And the leper, banned and isolated because of what mortal concept termed incurable and untouchable, was enabled through his faith, humility, and devotion to the Master to sever the bonds of the past and to come forth clean.

That this cleansing is symbolic of an exalted spiritual preparation is evidenced by the fact that in the Gospel of Matthew it occurs shortly after the giving of the Sermon on the Mount, and so belongs to the high phases of esoteric teaching. Mark includes it among the first works succeeding the Rite of the Baptism, and Luke places it immediately following the profoundly esoteric work of the Draught of the Fishes.

Not all the lepers who approached the great Healer were made whole again, as we shall see in the case of the Ten Lepers recorded by Luke. We can only understand this fact in the light of past causation. Some were not yet ready to break their bonds. No one can perform this office for us. Others can only point the way, we must do the work individually. It was not difficult for the Master to read the aura of a penitent before Him and so to know when he was ready for his freedom from just debts.

The Ten Lepers
Luke 17:11-19.

In this instance, the Master gave a demonstration of the fact familiar to all esotericists that man decrees his own sickness and his own time of healing. Ten lepers approached the Master and asked His mercy. His love and compassionate tenderness enveloped them all equally, but only one returned—healed.

Paracelsus attests to the universality of the Law of Healing when he declares, "No disease is incurable save when death is present. In the wisdom of the future all disease will have an end. Regenerative processes in illness are due to the Eternal in man."

The healing of the Ten Lepers is recorded only in the Gospel of Luke. Ten (10) is the number of equilibrium and Luke's Gospel is an important treatise on this subject for the esotericist.

The Capernaum Demoniac
Mark 1:23-26.

There has been much controversy among biblical scholars as to the extent of the belief in demoniac possession current in Palestine during the time of Christ. The esotericist understands, however, and not without historical foundation, that demonology was a familiar subject to the Jews of that day, as was also the knowledge of its sinister and far-reaching effects. Members of the Sanhedrin were required to understand the workings of magic so as to be able to deal with questions concerning it. Demoniac possession was included in this category and was also well known as a cause of disease. Rabbis and priests were instructed in the arts of exorcism. So much was this the case that the word "Jew" was almost synonymous with "magician" throughout the Roman Empire, and this helps us to understand the charges of sorcery so often brought against the early Christian communities.

Obsession was so prevalent and its increase so marked in the entire ancient world (not in Palestine only) that prominent among the seven great reasons for the coming of Christ at this particular time was this one, to break the spell between man and evil discarnates and elemental spirits by cleansing and purifying the currents of the desire realm, and thus make humanity amenable to a new and higher evolutionary impulse. The casting out of demons consequently occupies a conspicuous place in the healing ministry of the Messiah and its importance is stressed as an essential of His disciples' high training.

The writers of the Gospels set obsession apart as an entirely different malady from any other described. Obsessions are still a prevailing malady among primitive peoples and are recognized often as such by modern missionaries, many of whom have discovered the power of exorcism in the use of the name of Christ Jesus. Miss Mildred Cable, a missionary in China, has made many interesting observations relative to obsession, as the following quotation gives evidence:

> Our first woman patient in Hwochou Opium Refuge became interested in the Gospel, and on her return home destroyed her images, reserving however the beautifully carved idol shrines which she placed in her son's room. About six months later we were sent for by special messenger to see the son's wife who had occupied this room. When we arrived the girl

was chanting the weird minor note of the possessed, the voice, as in every case I have seen, clearly distinguishing it from madness. This can perhaps best be described as a voice distinct from the personality of the one under possession. It seems as though the demon used the organs of speech of the victim for the conveyance of its own voice. She refused to wear clothes or to take food, and by her violence terrorized the community. Immediately upon our entering the room, she ceased her chanting and slowly pointing her finger at us, remained in this posture for some time. As we knelt upon the *kang* to pray, she trembled and said, "The room is full of givei," (a term used by the common people to indicate discarnates who receive from every family certain propitiatory offerings). "As soon as one goes another comes," she said. We endeavored to calm her and made her join us in repeating, "Lord Jesus, save me." After considerable effort she succeeded in pronouncing the words and when she had done so, we commanded the demon to leave her, whereupon her body trembled and she sneezed some fifty or sixty times, then suddenly came to herself, asked for her clothes and food and seeming perfectly well resumed her work. So persistently did she reiterate the statement that the demons were using the idol shrine as a refuge, that during the proceedings just mentioned, her parents willingly handed over to the Christians present these valuable carvings, and joined with them in their destruction. From this time onward she was perfectly well, a normal and healthy young woman.

Among the individual healings by Christ Jesus recorded in the New Testament seven are of demoniacs: five men, one boy, and one girl. In each of these cases the Master used different and specific methods in obtaining cures which are well worth the careful study of the spiritual healer. As mentioned before, Christ was engaged not only in healing the sick but was at the same time instructing His disciples in the performance of the same works which He did, and when He sent them forth two by two into wider fields of service He gave them power over unclean spirits. (Mark 6:7.)

The first act of exorcism is recorded by both Mark and Luke and was among the earliest events in the healing ministry. This occurred on Sunday in Capernaum of Galilee, in the synagogue. Capernaum has been called the city of Jesus because He adopted it as His home when He was driven from Nazareth. It was also the home town of four of His closest Disciples and the scene of many of His most far-reaching works.

The words in which the Master addressed the demoniac show that He spoke not to the man himself but to some other being who abode temporarily within the man.

It is indeed noteworthy that all the obsessing entities knew the Christ, recognized His power over them, and felt that they must acknowledge themselves subject to Him at all times. This entity calls out: "Let us alone; what have we to do with thee, Thou Jesus of Nazareth?" But in response to the firm command of Christ, "Hold thy peace and come out of him," the entity obeyed His words and according to Luke, the physician, left the man unhurt. Whereupon the people who saw this, talked together of a new authority, and the law of healing introduced by the Christ, for, said they, "He commandeth even the unclean spirits and they obey Him."

In this case, the obsessing spirit seems to have been a human intelligence, still clinging to the earth and the pleasures of the senses, which it could enjoy only by usurping the sense organs of an embodied ego. It could therefore use the human larynx to produce speech, and used in ways recognizably human, though malevolent, the body which it had taken.

The Deaf and Dumb Demoniac
Matt. 9:32-33.

In the case of the deaf and dumb demoniac the possessing demon controlled the man's organs of speech and hearing, depriving him of their use. As soon as the evil spell was broken, the man could speak and was his normal self again. Hence the people who heard of these healings began to call Jesus both the "Son of Daniel" and the "Son of God."

The curing of obsession or casting out of devils will again, as in the time of Christ, become one of the chief ministries of healing in the New Age. Obsession is seldom healed at the present time because it is so little understood, usually being classed erroneously with insanity and various nervous disorders. To deal successfully with this form of disease, the healer must be one possessing the highest state of spiritualized consciousness. Many persons confined today in insane asylums are pitiful examples of obsession. Generally this terrible malady is the fruit of past causation and often the direct result of the practice of hypnotism. There is no sin bearing a heavier causation than that of depriving an ego, even momentarily, of its free will, its most priceless heritage.

The Demoniac of Gerasa; Their Name is Legion
Matt. 8:28-32. Mark 5:1-16. Luke 8:26-39.

"Their name is Legion." This healing is of special interest since it is described in Matthew, Mark and Luke, with slight variations in accordance with the phase of development each writer desires to emphasize. Paul admonishes neophytes to pray without ceasing, and again, to put on the whole armor of God or in other words, to keep oneself enveloped in an aura of prayer. This is most necessary for the aspirant when he first begins investigations upon the inner planes. He then finds himself confronted by much more subtle tests than those which confront him in the outer physical world, where evil impacts are somewhat deadened by dense matter. On the inner planes there is no such protective barrier. The legion of negative thoughts, words and deeds constantly being generated and set into motion on earth find embodiment on the lowest plane of the Desire World. Some of these are ensouled by elementals while others are fortified and used as magnetic channels of approach by earthbound spirits who are yet enmeshed in the evil of their recent earth lives.

Often these entities succeed in obsessing one who does not know how to command and control them. The aid of a Teacher is then necessary as in this biblical instance. "Come out of the man, thou unclean spirit," commanded the Christ. Evil spirits cannot harm one who is fearless and loving or who understands how to use the Name of Christ Jesus, that sacred NAME which is a talisman on both the inner and outer planes.

As soon as the Master had the *name* of the obsessing discarnate, it was completely under His power, and had no choice but to obey Him. This was a more difficult case than the ones previously discussed, and the great Teacher was also instructing His disciples in the secret power concealed in names (vibration) and how this power may be used for healing and upliftment.

The man at Gerasa (or Gadera) was controlled alternately by many demons, all exhibiting the most ferocious and destructive characteristics. The poor victim in his agony and despair had cut himself with stones and had slashed and lacerated his body. The transformation was instantaneous and complete: From a wild, demented beast whom all feared and shunned, he changed into a normal human being, and sat down like a child at the feet of Jesus. When the Master returned to the boat, he followed, asking only that he might remain near the wonderful Presence. Recognizing his utter dedication, the Master appointed him as His apostle and witness among the peoples of that area; and in obedience to the Master's wishes, he testified in Gadera and all the other cities of Decapolis the wonderful things that he knew of Christ Jesus and His works.

Swine in ancient Egyptian symbolism were identified with Mars, the lower or passional nature of man. The presence of the herd of swine in this case is perhaps more reminiscent of a healing ritual for obsession in ancient Babylon, in which an image of an animal, usually a pig, was placed beside the patient before the healer began his exorcisms; these included the command that the demon enter into the image, which was later destroyed. The great Lord of Life and Love would not condemn innocent animals to death. What He did was to return the evil spirits to their own element, symbolized in the herd of swine. He came not to destroy evil, but to teach man how to transmute it, to lift it up into a greater power for good, so that the greatest sinner may become indeed the greatest saint.

The casting out of the legion of demons occurred shortly after the Master had proved His high Initiate powers in stilling the waters and calming the storm.

The Healing of the Demoniac at the Foot of Mount Hermon

Matt. 17:14-21; Mark 9:14-29; Luke 9:37-42.

Immediately after the glory of the Rite of Transfiguration (which was witnessed only by the most advanced of the Disciples, Peter, James and John) occurred the most difficult of all the healings of obsession, and one which the Disciples themselves were unable to achieve.

Although the Disciples had already exorcised many evil spirits successfully, they found themselves powerless before this one. "Ofttimes it hath cast him into the fire and into the waters to destroy him." Here is the mystic key. This boy had in former lives been a follower of the Mysteries, working in the Temples with both the elements of fire and water. He had doubtless misused his powers and turned to black magic, hence in this life, "from a child," he had been under the control of powerful evil forces emanating from the center of the Black Brotherhoods. For this reason the Disciples, despite their high attainment, could not loosen this hold. Only a Master superior to the black arts could accomplish it.

"Why could we not cast him out?" the Disciples asked Him when they were come. "This kind can come forth by nothing but by prayer and fasting." In other words, it is only by the most complete life dedication through purity that the tenacious grip of the black magician can be broken.

This case has generally been taken to be one of epilepsy. It is significant in this instance to note that Aretaeus in his treatise on chronic diseases states that epilepsy is considered a disgraceful disease, for it is thought to be inflicted upon persons who have sinned against the *moon.* Galen in his book, *Critical Days,* asserts that the moon governs the period of epileptic seizures. (*Miracles and the New Psychology,* Micklen.)

The Man Healed of Palsy
Matt. 9:2-7.

Throughout the pages of the Bible the teaching is explicit that sin or wrongdoing is the direct causation of disease. According to Leviticus leprosy was the result of slander. Miriam was once stricken with leprosy following words of evil spoken against Moses during the years in the wilderness.

Among the early Christians it was believed that "Diseases come from seven sins: for slander, shedding blood, false oaths, unchastity, arrogance, robbery and envy." Christ Jesus emphasized the same truth often in His talks with the Twelve, as in the question He put to them after He had healed the paralytic by saying: "Have courage, my son, your sins have been forgiven. Arise, take up your bed and go to your home." He asked: "Is it easier to say *thy sins be forgiven thee,* or to say *arise and walk?*"

Permanent healing comes only at the end of a cycle of causation of which the illness is the concluding portion. Christ Jesus could easily, by His own cosmic powers, have instantaneously healed anyone of any disease whatsoever. However, if the sufferer had not learned the soul lesson involved, his infirmity would sooner or later have reappeared. It is only when the seed atom in the heart, which bears a record of the misdirected efforts (sin), has been cleansed by repentance, reform, and restitution that the Christ will say, "Arise, you are free." The Master can command, "Arise and walk," but only man himself can make it possible for Him to declare, "Thy sins are forgiven thee."

Paralysis, as all spiritual healers know, is the result of some form of fear. A deep and profound fear centered in the subconscious mind, perhaps for many lives, impedes and slows down the life functions, until ultimately the physical body becomes inert and unresponsive to the communications of the Ego: it has become paralyzed.

It was immeediately after this inspiring healing that there came the calling of Matthew, who, no doubt exalted by this sublime manifestation of the great Teacher's healing power, willingly renounced all things belonging to his former personal life and gladly followed Him. Later events in his life of glorious apostleship gave evidence of how complete and unalterable his dedication was.

The Healing of Peter's Wife's Mother
Matt. 8:14-15.

After the healing of the demoniac in the synagogue in Capernaum on the Sabbath Day, Christ Jesus returned home with Peter and Andrew, and they were accompanied by James and John. The house was in gala attire and the seven-branched candlestick was burning for the holy meal, the noon breakfast. This weekly festival was to be especially elaborate in honor of the presence of the beloved Master. However, when they arrived at the house, as Luke writes in his gospel, "Simon's wife's mother was holden with a great fever." He came and stood over her and rebuked the fever, and then took her by the hand and raised her up; and the fever left her, "and immediately she rose up and ministered to them."

In every instance of healing the great Physician used the Word of Power, and sometimes augmented this with the touch of His hand. The hands are messengers of healing and service. When the heart center is awakened, the hands become powerful channels for the inner healing forces.

Tears, colds, and similar physical conditions belong to the water element and may be traced to the lack of control in the emotional nature. Fevers relate to the fiery element and originate in a lack of control in the passional nature. Destructive or negative thinking, even insanity, pertains to the air element, and represents a failure to master the mental (especially the imaginative) processes which are closely linked with the creative energy. The physical body is but the sounding board of the inner vehicles which registers faithfully both their discordant and their harmonious notes.

Every infirmity is connected with one of the four elements. No fiery disease can exist in the water force, nor can any weakness connected with water exist in the fire element. All poisons are of fiery origin and have their center in the desire body, wherefore the spirit of poison can have no power when the lower desires have been transmuted. To such as the Disciples of the Christ who had accomplished the transmutation, the Master could say, "Thou shalt drink any deadly thing and it shall not harm thee."

Fever is a means of Fire purification, a process of cleansing the carnal desire nature. The experience of Peter's wife's mother was a dedicatory one for this woman who immediately arose and began to serve.

Love, service and sacrifice form the threefold path that leads to the spiritually creative work of true discipleship:

Healing the Syrophoenician's Daughter

Mark 7:24-30; Matt. 15:21-28.

Christ Jesus had gone into retirement for a time and desired that no one should know where He had gone. Mark writes that although Christ Jesus had thus sought seclusion, having "entered into a house, and would have no man know of it," yet, *"He could not be hid."* The compassion of His great heart always encompassed all sorrow and suffering so that He could not remain away when His succor was so much needed. Nor is He ever hidden from those who earnestly seek Him, nor heedless of any sincere call for help on any plane. "Lo, I am with you always," is His promise.

A Phoenician woman, whose name was Justa according to the Clementine writings, had journeyed one hundred and fifty miles or more in quest of His aid for her child. She was a follower of the cult of Astarte, the Moon goddess, but the fame of the Divine Healer had reached her in her far-off home, and when she had come to the place where the Disciples were she besought them to intercede with the Master for her.

At last she was brought into His Presence. In response to her pleas, He said, "It is not meet to take the children's bread and cast it to the dogs," and in these words we may perceive the spiritual status of this woman. She did not belong to the inner circle of students, therefore she was not ready to receive the bread (deeper teaching) of the children, (inner group). That she had, however, made the complete surrender of her personal life and was determined to walk in the Way leading to the inner circle is evidenced by her reply: "Yes, Lord, for even the dogs eat of the crumbs which fall from their Master's table."

Her dedication was accepted, and her daughter was instantly healed as the Master declared, "Oh, woman, great is thy faith, be it done unto thee even as thou wilt." These words hold high promise of the attainment that was later to be hers.

In this healing Christ Jesus demonstrated to His Disciples the truth that Spirit is all powerful and that it transcends the barriers of time and space. The girl was healed at His word, though miles stretched between her and the Christ, and He had had no previous contact with her.

Faith, humility and devotion without reservation will always open the door for every aspiring neophyte: "Great is thy faith, be it done unto thee as thou wilt."

The Man Healed of Dropsy
Luke 14:1-6.

Christ Jesus, the Lord of Love, centered His work in the supreme Law which is Love. He lost no opportunity of teaching and demonstrating this fundamental truth whenever He could and wherever He might be. On this occasion, as on a previous Sabbath, He sought to teach the literalists the pre-eminence of Love over the rigid and formal code which was the only Law they knew. This He achieved by healing a man of dropsy, in defiance of the Sabbatical laws which the literalists interpreted to prohibit anything in the way of labor on the Sabbath, even if it were the divine labor of healing.

The Sabbath observance was one of many customs which the Hebrews inherited from Chaldea. The Chaldeans observed five Sabbaths a month, and it was they who divided their month into the weekly period of seven days, dedicated successively to the Sun, Moon and five planets. This division of time was in use in Chaldea even so long ago as the time of Abraham, who, as a Chaldean Prince, must have been familiar with it before he heard the Voice of a New Revelation calling him to go forth into a new land. An Assyrian calendar explains that the Sabbath means "completion of work, a day of rest for the soul." It appears that it was unlawful to cook food, to change clothing, or even to offer sacrifice on the Sabbath; and the king was forbidden, we are told, to speak in public, to ride in a chariot, to perform any kind of military or civil duty and *even to take medicine* on this day.

As there were five Babylonian Sabbaths each month, there were sometimes more than one in a week. These Sabbaths, however, were not dedicated to any particular day, but came regularly on the 7th, 14th, 19th, 21st and 28th day of the month, regardless of the day of the week on which those dates fell. Thus all the star deities received homage in regular succession, and if any Sabbath was holier than another that was due to the special reverence felt for certain gods in localities sacred to them from remote antiquity. Not only the Assyrians and Jews but also the Phoenicians shared the Babylonian Sabbath observance.

It is significant that of these Sabbaths, the Jews selected for special observance only the Day of Saturn, or Saturday, the seventh day of the week. Seven is the number of completion, enfoldment, rest, assimilation. Thus in the course of time their Sabbatical laws expressed more and more the rigidity of the Saturnian principle in its negative, or formalistic, aspect. Christ Jesus came bringing a new pronouncement, the power and light of a New Day and a New Age, based upon the Solar Principle. It has been frequently remarked by astrological students of such matters that that the word "Satan" derives from Saturn, and in the Arabic language "Shaitan" means "He who despairs." Arabic and Hebrew bear much the same resemblance as we find between Spanish and Portuguese.

The Day of the Sun sponsored by the Christ bears a much

deeper significance than the average individual comprehends. The Sun is the center of life, light and love for the entire solar system to which this earth belongs. The Sun's Day therefore should be the day in which we dedicate ourselves to becoming miniature Suns, centers of radiating love, light and helpfulness as far as the radius of our influence extends.

Sunday is the first day, the New Day, the beginning of a new week, a time for the *assimilation* of the soul essences extracted from the experiences of the preceding week; and this assimilation is the starting point of a *new process,* for which it is the alchemical stone of tincture. The new Sun Laws of fellowship, equality and oneness which the Master championed, and which He immortalized in the Sermon on the Mount, are yet, even after two thousand years have elapsed, a center of controversy wherever an individual or a group have caught a vision of their meaning and have endeavored to introduce them into practical, everyday living. Had mankind followed the Sun Laws of Christ instead of the Saturn laws of the Scribes and Pharisees the world would not be the sorry place it is today.

On another Sabbath the Master tried to teach the supremacy of Love over Law when He healed the withered hand publicly. On this Sabbath day He endeavored to soften the Pharisaic obduracy by healing the dropsical man in the home of one of the leading Pharisees where He had gone to partake of the sacred Sunday meal. But minds and hearts were closed to His teachings, hence their ultimate destiny was the loss of all those *things* which they put before Christ. The same fate awaits the modern followers of pharisaical law, be they Jew, Christian or pagan.

In the lesson which the Christ gives immediately following the healing of the man with dropsy, He conveys a subtle intimation as to its cause and ultimate cure. This is to be found in the parable of humility wherein He admonishes those who come to the banquet to be content with the lower seats until invited by the host to come higher. He then adds the formula for true spiritual attainment which all Masters of Wisdom have handed down since the beginning of time, but which, even to this modern day, is the most difficult for the aspirant to accept and follow: "For whosoever exalts himself shall be humbled; and whosoever humbles himself shall be exalted" (Luke 14:11).

The Healing of the Withered Hand
Mark 3:1-5; Luke 6:6-10.

In addition to teaching profound occult truths through His healing works, the Master also gave some practical truths consistent with everyday living, as in the case of the man with the withered hand. His words and acts were not only for the people of His own time but are equally applicable to the needs of the moderns.

The Scribes and Pharisees are always with us and sometimes they are even within us. Intolerance and condemnation of the action of others is pharisaical. Living in such strict accordance with the letter of the law that we relegate mercy, compassion and love to the background is characteristic of those literalists whom the Master reprimanded so often and so sternly.

Because it was the Sabbath, the Pharisees objected to healing works being performed. The compassionate Lord was sad because of the hardness of their hearts and inquired of them, "Is it lawful to do good or evil on the Sabbath, to save a life or to destroy it?" They were silent before His question. Ofttimes the Christ power within us is hampered by rigid adherence to regulations which exclude the personal equation of pity and love and service outside the prescribed path.

In all spiritual healing, faith is the prime essential. Often the Christ used the word in His work; if not, then He caused the patient to demonstrate it. The man with the withered hand was commanded to "stretch it forth." With no thought of refusal, the effort was made—and the hand was moved and was whole again.

The annals of Mystic Masonry contain this same legend as related by Luke, who adds that it was the right hand which was withered or useless. The two hands symbolize the two paths of service in the occult world. Man in his present materialistic phase has virtually slain the Love power, allowing it to wither from disuse. When the Supreme Lord of Love appeared, He awakened the heart, and as the fires of the heart burned their path outward into the hands, the withered member was healed and made available once more for constructive work in the world.

It is significant in this connection that the withered hand was healed within the precincts of the Temple.

Healing the Centurion's Servant
Luke 7:1-10.

The story of the Centurion is recorded by both Matthew and Luke. This man, vested in military authority under the Roman government, had yet learned in his worldly contacts to practice the two principles which the Master enjoined upon all His disciples, namely, humility or self-effacement and active faith; truly an unusual achievement. Thus he was already qualified to become a follower of the Way, and to be made immediately the recipient of the Master's interest and benefits. "I have not found so great a faith, no, not in Israel," were the Master's words descriptive of the Centurion. The Centurion's bond slave, who was dear to him, was ill, and he had sent friends to ask the aid of the Great Healer, a request which was instantly granted. When the messengers returned home, they found the bond slave whole.

A supremely dedicated life centered in humility and service for others is the working formula for successful discipleship, and will always be productive of results, as exemplified in the response of the Master to the Centurion's request.

In this case, we have another instance of absent healing, as we saw in the story of the Syrophoenician woman and her daughter. Spirit permeates all things and all places in its active or positive manifestation, and matter itself is also Spirit, form being the result of crystallizations around the negative pole of Spirit, which is Space. Therefore the occultist declares that God is Spirit and that no man can be separated from Him in reality. Separateness of Man from God, Matter from Spirit, is but illusion; Unity is the reality, and as the concept of Unity is developed in consciousness, healing at a distance becomes possible. This is what Christ was demonstrating and teaching to the Disciples when He accomplished healings at a distance from the patient.

Verse eight is an esoteric description of a long and earnest preparatory training which leads to the conquest of self. The soldiers and servants are faculties within man himself. When the modern aspirant can affirm: "I say to this one, go, and he goes: and to another, come, and he comes, and to my servant, do this, and he does it," then he, too, is ready to receive the commendation and favor of the Master and to become aware that his life and his work have been found worthy to come into the aura of His divine and protective Presence.

Healing of the Infirm Woman
Luke 13:10-13.

Again the healing ministry was continued in the synagogue on the Sabbath day, and yet again the blind leaders of the blind continued to remonstrate, rigid in their adherence to the letter of the law while altogether oblivious of the Spirit contained therein.

This healing concerns a woman who had been unable to straighten her body into a natural, normal position for eighteen years. Esoterically, the healings which occur within the synagogue and Temple precincts all have a special hidden meaning not ordinarily found in the other healings. Kabbalistically, eighteen yields the number of nine, which is the cipher of freedom, of liberation and illumination. This woman had been inclined toward the earth (mortality) but now having found the Christ she is free, uplifted, centered no longer in the mortal life but in the way of Spirit, "He laid His hands on her and instantly she became erect and glorified God."

In the choosing of His disciples, invariably the Scriptures state: "He called unto them and they came to Him." In this statement we discover the first requisite of discipleship. He called, and this woman came, and she found the "Light which lighteth every man." He called to her, He spoke to her, He touched her. These are the first three steps taken by one who is ready to receive a higher unfoldment of consciousness, and they indicate the opening of the spiritual sense faculties by means of which the neophyte discovers a new world within himself and within nature.

The Woman Who Touched Him
Matt. 9:18-25; Mark 5:25-34; Luke 8:43-48.

Matthew, Mark and Luke all tell the story of the woman who had suffered with an infirmity for twelve years, and who was among the multitudes pressing and thronging about the Master as He passed on the way to the house of the nobleman, Jairus.

"If I but touch His garments I shall be made whole." These words ascribed to the woman are a part of an initiatory mantram. The garment represents the soul body in contradistinction to the personality. To become whole is to be able to pass through the portals of Initiation where one no longer "sees through a glass darkly, but face to face."

This woman and her healing represent the lifting of the feminine pole and rightfully belongs to the initiatory processes symbolically described in the raising of the daughter of Jairus. In the same way the raising of the Son of the Widow deals with the lifting of the masculine pole and is a part of the initiatory process described in the Resurrection of Lazarus.

The daughter of Jairus was twelve years of age. The infirm woman had been afflicted for twelve years, The two instances are related together in all three of the synoptic Gospels.

In order to understand the esoteric meaning underlying the healing of this woman who had been afflicted with an issue of blood for the greater part of life, we look to the ancient teachings on the mystery of the blood. "The blood is a most peculiar essence," Goethe tells us, and its vibratory rate indicates the esoteric status of the individual. The flowing of blood is a great cleanser and purifier of the desire nature. One who is ready for high spiritual work as prophet, teacher or healer, often undergoes some experience whereby a great loss of blood ensues. After this cleansing, he finds it less difficult to still the sense nature, and to silence the clamoring of appetite. Red blood represents man's carnal and materialistic nature. Eventually, through transmutation, blood will become a shining white essence.

All blood diseases are correlated to the element of Fire, and usually result from an overly stimulated desire body, either in the present embodiment or in some previous one.

The Initiator is always very solicitous of His charges as He instructs them in these veiled truths. This is the only recorded instance where Christ Jesus addressed a woman as "daughter." The Teacher becomes in very truth the father and protector of the "new-born" one.

Matthew records His salutation to her as, "Be of good courage." Mark and Luke, "Go in Peace," or "Go into Peace" —that Peace which passeth all understanding, for it has found its center in Omnipotent and Omnipresent Good.

Eusebius in the seventh book of his *Ecclesiastical History* states that he saw at Cesarea Phillipi a statue erected by this woman at the gates of her house, representing Christ standing with His hands outstretched to her kneeling before Him "like one entreating."

Raising the Daughter of Jairus

Matt. 9:18-19,23-26; Mark 5:22-24,35-43;
Luke 8:41-42,49-55.

This beautiful story, which veils the processes of Initiation from the general reader, is outlined in the three Gospels of Matthew, Mark and Luke.

Initiation is truly a dying to the old, personal life and being born anew. Luke says that the daughter of Jairus, a twelve-year old girl, "lay a-dying." But Christ said, "The maid is not dead but sleepeth." These are not contradictory statements when interpreted in the light of the Mystery Teachings, but have reference to the same experience.

Christ Jesus endeavored to demonstrate for the Disciples the healing of many and various forms of disease, their pre-existing cause and the method of dealing with it. In the presence of the most advanced of His Disciples He assisted three others to pass into the illumined state of Initiation.

The ego which inhabited the body of the daughter of Jairus was a very advanced one. In her we find an Initiate of the ancient Mysteries, returning as one of the earliest pioneers of the Christian Dispensation. She had been liberated on the inner planes, receiving the holy teachings pertaining to a higher awakened consciousness while her loved ones kept sacred vigil beside her physical casement. At the proper time, Christ, in the presence of the sleeping girl's father and mother and of Peter, James and John, (evidently the only ones present who were ready to understand these inner truths) assisted the maiden in returning and re-entering her physical body.

The Master greeted the girl when she returned with an expression of infinite beauty and tenderness revealing a wealth of inner meaning to the esotericist. Mark tells us that He said, *"Talitha cumi."* The word Talitha is an Aramaic diminutive meaning "little lamb." His words to her were, "Little Lamb, arise." Lamb or sheep is used throughout both the Old and New Testaments to describe the Initiate. The majority of high seers in the Mosaic era were "Shepherds." The Master Himself came as the Lamb of God, and in the later Initiation of Peter, His keynote is sounded in "Feed my sheep."

In the life cycle of the individual, the symbolic age of twelve is the crucial point for the child. It is then that the youth's desire nature begins to awaken, and the proclivities of past lives begin to manifest themselves. In an instance such as this of Jairus' daughter, an "old soul," one who has known many lives of experience in the earth school, this age marks a definite development of the spiritual nature. Instead of the awakening of the physical desires, there is a definite quickening of the accumulated soul powers of the past. Such a one has worked definitely and consciously with the processes of transmutation for many past lives. This was the case with the child Samuel when he began to prophesy, and the Master Jesus who was also twelve years old when He taught the elders in the Temple. Inspirational experiences are fairly common even among ordinary adolescents, and psychologists have observed that if an individual does not undergo a religious conversion during this period of life it is likely he will never have such an experience.

It is significant to observe that in all three of the synoptic Gospels, the raising of Jairus' Daughter is preceded by the exorcism of evil spirits.

In the experiences of the Initiate himself the expulsion of devils has reference to passing the Dweller on the Threshold, which is an entity formed of the essence of all evil and negative deeds of past lives, and which the newly initiated must face, conquer and dissolve (partially at least) by transmutation before he can pass into "realms of light" to be hailed as a "new born."

Jairus was a nobleman, a ruler in the synagogue, and therefore a man of high authority. When anyone attains the degree to which this girl Initiate had attained, such are always the sons and daughters of the king, for having found and claimed the rightful heritage of Spirit, one demonstrates true kinship with the Father, "All that the Father hath is mine."

All scriptural references to raising the dead to life refer to the latent divinity within man, which when awakened causes him to become an illumined or enlightened one. Many biblical references to persons being "dead" or "asleep" refer to the materially-minded.

When the silver cord which links the ego to the body has been severed, it is no longer possible to re-animate the body. The Master stated clearly for those who have eyes to see and ears to hear. "the maid is not dead, but sleepeth," indicating that the ego was still linked to the body, which was therefore yet alive.

The Nobleman's Son
John 4:46-53.

As we have seen, the Gospels of Matthew, Mark and Luke contain the story of the healing of Jairus' Daughter, which occurs comparatively early in the Gospel narratives because it symbolizes one of the first and most important of the purification works to be accomplished. There is, however, no mention of this event in John, for his Gospel, the most deeply esoteric of the four, deals with work of still higher import. Instead of the raising of Jairus' daughter, John substitutes that of the Nobleman's Son.

The Gospels as studied occultly reveal the path of Initiation in the Christian Mysteries, each character representing some particular attribute in process of development. The Nobleman's Son is not mentioned in the works of Matthew, Mark or Luke. The reason for this is to be found in the fact that in the process of spiritual attainment, the feminine principle must first be lifted and restored from its fall, as noted in the restoration of Jairus' Daughter. When this is accomplished, then follows the establishment of its equilibrium with the masculine. The first three Gospels are concerned with the former, John with the latter.

The mystic wedding feast at Cana of Galilee with which John opens his Gospel contains deeper teachings regarding the harmonizing of these two principles within the body of the aspirant for Initiation. The Nobleman's Son represents one who in his own life was demonstrating the work given by the Christ, The Scriptures state that after this raising, the nobleman and all of his household became followers of Christ Jesus.

Throughout the Bible the deeper teaching is symbolically concealed beneath the literal record which forms the basis for most of the current creeds.

When the masculine principle (the head; Hermes) represented by the raising of the Nobleman's Son, *who was not dead but at the point of death*, and the feminine principle (the heart; Aphrodite) typified by Jairus' Daughter, *who was not dead but asleep,* are again in equilibrium, the Cross will no longer be the symbol of Christianity, It will be represented by the two upright pillars, the Yachin and Boaz that adorn the entrance of the Temple of Solomon and represent the Divine Hermaphrodite. The neophyte or candidate will no longer be the "Widow's Son" but will become the Master who has found the Light in the East.

The Resurrection of Lazarus
John 11:1-44.

The nine Lesser Mysteries, also called the Lunar Mysteries, have been given in some form throughout the history of man. The advent of the Christ introduced the new or Solar Initiations to the world and it is to these higher truths, destined to serve humanity during the Great Sidereal Year beginning with the Sun's last precessional passage through Aries, that these Mysteries pertain. The religion of the Lamb bears a deeper and more far-reaching significance than is at the present time generally understood.

Lazarus was the most spiritually advanced of all the disciples who were under the tutelage of Christ Jesus. (The others did not reach this attainment until the Day of Pentecost.)

Exoteric religionists are puzzled to account for Christ's delay of two days before going to the aid of Lazarus. The esotericist knows that Christ was aware that only the body of Lazarus was in the tomb, whereas his spirit was on the inner planes receiving the initiatory work that gives entrance into the deeper Christian Mysteries. The Master Jesus was initiated into these Mysteries in the Rite of the Baptism, and Lazarus, the next in spiritual attainment, at the time of his supposed death.

Christ Jesus described this Initiation in the words, "This sickness is not unto death but for the glory of God." In other phraseology, Lazarus now becomes a more perfect channel for receiving and disseminating the glories of God upon the earth.

Mary and Martha, the two sisters of Lazarus, were among the highest in development of the women disciples of Christ. They were thus able to take part in the initiatory or Resurrection Rite of their brother, as did the father and mother of Jairus' Daughter. Mary symbolizes the mystic path, or the faith of the heart; Martha, the occult path, or the reasoning of the mind. The union of heart (love) and head (understanding) produce *Wisdom,* the true essence of the soul. Lazarus represents this twofold blending, which lifts the neophyte to a state of consciousness far transcending that possessed by ordinary humanity.

"Martha went out to meet Him, but Mary sat still in the house" (John 11:20). Martha, the mind, is ever seeking light through externalities. Mary, the heart, in stillness turns within to find the kingdom of heaven.

Christ Jesus said unto Martha: "I am the resurrection, and the life: he that believeth on me, though he die, yet shall he live; and whosoever liveth and believeth on me shall never die. Believest thou this?"

And Martha made reply, "Yea, Lord: I have believed that thou art the Christ, the Son of God, even He that cometh into the world."

And when she had said this, she went away and called Mary her sister secretly, saying, "The Teacher is here, and calleth thee."

These words of the Master to Martha have been called the human passport to immortality. They are not words addressed only to Martha, the sister of Lazarus; they are the call of the Christ to the reasoning or concrete mind of all humanity. "Be ye transformed by the renewing of the mind." This is accomplished by linking the mind with the "I Am" consciousness wherein dwells the realization of resurrection into eternal life.

The glorious message of New Age Bible interpretation is that this consciousness can be awakened here and now; it is not necessary to await death to work this transformation. "He that believeth in me, though he were dead [in materiality] yet shall he live again"—in renewed body, environment, and concept of life—a resurrection into a new being on every plane of consciousness. Truly a human passport to immortality.

John 11:38-39; 41-44.

Jesus therefore again groaning cometh to the tomb. Now it was a cave, and a stone lay against it. Jesus saith, Take ye away the stone. So they took away the stone. And Jesus lifted up his eyes, and said, Father I thank thee that thou heardest me. And I knew that thou hearest me always: but because of the multitude that standeth around I said it, that they may believe that thou didst send me. And when he had thus spoken, he cried with a loud voice, Lazarus, come forth. He that was dead came forth, bound hand and foot with grave-clothes; and his face was bound about with a napkin. Jesus saith unto them, Loose him, and let him go.

All higher birth must take place in a cave or stable: the Christ can be born within only through regenerative work upon the lower man. In Capricorn the Christ is born in the cave of the lower nature by purification. In Virgo He is born in the cave of the heart through transmutation. "Lazare deuro exo—Lazarus hither out! Loose him and let him go." These mystic words bear the message of the spiritual victory of Lazarus.

The Pharisees and priests were cognizant to some extent of the Mystery Teachings. Indeed, Arthur Weigall, the world-renowned Egyptologist, now deceased, declares that his researches in ancient religions have convinced him that the New Testament describes a ritual in which a condemned criminal was executed as a sacrifice, as in ancient Babylon, and that Jesus, when condemned to death, was crucified in accordance with the ritual demands. Dr. Rudolf Steiner stated that the Master Jesus was an Initiate in the Hebrew Mysteries but made them public (according to His own declaration, *Whosoever wills may come*) and as death was the penalty among all ancient nations for revealing the secrets of the Mysteries, He was immediately condemned to death.

A like case in Greek history is that of Aeschylus who, though called in a dream by Dionysius himself to write tragedy, was nevertheless threatened with death by an angry mob in a theater where one of his plays was produced, on the charge that he had revealed certain inviolable secrets from the Mysteries. He saved his life by taking refuge at the altar of Dionysius in the orchestra, and later was successful in proving before the Areopagus that he had not known that what he said was secret. Jesus, however, made no attempt to vindicate Himself, since He purposely revealed the Secrets of Israel, and willingly suffered the extreme penalty.

The Raising of the Widow's Son of Nain
Luke 7:11-15.

The raising of the Widow's Son as recounted by Luke contains also the outline of Lazarus' illumination or Christing. *Nain* (the name of the village) means Nine, and *the death of the Widow's Son* is mystic phraseology descriptive of one who has traveled the tortuous Way which leads through death (of the personal) to resurrection (into the impersonal). Such an one is no longer "the son of a widow." Luke explicitly states that after he arose Christ "delivered him to his mother." Equilibrium between the two poles of Spirit, masculine and feminine, was established. This is the supreme attainment of the Christian Mysteries, foreshadowed in the Rites of ancient times but consummated in the Mysteries established by the Christ. Thus it is that Christ is the Light of the World, the goal of all ancient Teachings. Equilibrium in Spirit had been lost under the old regime; even the Mysteries had degenerated into almost meaningless (and frequently cruel) ritual in many instances. Christ Jesus came pointing the way back: "I am the Way, the Truth, and the Life." To become Christed or initiated in *His Name* is the supreme purpose of earth evolution.

The son of a widow is an allegorical phrase that has reference to one who is attempting to develop the polarity of Spirit within. From the days of ancient Egypt to the present, members of the Masonic Order have been so styled.

The "widow's son of Nain" refers to one who has passed through the nine Lesser Mysteries and is now prepared (as was Lazarus) to be raised by Christ into the Greater or Christian Mystic Initiations. This is the ultimate of the 33rd degree ($3 \times 3 = 9$). It is foreshadowed in the 18th degree ($8 + 1 = 9$).

Beginning with the Degree of the Rose Croix (18th degree), and continuing through the 33rd degree, the Candidate is working definitely on the completion of his own selfhood, that Temple made without hands, but eternal in the heavens. This is his golden wedding garment, or perfected soul body. With the consummation of this Work he is no longer the Widow's Son. Polarity is attained, and his "healing" is complete.

The Deaf and Dumb Man Healed
Mark 7:31-35.

We are in bondage under the Law so long as we remain in ignorance of its true nature, but in the wisdom of the Christ we become free, because there is no longer any dissonance between our individual keynote and that of the Universe. This is the meaning of the teaching of Paul, the great biblical metaphysician.

"Behold I make all things new," declared Christ. When we are worthy to be freed from past karmic bonds, we contact the Law of Liberation. The choice is then ours, to reject or to accept, to remain under bondage or to be free. All biblical healings were so ordained by the worthiness of the recipient.

"The soul's faults of today crystallize into the body's ailments of tomorrow. Spirit is always the builder of the body. The miracles of the Master's healings are only for those who have ears to hear and eyes to see." Thus wrote the great Paracelsus.

Impediment of speech follows upon a misuse of the sacred life force. An injury or loss of the tongue is a consequence of blasphemy, the injury of others through gossip, or the betrayal of a sacred trust. "The tongue is a little member full of deadly evils." Other illustrations of the Law may be observed in the loss of fingers, as the karmic result of unfair and dishonest practices; loss of hands, as a result of committing wanton destruction as frequently occurs in war, for instance; loss of feet, resulting from walking in paths of wrong-doing and leading others therein; bodily deformity resulting from the perpetration of cruelties such as the hideous punishments of the horror chambers of the Inquisition; spinal trouble, through using spiritual forces for purposes of black magic and the like; stomach and digestive troubles from a gluttonous and debauched appetite;

heart trouble through intense selfish and personal love which failed to regard the welfare of others; and tuberculosis resulting from materialistic thinking and living. Sometimes the karmic consequences of violation of cosmic law follow within one lifetime; more often they occur in later incarnations, after an interval of death, so that an individual may be born innocent in respect of the one lifetime known to him yet suffer these karmic retributions carried over from the past.

In the case of the deaf and dumb man described in the gospel of Mark, Christ Jesus touched the man's ears and his tongue, and looking up to heaven (the symbol of the Eternal), He said, "*Ephphatha,*" which means, "Be opened." He had chosen to follow Christ into the heaven of a new life, freed from the limiting restrictions of the old. His choice may be ours with the same results.

Ephphatha, "be thou opened," refers esoterically to the development of clairvoyance, clairaudience and the power of the spoken Word awakened in the disciple. This symbolic act of the Christ has been commemorated in both the Greek and Roman churches in the Baptismal Rite where the priest touches the ears and mouth of the penitent with a finger which has touched his own lips, and pronounced the word, *Ephphatha.*

The early Church referred to *Ephphatha* as the mystery of the *Apertio,* or Opening, and connected it in the Mysteries of Christ Jesus with the Rite of Baptism wherein the disciple also received the powers of extended sight and hearing. It was possible for the Archangel whom we know as the Christ to permeate all crystallized atoms with the powers emanating from His own home world, the realms of Life Spirit (the Buddhic Plane), where all is life, light and love. Because of this, healings were instantaneous in all cases where He chose to make them so. Such were the forces resident in Him, whose radiations were so powerful that even those who touched His garment were made new again. This fact was again evidenced in the healing of Malchus' ear at the time of the arrest of the Master in Gethsemane.

After the prolonged exercise of His powers, the glorious Christ Spirit would depart for a season of solitude in an Essenian retreat, in order that His mighty vibrations should not completely shatter the human body of Jesus which He had assumed at the time of the Baptism and used throughout His ministry on earth. During these retreats from the public ministry, He withdrew from the mortal body, leaving it in the care of the Essenes, who worked upon it in His absence. This was a specialized work the Essenes were able to do because of their own high spiritual powers which they radiated from themselves. Advanced souls invariably work by projecting their vibrational powers. Thus also did Christ cast out the evil spirits with a word, and healed all that were sick and whose karma entitled them to healing, that it might be fulfilled which was spoken by Isaiah, the prophet, saying, "Himself took our infirmities and bore our diseases." (Matt. 8:17),

Paracelsus admonishes us to remember that the subject of disease and healing can be understood only when considered in the light of karmic law, and this affects not only the physical body, but also the several interpenetrating invisible vehicles of man. "There is a twofold power active in man," he says, "a visible and an invisible. The visible body has its natural forces and the invisible body has its natural forces—and the remedy of all disease and injury that may affect the visible form are contained in the invisible body, because the latter is the seat of power that infuses life into the former and without which the former would have no life."

Visible and invisible body building is divided into cycles of seven. The first cycle of seven is concerned chiefly with the building of the physical and vital bodies, which correlate to the development of the glandular system. The second cycle is concerned with the development of the desire body. It is fiery, and correlates with the chemistry of the circulatory blood system. The third cycle is given over to the development of the mental body. It is airy. Thought now becomes the supreme creative power. In the subconscious it establishes habits, the tendency of which is to crystallize the etheric or vital body. The fourth cycle summarizes or synthesizes the preceding septenates. It recapitulates the past, and in so doing frequently touches karma that has been carried over from previous earth existences, and which is now scheduled for payment.

The age of twenty-eight marks the completion of the fourth septenary cycle when, in the occult sense, the true mental life of the ego is considered to have begun. It marks the final maturation of the four etheric "sheaths" which are the matrix of physical growth.

"For ye should comprehend that there be seven lives in man, of which not one attaineth to the true life which is in the soul." These seven lives are the seven septenary periods from birth to forty-nine years of age, which is the "Middle Age" of the occultist, and marks a time of profound and fundamental change leading to new vision in one who has found "the *true* life which is in the soul." The seven must be transformed before the fullness of development is realized. Christ Jesus cast seven devils out of Mary of Magdala, which has reference to this sevenfold attainment. After this experience she became the foremost woman disciple of the Master and was the first of them all to be able to lift herself sufficiently high in consciousness to recognize Him when He returned on the blessed Easter Day.

"The true physician must both understand and perceive," writes Paracelsus further. "If he does not see the patient's astrality, he cannot prescribe that which being the curative opposing force, must be roused within the patient's spirit. The true healer looks not for causes in the visible, but seeks to understand the invisible." Truly, man will never know perfect health until he learns to live in harmony with the laws of life. Again in the words of Paracelsus: "Sickness is the expression of a fight that is being waged by the occult man against the degenerate conditions of his nature."

All truth is one and eternal, and the teachings of the Christ have reached down the centuries in the testimonies of the wise and the virtuous to our own day. The following words of a truly New Age teacher, Doctor Alexis Carrel, in his popular book, "Man the Unknown," are to the point: "Science," says he, "studies intensely man's liver, kidneys, all his physical functions, everything except the only important function, which is Thought." This sounds the keynote of the regenerative processes of the New Age. Christing the mind, Paul called it. When this is done, the purification and the perfecting of the body follow. The chains of past causation and the bondage of heredity hold us only so long as we permit them to do so. We are in bondage under the law; we are free in Christ.

"Go and sin no more lest a worse thing come upon thee." These words well express the close connection existing between disease and sin, sin being all that which is not in accord with the constructive powers of nature, or in other words, with divine Law. Illumination and regeneration are one in the processes of healing. To know continuous radiant health is to live in constant communion with the divinity within. This was the message of the Christ as it is of all true teachers who have both preceded and come after Him.

The physical body is a reflection of the Divine Plan as it manifests in the universe about us. It is composed of molecules ensouled by a central point of light or spiritual power, which controls its vibratory rate or motion. Every element in the universe is within man. The microcosm is the child of the macrocosm. Inharmonious interaction, or disease, manifests in the etheric body before it registers in the physical. The tone of the vitalizing vehicle is lowered; it is "jangled out of tune" by ceasing to vibrate in harmony with the keynote of its archetypal pattern.

Positive affirmations and constructive thinking rapidly restore the normal tone of the etheric body and contrariwise, fear is the greatest deterrent to the restoration of health. The Twenty-third Psalm holds a magical power for the alleviation of fear. Let the rhythm of its declarations impart their harmony and strength into the whole being. It will make for health and wholeness. "The Lord is my shepherd, I shall not want." "I will fear no evil for Thou are with me."

The true spiritual healer possesses faculties with which the inner bodies of the patient and their relation to the physical vehicle may be examined. "If our medical students," writes Franz Hartmann, the noted occult writer and physician, "were to apply a part of the time which they employ for the study of external sciences which are practically useless to them, to the development of their interior perceptions, they would become able to *see* certain processes within the organism of man which are to them at present a mere matter of speculation and which are not discernible by physical means."

The day is not far distant when orthodox medicine, like orthodox science as a whole, and also orthodox religion, will experience a spiritual awakening that will lift it to new heights of service. The quickening activity is under way. Ever greater are the numbers of awakened souls earnestly striving toward the ideal enunciated by the Blessed Lord Himself when He said:

> "Be ye therefore perfect, even as
> your Father which is in heaven is perfect".
> Matt. 5:48

CHAPTER II

The Parables of Christ's Ministry

The Parables of Christ Jesus have been termed the finest literary art of the world, combining, as they do, simplicity, profundity, human emotion and spiritual intensity.

St. Augustine says that Christ's miracles are acted Parables and that His Parables are miracles of beauty and perfection.

The Greek meaning of Parable is *to place beside for the purpose of comparison.* Those who assert that there is no secret or inner meaning in Christianity must forego entirely a study of the Parables, for the Saviour explicitly declares as their purpose, "seeing, they may not see and hearing, they may not understand."

One of the distinctive characteristics of St. Luke's Gospel is the importance he accords the Parables. Of the thirty or so which are most familiar to the Bible student, eighteen are narrated only in the Lukan Gospel. For purposes of esoteric interpretation we have grouped the Parables into sections as they relate to one or another of the specific aspects of the Christian Mysteries.

Parables of the Old and the New

The great wisdom of the Supreme Master caused Him to emphasize the necessity of embracing the pioneer truths of each new age inaugurated by the precession of the Equinoxes from one zodiacal sign into another. This brings an ever-recurring conflict: The conservatives cling to the old. Those ready for advancement accept the new. That it is the part of wisdom to accept the new the Christ makes plain in the Parable of New Wine and Old Wine found in Luke 5:37-39, Matthew 9:17, and Mark 2:22; also in the Parable of Treasures New and Old in Matthew 13:52, and Parable of the New Patch on the Old Garment in Luke 5:36, Matthew 9:16, and Mark 2:21.

The life and teachings of Christ Jesus are a constant protest against so strict an adherence to form that it becomes stereotyped and causes the spirit to be obscured. "Before Abraham was, I am," was His challenge to His own age. New cloth must be fashioned into new garments; new wine, if it is to remain pure and unpolluted, must not be poured into old wine skins, but into new.

The Piscean Age, influenced by Pisces and Jupiter, has established churchcraft founded upon creed and dogma. The religion of the new Aquarian Age under Uranus will be untrammeled. As the Master observed:

Matthew 13:52.

"Therefore every scribe which is instructed unto the kingdom of heaven is like unto a man that is an householder, which bringeth forth out of his treasure things new and old."

If any man is born in Christ he is a new creature, asserted Paul, speaking from his own personal experience.

St. John, from the exaltation of his high Initiate-consciousness, declared: "Behold, I make all things new" for "the former things are passed away."

The mystic Tennyson sings in his inspired song of Initiation, *The Idylls of the King:*

The old order changeth, yielding place to new,
And God fulfills Himself in many ways.

PREPARATION FOR DISCIPLESHIP

Parable of the Pearl of Great Price } Matthew 13:44-46.
Parable of the Hidden Treasure }
Parable of the Mustard Seed. Mark 4:30-32, Luke 13:18-19
Parable of the Leaven. Luke 13:20-21.

The Pearl of Great Price and *The Hidden Treasure* are twin Parables. Each recounts the same truth, namely, the necessity of entire and complete dedication to the quest of the spiritual life. This full allegiance is the primary requisite of the Path of Discipleship. Nothing less will suffice than that the *whole* energy of mind, soul and body be sent in *one* direction.

The Parable of the Mustard Seed teaches us once more that we are all Christs-in-the-making, and that each one of us must, in a small way, make our lives a replica of the life of the Christ. The mind is the path; therefore the beginning of the resurrection within our own lives must be accomplished by establishing within ourselves a new mind through the creative power of thought. The Master knew this truth and gave it to His Disciples and to the multitudes gathered around Him. He likened the attainment of the kingdom (within) to the planting of a seed in the ground. As the seed lies embedded in darkness, hidden away from the light for a time, apparently inert and lifeless, so it is with the aspirant when he begins to live the spiritual life. For a time it may seem that he is making no progress. He is beset with trials and temptations and enveloped in darkness, and knows not how it is possible for the seed of the Spirit to spring up.

Jacob Boehme describes this place on the Path so aptly that it finds an echo in the heart of everyone who has passed this way. He says: "It is not so easy a matter to become a child of God as men imagine . . . To *turn the mind* and *destroy self* there is a strong and continued requisite, and such a stout and steady purpose that if the body and soul should part asunder by it, yet the will would persevere constantly and not enter again into the self. A man must wrestle until the dark center that is shut up close breaks open, and the spark lying therein kindles, and from thence immediately the noble lily branch spouteth—as from the divine grain of mustard seed, as Christ saith. A man must pray earnestly, with great humility, and for a while become a fool in his own reason and see himself void of understanding therein until Christ be formed in this new earth incarnation."

If we possess ourselves of this strong and continued earnestness of purpose we may rest assured that we shall come to know the truth of the Master's words: "The earth bringeth forth fruit of herself; first the blade, then the ear, after that the full corn in the ear."

The power of the Christ-life that is within the seed causes it to push its way up through the darkness until at last the tender, green blade breaks through the earth and finds the sunlight. The power of the mind being renewed may be likened to the new blade in that it is but a small beginning, and shows but little promise of its future wondrous attainment. As we grow in Christ power, there comes the ear or the fruit. "By their fruits ye shall know them," said the Master. And finally comes the full corn in the ear, or the wondrous fulfillment of the Christed mind, the powers of Initiation, producing a man whose light shineth, as Jacob Boehme put it.

Again we may liken the seed planted in the ground to the student who is just beginning a study of esoteric Christianity; the green blade to the novice who has begun to demonstrate power through good works or the apprentice in Masonic ceremonialism; the ear to the disciple who has progressed even farther upon the Path, or the fellow craftsman of the Lodge; and the full corn in the ear to that lofty attainment we call Initiateship, which makes a man a Master.

The Christ likens the kingdom to a grain of mustard seed which when sown in the earth is less than all the seed that be in the earth. Here He is telling us that the gateway to the kingdom of the new consciousness, the kingdom of heaven within, is *humility*.

Again Jacob Boehme, that disciple of true humility, tells us from his own experience: "When the outward reason (concrete mind) triumpheth in the light, saying, 'I have the true child,' then the will of the desire must bow itself down to the earth and bring itself in the deepest humility and say, 'Thou art foolish and have nothing but the grace of God.' Thou must wrap thyself up in that belief with great humility and become nothing at all in thyself, and neither know nor love thyself. All that thou hast or is in thee must esteem itself as nothing but a mere instrument of God."

This is the lesson that Gethsemane holds for each neophyte. It is only as he forgets self, and thus makes himself a fit instrument through which the Christ power may work, that he may be lifted to know the joys of the resurrection.

Christ Jesus said, "But when it is sown, it groweth up and beareth greater than all herbs, and shooteth out great branches so that the fowls of the air may lodge under the shadow of it." And many such parables spake He unto the people as they were able to bear them, that is, as they were able to understand His meaning; but when He and His disciples were alone, He explained all these things to them.

The farther we progress upon His Way, the more illuminating do His words become and the more able are we to understand His mystic message.

In the Parable of the Leaven the great Teacher is treating

of the far-reaching power of transmutation, the most subtle and the most potent of all forces.

Leaven is a silent agency, its workings are unseen and unobserved by outer sight until the manifestation is completed. "Three measures" was an ephah of flour, the amount ordinarily used for the family baking. In order that the bread be of the required consistency and lightness the leaven must penetrate the entire mass. The three measures, spiritually, refer to body, mind and soul which must each one become infused with the light of Spirit before the transmutation processes can be effected.

Paul gave in a few words an arresting description of what happens to the disciple when "the whole"—namely, body, mind and soul—"has been leavened," in the statement, "In Him we live and move and have our being."

The Christ leaven is at work in the world and its activities will not cease until all mankind walks in the light as He is in the light and all nations come to know the glory of one vast fellowship together.

SYMBOLS OF DISCIPLESHIP

Parable of the Chief Seats—Luke 14:7-11.
Parable of the Pharisee and Publican—Luke 18:9-14.
Parable of the Laborers and Hours—Matthew 20:1-16.
Parable of the Talents—Matthew 25:14-30.
Parable of the Pounds—Luke 19:11-27.
Parable of the Good Samaritan—Luke 10:25-37.
Parable of the Sower—Mark 4:3-20.

The seven Parables are lessons pertaining to the teachings on humility, compassion and service—the three columns found in every initiatory Temple.

It is by demonstrating daily these three character attributes of humility, compassion and willingness to serve others, that the disciple gives proof of worthiness for further inner-plane instruction and work. One who thus faithfully practices these qualities earns the privilege of hearing that treasured promise recorded in Isaiah 48:6, *"I have shewed thee new things from this time, even hidden things, and thou didst not know them."*

The need for humility is the keynote of the Parable of the Chief Seats and the Parable of the Pharisee and the Publican.

That it is the humble who shall be exalted, Christ Jesus taught as a fundamental truth of the spiritual Way. Perhaps the most beautiful example of the importance which He attached to the cultivation of humility is found in the Rite of the Foot Washing. Here the Master declared emphatically that he who does not observe this Rite (meaning one who does not measure the deeds of his daily living by the gauge of humility) "can have no part in me."

The Parable of the Laborers and the Hours is one most profound and far-reaching in its application to human life upon the physical plane.

The great, eternal and immutable Cosmic Law which governs the universe is centered in the Spirit of Oneness. Every human being is a child of God (All-Good) which means that all are inherently divine and consequently each has a right to an equal share in the inheritance of the Father's kingdom. The Law operates impartially. An equal share awaits each ego; it is his for the claiming and the taking. Many there are, however, who do not realize this truth and so do not receive the full share of their divine inheritance. "Many bear the burden of the day and the scorching heat," they live, that is, in accordance with the laws of materiality, as yet unawakened to the Law of Spirit by which "all that the Father hath is mine."

The vineyard is the earth plane. The laborers are our evolving humanity and the householder is God or Cosmic Law. Ofttimes in the working of this great Law one who is first in the eyes of men is last in the sight of God.

Those who are unaware of the impartial measures of Divine Law are the complainers against the householders (the Law in operation). Theirs is the eye that is evil (limited) so that they do not recognize that "I am good." They do not see that when man prepares himself to receive only the highest manifestations of Divine Law, he will know and demonstrate only All-Good. The limitations of disease, poverty, and even death, will be dissolved amid the mists of the evanescent and the unreal. Man will come to inhabit a new world in which Equality, Fellowship, Love and Life shall reign supreme and for all time.

Parables of the Talents and the Pounds

The stories of *The Talents and the Pounds* as related in the Gospels of Matthew and Luke are twin Parables centered primarily in the twin laws of rebirth and causation. The "old soul" possesses many talents (ten), the "young soul" possesses but few (one). The majority of humanity is represented by the man possessing five talents. The five-talent man typifies the race at its present midway station upon the great evolutionary arc.

As man sows in one life, so he must reap in the succeeding incarnation. "I will judge you from your own mouth," has reference to the just action of the law of causation. The "young soul," one who is immersed in material interests, is unaware of this great karmic law, and asserts, "I reap what I have not sown." It is through lives of sorrow and travail that a true understanding of the justice of the karmic law is achieved.

The Parable states that *"unto everyone that hath"* it shall be given, and from *"him that hath not"* it shall be taken away even that which he has. *"One that hath"* refers to those who have learned to abide in the light of the Spirit. The argument of this story is that divine righteous judgment is made *not* according to the work accomplished but according to the measure of opportunity. No judgment can be right or just which is not made in the light of past causation and the fruitage of previous lives lived upon the earth.

We further perceive in this Parable the action of the law according to which like attracts like. The truth of this law is everywhere observable in the physical worlds. It is equally so in the superphysical worlds. The gamester will associate with his kind; musicians will be drawn together by their common profession, and students will seek the opportunities afforded by libraries. Death does not change the real man. Christ Jesus was enunciating this law of attraction in the Parable of the Pounds.

Ten is a number of power and of the deepest occult significance. It is a most important number in the Old Testament. The man who acquired the ten pounds is representative of one who through previous lives has attained to high spiritual power.

The number five indicates lower spiritual status; it is the number of intellect and that stage of development where all the five senses are awake and active. Thus the man who had gained five pounds was one who was on the path of intellect, but who had not yet awakened the higher spiritual centers.

The man possessing only the one pound, which he hid, is the man who is entirely material, one who has not started on the spiritual path and who, moreover, does not even know that such things as occult training and esoteric development exist.

The man possessing only one pound of which he made no use was the young soul who had lived only a comparatively few lives upon earth and had not learned how to forget himself in service for others. The man possessing five pounds had been longer upon the way; he had begun to learn the lessons of service and brotherhood, and to consider the welfare of those about him. The man possessing the ten pounds, and to whom an extra one was given (eleven signifies polarity), was the old soul who through many lives of love and service had built the "golden wedding garment." He represents the nobleman who had journeyed to a far country and was ready to return, having received for himself a kingdom.

Parable of the Sower

The Parable of the Sower was given during the second year of the Ministry, upon the shores of the Sea of Galilee, probably at Capernaum. On account of the great multitudes surging about Him, some attracted by His words and others seeking to be healed, the Christ was compelled to set out a short distance from shore in a small boat in order to speak to them.

Christ Jesus used Parables freely in His teachings because they were so easily adapted to the varied nature of His audiences. A child could see the profoundest truth in this charming story setting, while those who were ready for the harder things found there many pearls of wisdom. Here the seed represents the mighty power of Truth always waiting for man to receive it—that Truth which is the corner stone of the Temple of Evolution, yet is ever rejected by the multitudes. The sower represents those who give out spiritual Truth. "As he sowed, some fell by the wayside and the fowls of the air came and devoured it up." The seed which fell by the wayside and was devoured is a picture of the emotionally inconstant type of person, one who receives spiritual teaching with avidity, who is lavish with promises and enthusiastic to meet the hardest tests that the spiritual life can give; but who, when these tests come (for they must always come) loses courage, and in the wane of enthusiasm he departs from the Way. Perhaps it is the call of the world which is heard. Frequently it is another school of thought offering what appears to be a more attractive, or, in many cases, a quicker, method of development; and so he flits from one thing to another, always seeking, never finding, never building a foundation anywhere. For him the seed of Truth has in this life fallen by the wayside indeed and the birds of the air have come and devoured it.

"And some fell on stony ground, where it had not much earth; and immediately it sprang up, because it had no depth of earth; but when the sun was up, it was scorched; and because it had no root, it withered away." The Master here was referring to the purely mental type of person whose heart has not yet been awakened. This person can give an excellent discourse on the meaning of religion and the living of the spiritual life; he can perhaps repeat accurately passages of philosophy upon the subject, and quote verbatim whole chapters from the Bible. But when put to the actual task of living the life, when the opportunity comes to really give up self in the service of others, he is generally found wanting. It is love that teaches the selfless life. The purely mental person can tell others how to live the life that leads to Christ, *but it is only the one who has learned to love purely and unselfishly who attains unto this goal himself.*

"And some fell among thorns, and the thorns grew up, and choked it, and it yielded no fruit." The thorns represent the lower desire nature. Since that far-off Atlantean time when the link of mind was first given to general humanity and this mind coalesced with the desire body, the power of the desire nature has been the most fruitful source of evil in the world. Knowing this, the Master of occult wisdom gave a lesson to His disciples and preached a sermon to the multitudes, in which He stressed the dire consequences which follow the wrong use of the creative force. He here states that the misuse of this force within man causes a life to yield no fruit. The fruit is the perfection of the tree and fruit trees are the most advanced life of the plant kingdom. It is the power of the purified desire nature that causes man to become the perfected fruit of our scheme of evolution. This great truth, so little understood at the present time, will be basic to the Aquarian religion. What is now taught esoterically will in Aquaria be shouted from the housetops. Christ Jesus more than two thousand years ago made this spiritual fact the pivot of each of His messages to humanity.

"And other fell on good ground, and did yield fruit that sprang up and increased; and brought forth, some thirty, and some sixty, and some an hundred." The good ground represents the united powers of head and heart—the ideal attainment for those who seek to know the mysteries of the Kingdom of God. It was this attainment *alone* which yielded growing and increasing fruit. Such fruitage is proportional to individual ability and capacity for growth. There are some who have earned a wider sphere of usefulness than others, and God's love may be depended upon to mete out impartially to each one exactly what is his just desert under the law of causation. Meditation on this Parable will yield deep mystic meaning. "He that hath ears to hear, let him hear."

Parable of the Good Samaritan

In the Parable of the Good Samaritan, Christ enunciated the truest definition of discipleship as loving, self-forgetting service. It is not enough to be a priest and minister only to the souls of men. It is not enough to be a Levite and officiate in the Temple service. True discipleship demands of us also practical service in the physical betterment of humankind. This means true neighborliness, the giving of one's time, one's substance and oneself for the welfare of others.

Love thy neighbor (whomsoever it is given thee to serve) *as thyself,* is the supreme commandment.

"Though buried deep or thinly strown,
Do thou thy grace supply;
The hope in earthly furrows sown
Shall ripen in the sky."

OBSTACLES ALONG THE WAY OF ATTAINMENT

Parable of the Unmerciful Servant—Matthew 18:35
Parable of the Young Ruler—Matthew 19:16-30.
Parable of the Rich Fool—Luke 12:13-21.
Parable of Lazarus and the Rich Man—Luke 16:19-31.
Parable of the Prodigal Son—Luke 15:11-32.
Parable of the Lost Coin—Luke 15:8-10.
Parable of the Lost Sheep—Luke 15:4-7.
Parable of the Rejected Cornerstone—Matthew 21:42-45.
Luke 20:17-18.
Mark 12:10-11.

Parable of the Cruel Vine Dressers—Matthew 21:33-41.
Mark 12:1-9.
Luke 20:9-16.
Parable of Children at Play—Luke 7:31-35.
Parable of the Empty House—Matthew 12:43-45.
Parable of the Unfinished Work—Luke 14-28-30.
Parable of the Great Renunciation—Luke 14:31-33.
Parable of the Bond Servant—Luke 17:7-10.
Parable of the Barren Fig Tree—Luke 13:6-9.
Parable of the Tares—Matthew 13:24-30, 36-43.
Parable of the Last Judgment—Matthew 25:31-46.

In the Parable of the Unmerciful Servant, Christ enunciates principles of the social code belonging to the Aquarian Age in which compassion, mercy, and the spirit of charity and true brotherliness are manifested. In sharp contrast with the beauty of this picture is shown the hard, arbitrary and inhuman approach of our own time.

Those who have glimpsed the high concepts of this dawning New Age have been scored by sceptics and materialists as Utopian idealists and dreamers. Aquarian idealism, however, is actually based on the teachings of the Christ who looked far beyond His own day and, in the midst of a hostile world, dared to proclaim truths belonging to a new and a brighter tomorrow.

Parable of the Young Ruler

In the Parable of the Young Ruler we are taught that the tests and temptations of life are individual, because the path which leads unto Eternal Life is different for each. The Sufi mystics have said that there are as many paths to God as there are souls to seek Him, that every soul is itself a path—an ancient truism which the Bible illustrates in the story of the young ruler who came to Christ Jesus.

Matthew 19:16-30

And, behold, one came and said unto him, Good Master, what good thing shall I do, that I may have eternal life?

And he said unto him, Why callest thou me good? There is none good but one, that is God; but if thou wilt enter into life, keep the commandments.

He saith unto him, Which? Jesus said, Thou shalt do no murder, Thou shalt not commit adultery, Thou shalt not steal, Thou shalt not bear false witness.

Honor thy father and thy mother; and, Thou shalt love thy neighbor as thyself.

The young man saith unto him, All these things have I kept from my youth up; What lack I yet?

Jesus said unto him, If thou wilt be perfect, go and sell that thou hast, and give to the poor, and thou shalt have treasure in heaven; and come and follow me.

But when the young man heard that saying, he went away sorrowful; for he had great possessions.

Then said Jesus unto his disciples, Verily I say unto you, That a rich man shall hardly enter into the kingdom of heaven.

And again I say unto you, It is easier for a camel to go through the eye of a needle, than for a rich man to enter into the kingdom of God.

When his disciples heard it, they were exceedingly amazed, saying, Who can then be saved?

But Jesus beheld them, and said unto them, With men this is impossible; but with God all things are possible.

Then answered Peter and said unto him, Behold, we have forsaken all, and followed thee; what shall we have therefore?

And Jesus said unto them, Verily I say unto you, That ye which have followed me, in the regeneration when the Son of Man shall sit in the throne of his glory, ye also shall sit upon twelve thrones, judging the twelve tribes of Israel.

And everyone that hath forsaken houses, or brethren, or sisters, or father, or mother, or wife, or children, or lands, for my name's sake, shall receive an hundredfold, and shall inherit everlasting life.

But many that are first shall be last; and the last shall be first.

This incident does not mean, as many have concluded, that the possession of material wealth is in itself a wrong, but that it becomes so only when misused or given undue importance in the consciousness of its possessor. Each neophyte discovers that he retains some particular besetting sin—pride, envy, arrogance, lust, ambition, greed for power and position, love of wealth, or the joy of amassing it. Any one of these may be the particular weakness that must be overcome and eradicated as the chief barrier to attainment. In the incident of the young ruler it was the love of his material possessions; hence the Master, knowing this, presented him with that which would be his most difficult task, "Go sell all that thou hast and give to the poor."

"Thou shalt have no other gods before me" is an important commandment and the one most often disregarded. The kingdom and its fruits must occupy the paramount place in the life of the aspirant. To one who succeeds in this quest, the Master has given the promise that he shall receive an hundredfold and shall inherit everlasting life.

To another possessing vast earthly wealth, but who regarded himself only as a steward to dispense it for the benefit of man and to the greatest glory of the Christ, another test dealing with some weakness not yet overcome would be necessary.

The command to forsake houses, land, and family for the Master's sake simply means that the love of the Christ and the service of His Kingdom must needs be kept as the first dedication. Neither personality nor possession may interfere if Life Eternal is to be won. It is this which makes the way so difficult and causes the Christ to say: "So the last shall be first, and the first last; for many be called, but few chosen."

In the Parable of the Rich Fool the Master gives expression to a truth almost entirely neglected in our civilization, but which must be made a prime essential in the education of the new generation if it is to pioneer a brighter and a better world.

Take heed, He admonished, and keep yourselves from all covetousness; for a man's life consisteth not in the abundance of the things which he possesseth.

This teaching reverses the educational methods of the modern world. For all too long the scale of measurement has been set to "things" rather than to character. Such superficial values can only be productive of a transitory good. In consequence of this substitution of the false for the true there is upheaval, chaos and world tumult. Humanity must return to an appreciation of *eternal* values before an enduring civilization can be established.

He that layeth up treasures for himself is not rich toward God. The great choice is between the mundane and the spiritual.

The Parable of Lazarus and the Rich Man paints in vivid colors the striking contrast in the world between the rich and the poor.

The first scene of this soul drama is laid in Palestine and depicts the ease and wealth of the rich man as opposed to the abject poverty of the beggar Lazarus who comes daily to beg for crumbs from his table.

The second scene is laid in the after-death state where the condition of the two men is reversed. Lazarus now enjoys the bliss of heaven; the rich man is undergoing the pangs of remorse in Purgatory in consequence of the thoughtless and self-centered life which was his while living upon earth.

The great lesson of this Parable is in its teaching that man is building for his after-earth life in the manner of his daily living here and now. It also suggests the purpose of suffering and sorrow in human evolution, shows how sorrow and joy balance one another in human experience. Fiona MacLeod (the pseudonym of the famous English writer William Sharp, drawn, it is said, from memory of a previous feminine incarnation) writes: "In Paradise there are no tears shed, although in the remotest part of it there is a grey pool, the weeping of all the world, fed everlastingly by the myriad eyes that every moment are somewhere wet with sorrow or vain regret. And those who go there stoop and touch their eyes with that grey water and it becomes a balm to them and they go upon their way healed. Their songs thereafter are the sweetest that are sung in the ways of Paradise."

Sorrow is the great solvent and equalizes all things, so says the Great Teacher of all mankind. Most frequently it is sorrow's lessons that awaken the "young soul" and set his feet upon the Shining Way whereon are evolved the compassion, the humility, and the power to serve selflessly, which are the soul signatures of true discipleship.

Parable of the Prodigal Son

The Prodigal Son is perhaps the most familiar of all the Parables. It has been termed the *"evangelium in Evangelio,"* the Pearl of the Parables. Christ gave this Parable together with two of a similar nature upon receiving the reproach of the Pharisees because of His intimate and tender association with outcasts, winebibbers and sinners.

This beautiful trilogy, made up of The Prodigal Son, The Lost Coin and The Lost Sheep, has been interestingly described as representing not three separate and distinct stories but three united and continuous chapters in the soul drama of man. They are interblended like the three primary colors which merge in white light. The story of the Lost Coin represents the lower red ray, the story of the Lost Sheep typifies the yellow ray, and the Lost Boy the blue ray. Together they unite and are dissolved in the luminous radiance of the White Light of Spirit.

None can ever sink so low into degeneracy but that he can be lifted and transformed through the love of Christ. These three Parables beautifully exemplify His words: "I came to seek and to save that which is lost."

The Parable of the Prodigal Son contains the whole story of our human evolution. Within every individual are the two natures of contrary tendency, as Faust laments, represented in this Parable as the two sons. The Higher Self never fails. As the Father says, "Thou art ever with me; all that I have is thine." The younger son represents the lower nature, which in our present stage of evolution has taken a journey into a far country and there wasted its substance (life force) in riotous living. In that far country of materiality we all feed upon the husks with the swine. We wander as prodigal sons in the material world, far from the light of the Spirit, until, surfeited with the things of the world, we hear within the "still, small voice" which called Elijah and which is calling within the heart of every man and woman in the world today. This voice is never heard until the soul realizes with Paul that "things that are seen are temporal, but things that are unseen are eternal." It is then we realize the mighty famine that there is in the land. The spirit longs for its eternal home, and heeding the call within retraces its steps toward the Father's house. It has sorrowed enough, and in utter humility it confesses, in the words of the prodigal: "I am no more worthy to be called thy son; make me as one of thy hired servants." It is then that he is given the prodigal's joyous welcome as described by Luke.

Since the story of the prodigal son is the story of all mankind, it is found in varied forms in many religions. In a curious old book by Lambspring, a medieval alchemist, we find this passage: "When the son entered his Father's house, the Father took him to his heart and swallowed him out of excessive joy."

Albert Pike, in his Christian interpretation of the First Degree of the Masonic Blue Lodge, relates a similar story. It tells of Man who, after the fall, went wandering blindly in the darkness of war, famine, and pestilence, with feet naked and bleeding, until sorrow and suffering at length began to work a repentance and reformation in his heart. This brought him at last into the light of the Worshipful Master, the power of the Spirit within.

The work of the Earth Period is the redemption of the fallen nature within man, exemplified by Adam and Eve in the Garden of Eden story, and variously described throughout the different books of the Bible. The transmutation of the lower nature and the blending of the higher with the lower (the two sons of this Parable), correspond to the Marriage of the Bride and the Lamb of the Book of Revelation, and represent the perfected state which humanity will have attained at the end of the Earth Period. (The purpose of evolution is to raise even the lowest, and to make those who are spiritually dead alive again.)

The Parable of the Prodigal Son portrays the path of involution, by which egos descended from the World of Virgin Spirit to the physical world, where the awakening of the spirit turns involution to evolution. The divine powers within lead us beyond the plane of alternating life and death, and again we come to know the Eternal Life of the World of God. Hence the great rejoicing mentioned in the Parable over the return of one who has completed the earth-round and again entered his heavenly home, to be reunited with that higher self which has never at any time been absent from the bosom of the Father.

The Parable of the Prodigal Son also refers to the journey of the ego through its many embodiments upon the physical plane, as the Spirit makes its pilgrimage through matter. The nadir of materiality having been reached, the inherent divinity calls out to it to return to the Father's house, to know the joy of conscious communion with God. Then, as neophytes, we enter the straight path of Initiation, and to our amazement the Father meets us from afar off, for the great eternal love of God is ever waiting to gird about our incompleteness with His presence, our restlessness with His rest.

Parable of the Lost Sheep

In the Parable of the Lost Sheep the digits of the numbers ninety and nine total eighteen or nine, the number of all mankind. *All* must be eventually saved. No one can be permanently "lost," for each is part of God.

The one whom the Great Teacher bends down to help is the brave and dauntless aspirant to Initiation. Such a one always has the help and protection of the Masters of Wisdom, who have travelled this same way themselves. There is always much rejoicing in Heaven when any neophyte makes the grade which earns for him the blessed privilege of the consciously eternal life.

The Parable of the Rejected Corner Stone is symbolic of the Christian Mysteries, the highest initiatory rites which have ever been brought to earth. "The same is the head of the Corner." Its companion Parable is that of The Cruel Vinedressers, which depicts the coming of the great Christ Spirit and of the Initiate Messengers who preceded Him to prepare the way for Him.

The reception and treatment accorded these exalted Ones have its reflection in world conditions today. If humanity continues to fail in measuring up to their high teachings, the vineyard (earth) will be let out to other husbandmen, meaning another and more advanced life wave.

In the Parable of the Wise and Foolish Builders, Christ likens human life to a house builded either upon the sands of shifting emotions or upon the rock of spiritual understanding. In one instance the foundation is unstable, the goal of life correspondingly uncertain and insecure. The life (or house) built upon the rock of Spirit remains firm and steadfast and, though "the floods came and the winds blew, it fell not." The builder of such a house affirms with St. Paul, "None of these things (of the outer world) move me."

Those who have builded their houses upon the sands, the Master likens to children at play; as children who sit in the market place and pipe to one another, so He describes them. This picture remains an apt simile of the superficial, frivolous lives of the unthinking multitudes even of the present age.

The aspirant of the Mosaic Dispensation was admonished that "he that putteth his hand to the plow and turns back is not worthy of the Kingdom."

The same instruction is given by the Saviour in the Parable of the Empty House: again a grave warning against attempting to turn back to the life of the world after entering upon the Path.

After the rhythms of mind and body have been attuned to spirit vibrations, if one descends again into material living, the result is often both a physical and a mental derangement. The Master spoke truly when He said: "The last state of that man becometh worse than the first."

The chief requisite for discipleship, and also the principle obstacle to its successful attainment, the Supreme Teacher shows in the Parables of the Unfinished Work and the Great Renunciation.

Luke 14:26-27.

If any man cometh unto me, and hateth not his own father, and mother, and wife, and children, and brethren, and sisters, yea, and his own life also, he cannot be my disciple.

And whosoever doth not bear his own cross, and come after me, he cannot be my disciple.

The Master's words do not mean that we must hate our own beloved in a literal sense. He has reference to the living of the impersonal life. One's own become even dearer, but the affections are no longer circumscribed. All the world becomes one's home and every human being in it a brother.

The Path of Discipleship has been fittingly compared with the church steeple, narrowing toward the summit where the cross stands alone against the sky. This marks the supreme testing place of the aspirant. "This man began to build and was not able to finish," is said of many neophytes at this place.

The Master's words are explicit and allow of no compromise: "So therefore whosoever he be of you that renounceth not all that he hath, he cannot be my disciple."

The Parable of the Bond Servant is a challenge to the endurance, the loyalty and the unswerving allegiance of the disciple. In this Parable he is told that he is not to expect material compensations and worldly recognition for spiritual work. He will not sail into heaven on flowery beds of ease, as the old hymn goes, nor be attended by the adulation of thronging multitudes.

His compensations will be spiritual ones and recognition of his worth will be made upon the inner planes. Ridicule and persecution may follow his outer life as it did that of his Master. Will he be content with this? Again the challenge of renunciation, the challenge of discipleship, flames clear and high: "We have done that which it was our duty to do."

THE TEACHING OF REGENERATION

In the Parables of Regeneration are given the highest teachings of discipleship and the final testing upon the Path. Foremost among these is the Parable of the Barren Fig Tree.

Matthew 21:17-21.

And he left them, and went out of the city into Bethany; and he lodged there.

Now in the morning as he returned into the city, he hungered.

And when he saw a fig tree in the way, he came to it, and found nothing thereon, but leaves only, and said unto it, Let no fruit grow on thee henceforward for ever. And presently the fig tree withered away.

And when the disciples saw it, they marvelled, saying, How soon is the fig tree withered away!

Jesus answered and said unto them, Verily I say unto you, If ye have faith, and doubt not, ye shall not only do this which is done to the fig tree, but also if ye shall say unto this mountain, Be thou removed, and be thou cast into the sea, it shall be done.

It is a modern mystic who says: "Every city mentioned in the Bible is to be found in the heart of man, and every period of time mentioned in the Bible is now." The name Bethany means a house of dates or figs. Both fruits esoterically mean fructification, increase, and also symbolize the feminine principle of humanity. It becomes the Christ principle in man when his lower nature has been purified and his human or concrete mind spiritualized. It was in Bethany that our Saviour performed many of His wonderful works of loving service, and it was while lodging there that He raised Lazarus from the old life into the new, thus beginning an advanced epoch for our human life wave.

When He returned to the city He hungered—not for physical food, for He said, "I have food that ye know not of." But He hungered to help humanity, to assist it in the process of purification, and to raise the feminine principle which lies fallen within the nature of each and all.

The fig tree symbolizes the power of generation. The Lord of Love and Life would never have cursed any form of life, for He is a part of all that lives. He was speaking here to His Disciples, of the misuse of the power of generation and of its ultimate results. Generation is but a temporary phase of our present state of evolution. We know that the organs of generation will eventually atrophy, and that even now the male organ is separating from the body. When the seven spiritual centers awaken within the body, the heart and larynx will be the organs of generation. It was for this divine consummation of human power that Christ Jesus hungered as He went out of the city unto Bethany.

In the Parables of the Tares and of the Last Judgment, the Great Teacher is recapitulating all the experiences of an earth life and pointing to the impress made upon the soul which determines the path of progression or retrogression when through death it enters the inner planes.

The Last Judgment is the record of the life just ended, which has been impressed upon the individual Book of Life, the "seed atom" of the heart.

In some Parables Christ has given definite steps of occult development. In others He has contrasted the Way of Evolution (for the masses) and the Way of Initiation (for the few), and again He shows what the attainments of Initiation are.

In these closing Parables He stresses the fact that the most important of all teachings for all time is that teaching which we *live* in our daily intercourse with our fellow men. No amount of spiritual instruction will avail to give us the Kingdom unless we practice in our daily lives the precepts which the Masters have implanted in our minds. "By their fruits ye shall know them."

Sheep and goats belong astrologically to the Christian Mysteries. Capricorn (goat) is the Birth sign of the Master and Aries (sheep) the Resurrection sign. Christ's first Ministry occurred during the last quarter of the Arian Age. The second Ministry will perhaps take place in the Capricorn Age.

Syrian sheep were white (Aries) and goats black (Capricorn). It is the profundity and mystery of Capricorn which has been often associated with the darkness of evil and black death.

PARABLES OF INITIATION

Parable of the Wise and Foolish Virgins—Matthew 25:1-13.
Parable of the Great Supper—Luke 14:16-24.
Parable of the Wedding Garment—Matthew 22:11-14.
Parable of the Wedding of the King's Son—Matthew 22:2-10.

The Parable of the Ten Virgins was one of the teachings of Passion Week, the period when the most profound instructions were given to the inner circle of the Disciples. The virgins are awaiting the Bridegroom, who has been delayed, but when he comes, unexpectedly, at midnight—that most mystical hour of the soul's night!—five of them have no oil for their lamps. "And the foolish said unto the wise, Give us of your oil; for our lamps are going out."

The Virgins represent those who have found the path of discipleship and are ready for the deeper work that leads to liberation from the physical body, with freedom to function in the radiant golden wedding garment of the soul. Five is the number of the physical senses. Five are the nails which hold the foolish Virgins to the cross of matter, and these same five nails, when "pulled," bring the resurrection of a new life to those who are wise. The truly wise one eventually becomes a "five pointed star." "I am the Light of the world," proclaims the Supreme Master of the new Christian Mysteries. Some of the miracle or mystery plays of the thirteenth and fourteenth centuries were based upon this Parable.

The oil is the holy life force, the Christ Light within the body of the disciple. The dissipation of this force is the sin against the Holy Ghost, that sin which cannot be forgiven, but which must be expiated through lives of weakened and imperfect bodies, such as may be seen all about us today.

The foundation of all true esoteric teaching is based upon the conservation of the life force within the body. When this oil is lifted up the spine it awakens the pineal and the pituitary glands in the head, causing the third ventricle to glow with a lambent flame. In one who has attained to Sainthood, this light radiates as a halo around the head and envelops the body in an aura of golden light. It constitutes the lamp (or torch) which heralds the coming of the Bridegroom. "When the pupil is ready, the Master appears." The disciple is instructed how to liberate the spirit from the body, so that it may travel at will in "foreign countries" or, as the Parable describes it, "they that were ready went in with him to the marriage and the door was shut." Only to those who weave the wedding garment through living the spiritual life is the door thus opened. A sensitive optic nerve will give etheric vision, an extension of physical sight, but the uplifted sacred fire within the body above can awaken the dormant organs of the head and give the power of true spiritual vision. "Watch therefore, for ye know not the day nor the hour."

The foolish virgins are those who, while understanding these things, do not live the holy life, but waste their substance—and their time—in riotous living. Like Esau they sell their immortal birthright for a mess of pottage. Many are called, but few are chosen; all have the opportunity, but few will submit to the discipline. Hence the Master's rebuke: "Verily I say unto you, I know you not!"

Avicenna, the celebrated Arabian philosopher, says: "If we may get at the Fifth we have arrived at the end. Through polarity, or the marriage of the masculine and feminine [the soul and spirit of the wise virgin], four children are born, two boys [Fire and Air] and two girls [Water and Earth]." When these four elements are properly blended and united, or absorbed again by the One, the White Stone of Revelation is complete, as is the Great White Work of the alchemists and the wise virgins of the Parable, who go out to meet the Bridegroom and to help establish His new Kingdom, through regeneration, upon the earth.

If we carefully and reverently study the life story of the Master, Christ Jesus, as it is given to us by His Disciples, Matthew, Mark, Luke and John, we shall find that He has given us light upon every problem that we, as neophytes, can ever meet upon the Path. From Him we may learn how to attain that consciousness wherein the mind becomes Christed, wherein we no longer see and judge with our finite minds, but lift ourselves, through the spiritual exercise of adoration, above the more personal likes and dislikes based on the illusory half-truths presented by way of the bodily organs. Then we are able to sense the divinity in everything that lives; to see, in the words of Elizabeth Browning, "every bush afire with God." It is only as we approach a study of the Bible in this manner that the veil is lifted and we find the inner meaning of its teachings. "He who lives the life shall know the doctrine.'

Parable of the Great Supper

Perhaps none of the Master's lessons makes so universal an appeal as does the Parable of the Great Supper, because it is so pertinent to the daily problems which confront every human being, while its inner meaning takes us back to the first commandment given to Moses upon Mt. Sinai and repeated by the Master to His disciples: "Thou shalt have no other gods before me." This commandment is the keynote of the Parable. When this commandment has become the foundation stone of the life of the aspirant, it will no longer be difficult for him to live the spiritual life.

The Great Feast represents the opportunities of the spiritual life that have been spread so bountifully before us. The guests bidden represent humanity for whom Christ Jesus made His great sacrifice, and for whom He has opened the way: "Come, for all things are now ready."

"And they of one consent began to make excuse." These words are as true of man today as they were on the day they were written. Many are eager to read books of mysticism and to attend classes and lectures upon these subjects, but when the great testing time comes, when they are required to give up worldly pleasures and personal advantages, we hear the same voice that has echoed down through the years ever since the Master gave this Parable to the people, "I pray thee have me excused." Many who appear most enthusiastic in the beginning turn away from the beautiful teachings of esoteric Christianity when they are required to discard furs and give up meat and nicotine. Yet these are only the most elementary sacrifices on the way of spiritual progress, the merest beginnings on the Path that leads to the Table of the Great Feast. The privileged having rejected Him and having neglected so great an opportunity, the command comes, "Go out quickly . . . and bring . . . the poor, and the maimed . . . and the blind" referring to the fact that the Way of Initiation (the understanding of the inner mysteries of spiritual things) is no longer trod by the priestly caste alone. At the coming of Christ Jesus the veil of Initiation was rent so that all who made themselves worthy might enter into the Holy of Holies.

The statement in Luke 14:26: "If any man come to me, and hateth not his own father, . . . he cannot be my disciple," obviously does not mean, literally, that we must reject our family, but it does mean that no one can really progress upon the spiritual Path who permits any personality to come between him and his love of the things of the Spirit. This is one of the most subtle temptations the neophyte meets. In that wonderful story of spiritual unfoldment, *Parsifal,* this place on the Path is symbolized by the flower maidens who tempt Parsifal and endeavor to win him from his pursuit of the Holy Grail. It is not spiritual, however, to shirk any responsibility or any family obligation already incurred, for one who does this incurs a heavy debt of causation for the future, which may endure perhaps for many lives. He may then hear the words, "None of those men which were bidden shall taste of my supper."

Those who have attained unto a full realization of the meanings of the concluding words of the Parable of the Supper know that they refer to the difficult lesson of learning to bear the cross. As taught in the Parables of the Unfinished Work and the Great Renunciation (Luke 14:28-33) he must be prepared to pay the full cost of the spiritual adventure upon which he has launched himself, without complaint or quibbling.

We must learn to be in the world and yet not of it, to bear persecution and insult, to bear doubt, suspicion, and misunderstanding, and yet give only love in return. Christ's words are very simple and plain: "If any man hate not his own life also, he cannot be my disciple." But after we have suffered and endured, after we have made ourselves worthy to hear Him say, "Come, for all things are now ready," and to sit at the Great Supper beside Him (which means to partake of the spiritual joys of the celestial realms), then we shall know that our sorrows and renunciations were but seeming, for His infinite love and wisdom will return to us in a thousandfold measure that which we renounced for His sake.

Parable of the Marriage of the King's Son

Our last two Parables are contained in the one account in Matthew 22:2-14. There we find a story which includes two very important features of the spiritual life. What we have termed the Parable of the Wedding Robe is found in the last four verses of the story of the Marriage of the King's Son.

Matthew 22:2-14.

The kingdom of heaven is like unto a certain king, which made a marriage for his son,

And sent forth his servants to call them that were bidden to the wedding: and they would not come.

Again, he sent forth other servants, saying, Tell them which are bidden, Behold, I have prepared my dinner: my oxen and my fatlings are killed, and all things are ready; come unto the marriage.

But they made light of it, and went their ways, one to his farm, another to his merchandise:

And the remnant took his servants, and entreated them spitefully, and slew them.

But when the king heard thereof, he was wroth: and he sent forth his armies, and destroyed these murderers, and burned up their city.

Then saith he to his servants, The wedding is ready, but they which were bidden were not worthy.

Go ye therefore into the highways, and as many as ye shall find, bid to the marriage.

So these servants went out into the highways, and gathered together all as many as they found, both bad and good; and the wedding was furnished with guests.

And when the king came in to see the guests, he saw there a man which had not on a wedding garment:

And he saith unto him, Friend, how camest thou in hither not having a wedding garment? And he was speechless.

Then said the king to the servants, Bind him hand and foot, and take him away, and cast him into outer darkness; there shall be weeping and gnashing of teeth.

The Marriage of the King's Son is the story of life in the physical world. The light of Truth is unperceived by the masses and the servants, or those who dedicate themselves as heralds of Truth, are persecuted, while the world goes lightly on its way, one man to his farm, another to his merchandise: the things of the world are paramount. Few have any knowledge of the true mission of the Christ and fewer still have any conception of how to prepare for His return (symbolized in the Marriage Feast). Only those who have the wedding garment will meet Him when He comes, the great majority will be greeted with the rebuke: "Friend, how camest thou hither, not having a wedding garment?"

This wedding robe incident conceals a formula for the Mystic Marriage Rites. The wedding robe is the soul body fashioned of the blue and gold of the two higher ethers which are attracted by the high aspiration and pure and holy living. This etheric robe is part of the spiritual equipment of every true disciple. Arrayed in it he can visit other planes and foreign lands as an Invisible Helper. The *wearing of the robe* marks one as a true Initiate. Only such pioneers in spiritual attainment will be worthy to welcome the Christ "in the air" (the New Air Age).

But great danger attends any attempt to enter the inner planes unprepared, as those do who take "short cuts," not having built a soul body through spiritual living. Insanity, and oftentimes death, follows upon such a course. The unfortunate pseudo-Initiate is literally cast into outer darkness where there is much wailing and lamentation. Holy things are for the holy. Any desecration of them brings its own deserved punishment.

Those, however, who weave the Soul Garment through purity, chastity and loving, selfless service, are here and now fitting themselves to become the pioneers of a new race which shall live and reign with the Christ in a New Heaven and a New Earth. Only such are worthy to be called Christian, or followers of Christ, for this term, when rightly understood, applies not merely to the Christian sect as such, but to those of every race and nation who are living a pure and holy life so that the wedding garment is in the making. The Christ came as the World Saviour, not to replace other great Teachers, but to supplement and extend their work. Many biblical teachings are duplications of the Ancient Wisdom and are to be found in other Bibles also. The story of Joseph is a legend of Initiation belonging to the earliest Egyptian Mystery temples; so is the Parable of the Prodigal Son and the Resurrection of Lazarus. The same resurrection theme is paralleled in the oldest of Hermetic and Masonic ceremonials and rituals.

The story of Daniel, and also Ezekiel's vision, are found in the Fire Mysteries of Persia. Many of the works and words of the Christ, including the record of the Disciples, the Birth, Baptism, Transfiguration, Resurrection, and Ascension are duplicated in the lives of other World Saviours and their disciples. The Revelation of John conceals the formulae of the Grecian Temple Mysteries.

Any unprejudiced student of comparative religion must admit these facts. The work of the New Age Bible interpreters is not to conceal, but to reveal these truths. It is not for them to seek for differences between the teachings of the Christ and other World Teachers that tend to disparage the latter, but to look for the deep fundamental harmony which is the basis of all their work, and to proclaim that each in turn was an expression of the Cosmic Christ, preparing the Way for the coming of the Lord, the World Saviour who was to become the Planetary Spirit of the earth.

This Cosmic Christ is the basis of all spiritual progress, but His truth is revealed in an ever ascending scale as man progresses. The secret teaching of one age becomes common knowledge in the next. This fact is evident when studying the Sun's precessional passage through the twelve signs of the Zodiac, which mark progressive astrological cycles of development. As such, at some future time, they will be so considered in the study of comparative religion. Before the coming of Christ, the inner teachings were all termed Lunar Mysteries, because man then received his spiritual light from the Solar Logos only as it was reflected by way of the Lunar Race Spirits, or gods. Hence, in many early religions the Moon was worshipped, it being considered as superior to the Sun. It will be found that these religions were given during the age that the Sun by precession passed through a feminine sign, Taurus. It was then that Isis was worshipped as the mother goddess of Egypt and Astarte as that of Babylon.

All Lunar Mysteries deal with an external ceremonial describing the birth, life, death, and resurrection of spirit in its pilgrimage through matter. This is the ceremonial used in the Masonic lodge in connection with Hiram Abiff, the widow's son, and in the Church in connection with the life story of Christ Jesus. Both of these ceremonials are fragments of the Mystery teachings.

However, when the Christ came to earth, He brought a deeper teaching belonging to esotericism. In mystic terms, He rent the veil hanging before the Temple door. No longer are priests essential to the ritual or ceremonial. The deeper truths of the Christian Initiations are received directly by the man himself; the spiritual force reaches him direct from the Sun, for the Christ has opened the Way. The early Christians were followers and demonstrators of this Way, the Path of the Solar Mysteries. Their work parallels the preceding teachings, but on an ever ascending scale. Thus the events in the life of the Christ outline the identical steps of other Saviours, but with this important difference: Initiation is no longer an external process, but an inner one. Every event described in the life of the Christ becomes an inner workable power or faculty within the body and life of the Initiate. He becomes a Christed one; a beloved son in whom the Father is well pleased.

Everyone found worthy to receive the deeper Christian teachings becomes a child of the King and a brother of all who have attained, and Angels chant for him that same mystic chorus: "Peace on earth and good will among men." When a sufficient number of men shall have been thus reborn, the new regime of the Christ will be established upon the earth.

CHAPTER III

Christian Initiatory Teachings

The Calling of the Twelve

Before every important step that He took, the Christ went for a time into the silence of the desert. He knew that His work was to be accomplished within the short space of three years. He therefore chose the twelve most advanced of His followers to carry on the work of disseminating the new religion when He had gone. Immediately after choosing the Twelve, He delivered the Sermon on the Mount, His most sublime public utterance.

After conflict, trial, and temptation such as no other has ever known before or since, He returned from the wilderness to share with men the divine realization which was His. The physical body of Jesus was as a tool in His hand. Every feeling and emotion was subservient to His dual powers of spiritualized will and dynamic love. He returned to the world to bring to it the new message of redemptive Christianity. Through perfect self-control and an absolute dominion over Himself, Jesus the Christ performed works the world calls miracles. The fundamental tenet of His teaching is contained in His words, "The kingdom of God is within you." When we discover this kingdom within ourselves, we shall find it also in others, and in all things about us. *The Path of seeking must be the way of love.*

From the multitudes who surrounded Him, He chose the Twelve Disciples who made up His inner circle, among whom were several who had received esoteric instruction from John the Baptist in preparation for the call from the Messiah. These chosen Disciples were not ignorant fishermen as many have supposed. They were men whose esoteric training and attainments proved them to be ready for receiving and teaching the deeper truths of the Christian religion.

It was customary in the time of Christ for every rabbi to earn his livelihood at some gainful employment, even manual labor, in order that he might teach spiritual things free of charge.

Thus Jesus was taught carpentry and building. He was a practical as well as a spiritual Mason. Paul was a tent maker. In Hebrew eyes there was no indignity connected with common labor. It was the over-intellectual Greeks who despised all manual employment. While revering the beautiful works of the sculptors, painters, and builders they despised the workers who produced them! Incredible as it seems, the divine Phidias was looked down upon by Athenian aristocracy. Unfortunately, this blemish upon the otherwise lofty Grecian temperament has been reflected in Greek translations of the Gospels, giving us the impression that Jesus and the Twelve were ignorant laborers. While it well may be that not all were brilliant philosophers in the formal Greek sense, it does not follow that they were not highly cultured in the Hebrew wisdom with its marvelous Kabbala and astronomical theosophy inherited from ancient Chaldea whence came Abraham.

In America today we may observe a similar misapprehension. The brilliantly educated European scholar comes to our shores with but a limited English vocabulary and is ofttimes greeted as an "ignorant foreigner." The Hebrew Disciples of Jesus must have so appeared to Grecian eyes.

Andrew was the first chosen of the Twelve. He never became one of the innermost circle, but won special recognition through bringing his brother Peter to Christ. It is a wonderful privilege to carry the message of the Spirit to others. Both James and John were quiet and reserved, but possessed an intensity which caused the Teacher Himself to call them sons of thunder. This intensity accounted in part for the martyrdom of James who was the first Disciple to follow his Master to the Cross. A similar intensity, but softened by divine love, placed John at the head of the Disciples in spiritual attainment.

Philip, being materially minded and spiritually undiscerning, was slow to accept the divinity of our Lord. His inseparable companion, Nathanael, was a mystic and a dreamer. Christ Jesus, at His first meeting with Nathanael, promised that he should see the wonders of heaven; He made it clear, in fact, that Nathanael was to attain through Initiation, an experience that was gloriously fulfilled in his later life. Matthew was the fifth and the last of the Disciples to be chosen separately. The remaining seven were called out just prior to the Sermon on the Mount.

Mark 3:14-19.

And he ordained twelve that they should be with him, and that he might send them forth to preach.

And to have power to heal sicknesses, and to cast out devils:

And Simon he surnamed Peter.

And James the son of Zebedee, and John the brother of James; and he surnamed them Boanerges, which is, The sons of thunder:

And Andrew, and Philip, and Bartholomew, and Matthew, and Thomas, and James the son of Alphaeus and Thaddaeus, and Simon the Canaanite,

And Judas Iscariot who also betrayed him; and they went into an house.

The name Peter in the Egyptian language meant "the opened eye." In Greek, Peter (petra) means rock. One of the utterances of the Master was, "upon this rock I will build my church." A stone is universally used as a symbol of the Initiate. Initiation is the foundation of religion and is in that sense the rock upon which the Church is established—a fact to be generally recognized in the coming age.

Jerome states that the Jude of Luke, Lebbeus of Matthew, and Thaddeus of Mark, all refer to the same Disciple. This Disciple did not become prominent until after the Ascension.

Simon, Zelotes, belonged to the nationalist, patriotic sect of theZealots whose aim was to throw off the Roman yoke, restore the freedom of the Jewish State and then conquer the world under the banner of the Messiah, with fire and sword. Simon "the Zealot" was to learn, however, that the most effective weapon of all is the power of the Christ love and that it is the only weapon with which to achieve world conquest.

Information relative to Thomas is found chiefly in the Gospel of John and in certain apocryphal documents. Thomas was slow to believe. He was pessimistic and despondent. Yet so intense was his devotion to the Master that he was willing to die for Him. He was a skeptic yet he was filled with earnestness and aspiration, and later became one of the most glorious of the Disciples. He was particularly revered by the philosophically trained Gnostics.

Judas Iscariot was the man of mystery, the betrayer of the Christ. He came from Kerioth, which belonged to the tribe of Judah. This tribe is governed by Leo, the heart sign, and symbolizes one in whom the love nature is linked with the sense life. Judas portrays the state of the average man who daily betrays the Christ, the Higher Self, within. Each of the twelve Disciples represents a specific faculty or attribute of man himself: Judas, therefore, will play his role in human evolution until such time as the lower nature of the race shall be redeemed. He destroyed himself, as all evil ultimately destroys itself, and was replaced by Matthias, the symbol of the redeemed man of the New Age and the new race.

Judas Iscariot Replaced by Matthias

All that is known of Matthias is that he was in constant attendance upon Christ Jesus almost from the beginning of His Ministry. He is said to have been one of the seventy disciples sent forth by the Master. He and Barnabas were evidently the most highly advanced of the seventy, as they were the two recommended to take Judas' place. The choice eventually fell upon Matthias.

Eligibility for elevation to the rank of discipleship was determined, Peter states in Acts 1:22, according as one had taken the Initiations taught by John the Baptist, had followed the three years' work given by the Christ and had finally been accounted worthy to be among the Elect who participated in the Resurrection Rites.

An apocryphal gospel written under the name of Matthias is quoted by Clement of Alexandria in his *Traditions.* He is said to have met martyrdom circa 61-54 A. D. in Cappadocia.

Since so little is known of Matthias, the following legend about him is of interst as at least suggesting the course of his life and work.

When the Disciples were allotted the countries in which they were to work, it fell to Matthias to go to the land of the man eaters. Every stranger who entered this country was laid hold of and his eyes put out, after which he was made to drink a drug prepared by sorcery whereby the heart was altered and the mind deranged.

Such was the cruel treatment accorded to Matthias when he came to this people. However, the magical drug had no effect upon him and as he prayed his sight was restored. Jesus then appeared to him in prison and said: "Be of good courage, Matthias, for I shall deliver thee from all danger. Remain here twenty-seven days for the edification of all souls, and after that I shall send Andrew to lead thee forth from prison, and all who hear thee shall be saved." Then Matthias began to sing and to instruct other prisoners in the Mysteries of Christ.

When the twenty-seven days were fulfilled since Matthias was imprisoned, Jesus appeared in the country where Andrew was teaching and bade him take his disciples and go to the rescue of Matthias. The boat in which Andrew and his disciples sailed, the Angels who were their companions, the Master who was their pilot, and the visions of Paradise granted them, are in part descriptive of the experiences of Invisible Helpers upon the inner planes, in part a lesson on the Divine Immanence.

As Andrew and his disciples slept, the legend continues, the Master commanded the Angels to carry them to the city where Matthias was confined. Andrew made the sign of the cross upon the prison gates which then opened of their own accord. Entering, Andrew found Matthias singing, and they greeted one another with a holy kiss. Then as Andrew and Matthias prayed, they laid their hands upon the faces of the blind men in prison and their sight was restored and also their human reason. There were two hundred and seventy men and forty-nine women whom Andrew and Matthias released from prison on that day.

All were rendered invisible as they left the city by the eastern gate, pausing there to partake of nourishment from a great fig tree. Andrew then commanded a great cloud to descend, to take up Matthias and the disciples of Andrew, and to set them down upon a distant mountain where Peter was teaching.

The beautiful ministry of Invisible Helpers is thus clearly revealed in holy legend as it was known to the earliest Christians through the personal instruction of Christ's own Disciples.

The Twelve Disciples are of varied types, for they serve as prototypes of humanity in general and indicate thereby that there is room and work for all in the Master's vineyard.

Qualities and Attributes of the Twelve Disciples

Peter is the man of action; John, the man of prayer; Thomas, the skeptic; James, the aspiring; Nathanael, the dreamer; James, the methodical; Andrew, the humble; Philip, the commonplace; Thaddeus, the courageous; Matthew, the servant of Rome; Simon, the rebel against Rome; and Judas, the betrayer.

Twelve is the most important number of the New Testament, for twelve is the perfect number of Deity in a cycle of expression.

The new Holy City as portrayed in Revelation has twelve gates that are never closed. With the ending of the cycle of twelve a new manifestation of life begins on a higher round. Thus the incidents in the life of every Teacher who brings a cosmic message to humanity parallel the passage of the Sun through the twelve zodiacal signs.

There always have been twelve physical and twelve spiritual powers manifesting in humanity, corresponding to twelve spiritual centers in the body, which, when awakened, are symbolized by twelve lights, or the "flowers that bloom upon the cross." These centers are to be awakened as man progresses into higher phases of development; they represent the divine consummation of God's great plan for the entire human family at the end of the present Earth Period.

The following table correlates the Twelve Disciples with attributes of character and with the twelve signs of the Zodiac.

JAMES—Hope—Aries.
ANDREW—Strength—Taurus.
THOMAS—Doubt—Gemini.

NATHANAEL—Intuition—Cancer.
JUDAS—Passion—Leo.
JAMES (Son of Alpheus)—Method—Virgo.

THADDEUS—Courage—Libra.
JOHN—Regeneration—Scorpio.
PHILIP—Spiritual Knowledge—Sagittarius.

SIMON—Enthusiasm—Capricorn.
MATTHEW—Spiritual Will—Aquarius.
PETER—Faith—Pisces.

The twelve cosmic principles manifesting in the universe may be correlated with the Twelve Disciples thus:

1. Will—James—Hope.
2. Wisdom—John—Love.
3. Activity—Peter—Faith.

{ The perfect Trinity: "Now abideth Faith, Hope, and Love. But the greatest of these is Love."

4. Contraction—Thomas—Doubt.
5. Expansion—James, the Less—Growth of Spirit.
6. Attraction—Andrew—Strength.
7. Repulsion—Simon—Zeal.

8. Crystallization—Matthew—Custom.
9. Construction—Thaddeus—Courage.
10. Destruction—Judas—Passion.
11. Addition or Increase—Nathanael—Intuition—Imagination.
12. Reflection (As above, so below)—Philip—Spiritual Knowledge.

THE SERMON ON THE MOUNT

The Initiatory Key

The Sermon on the Mount holds a place in the New Testament corresponding to that of the Ten Commandments in the Old. The Ten Commandments are external laws imposed by external authority which man was taught to obey under the whiplash of fear. The Sermon on the Mount contains the law of love which man must inscribe within his heart and write upon his forehead, to use the familiar phrase of Paul. The general theme of the sublime message is *Love,* and the thoughts which the Master expressed in it formed the groundwork of His teaching and His living. Humanity has not begun to live these spiritual precepts because it has not yet learned that *the greatest of all powers is love.* Christ Jesus, the Lord of Love, demonstrated this power in His every word and deed while upon the earth. We can follow in His steps only as we, too, learn to live the life of love.

"Love thy neighbor as thyself;" "Seek ye first the kingdom of God;" "Be ye perfect, even as your Father which is in heaven is perfect;" "Blessed are the pure in heart for they shall see God." All these admonitions require the cultivation of the transcendent "power of love" for their successful accomplishment. Christ explained to His Disciples that in order to attain unto this state of perfection they must learn to cultivate the active qualities of humility, sympathy, compassion and purity, together with an intense desire for righteousness and courage even to suffer martyrdom. How well the Twelve chosen to be nearest Him followed the instruction given them on that Midsummer Day may be judged from the fact that, with the possible exception of John and Judas, each one went, after Him, to a martyr's death upon the cross. They learned the literal meaning of the words, "Greater love hath no man than this, that a man lay down his life for his friends."

"Do good to them that hate you, bless them that curse you, pray for them that despitefully use you." This is an injunction of the Christ that has been called impossible of fulfillment. It requires an utter renunciation of self, a complete self-mastery, and the awakening and functioning of the power of love as the dominant keynote of the life: a lofty ideal which only those wholly consecrated to the spiritual life are able to achieve. We call ourselves and our nation Christian; the degree to which we are entitled to be so designated may be determined by measuring our Christianity against the standard given us by the Christ.

"But whosoever shall smite thee on thy right cheek, turn to him the other also." Resist not evil; think not of the wrong suffered but of the course of action that will best help the wrongdoer. If punishment is necessary its motive must always be remedial and never tinged with revenge. Love must point the way and justice ever be tempered with mercy, else it ceases to be justice.

"And if any man take away thy coat, let him have thy cloak also." This means helpfulness—the active expression of benevolence. "Give to him that asketh thee." The gift need not necessarily be a material one; understanding, encouragement or loving kindness may be the greater gift. Help a man to help himself. It has been said: "A beggar is a challenge to the highest that is within us." It is for us to help the beggar to rise out of his beggary, and to teach him to find that divine power within himself with which to overcome poverty and all negative conditions that hamper the expression of the spirit within. Such a gift is of all the most priceless.

"Of him that taketh thy goods, ask them not again." There can be no quarrel if only one person is belligerent. All difficulties are to be settled out of court if possible; this done, let there be no bitterness to act as new causation for a debt to be liquidated in this or future lives. Bitterness creates a tie that binds man with man in future entanglements.

"All things whatsoever ye would that men should do unto you, do ye even so unto them." This is the most precious of all the sayings in this sublime Sermon on the Mount; it sets the standard for living the Christ life. *We are true disciples of the Christ only when we really live the Golden Rule.*

"Give and it shall be given unto you." If our consciousness radiates only truth, beauty, love and harmony, only such qualities will return to us. The vibratory power of spiritual qualities is built into the archetype in the Heaven worlds, and operates to give back to us again exactly what we put into it. "God is love, yet God is law."

The Sermon on the Mount is found in its most complete form in the Gospel of Matthew, chapters five to seven inclusive. These chapters might well be used for the daily study and meditation of every esoteric aspirant regardless of affiliation or belief.

There are many speculations regarding the second coming of Christ. Esotericism teaches that *the Christ will return only when humanity has learned to put into practical demonstration in daily life the great spiritual truths expressed in the Sermon on the Mount. Only then shall we be ready to "meet Him in the air,"* the place of attainment.

The raising of the daughter of Jairus, the healing of the demoniac boy, the stilling of the storm and the multiplication of the loaves and fishes were among the important works of the Master during the early part of His ministry. Aside from their interest as miracles, so-called, each one of these events holds also an esoteric meaning pertaining to Initiation and to the awakening of a larger spiritual consciousness.

THE MYSTERY OF THE SUMMER SOLSTICE

There is a planetary entity which is built by the thoughts and deeds of humanity. As man finds the path of redemption through chastity, the body of earth is correspondingly purified and refined. The earth's ultimate destiny is to become a ball of light floating in a sea of golden ether. The "redemption" of the earth, its future status, position and function, constitutes part of the work belonging to the exalted ninth degree of the Lesser Mysteries. This degree is celebrated on Midwinter and Midsummer nights; in fact, it is not possible to observe the celebration at any other time. The solstices mark the time when the earth's vibration is highest and when the cosmic rays of the Christ life are either entering or being withdrawn from it—the former occurring at the Winter Solstice and the latter at the Summer Solstice.

Christ, the Grand Hierophant of these Mysteries, after having called the Twelve, gave His Mysteries on Midsummer Day as the foundation work of the New Age religion, the fragments of which were gathered together in the Sermon on the Mount. The Great Work was permeated with the spirit of love, unity and harmony which emanates from the home world of the Christ. Consequently, to such as have not touched the Christ world of unified consciousness the Sermon on the Mount seems illogical, sentimental and impractical. But to such as have contacted the Christ realm it strikes the very keynote of the true Christian dispensation.

Matthew 5:1-2.

And seeing the multitudes, he went up into a mountain; and when he was set, his disciples came unto him; and he opened his mouth and taught them.

"He went up into a mountain." This was the mountain of spiritual consciousness, the inner planes where are located all true Mystery Temples. Churches, schools, study groups—organizations of any kind on the physical plane—are but preparatory agencies which aim to fit disciples for entry into the deeper spiritual work. The spiritual work itself, however, lies beyond their scope. No man becomes an Initiate by merely joining this or that body; but when he has prepared himself properly an esoteric teacher or emissary from a Mystery Temple approaches him. At this point he may be said to have "graduated" from the preparatory agency with its exoteric teachers and instruction although he may, in a spirit of humility, continue work with that group in order to serve those less advanced than himself.

He is not yet an Initiate though he has been *called out* by his esoteric Teacher; he has, so to speak, matriculated in the University of Spirit where the course of work occupies thousands of years and uncounted lifetimes. Through continued work he eventually qualifies for Initiation.

In the Christ story this is the time when *the disciple follows the Master up into the mountain.* The body is no longer a prison house. He is free to work with the Christ on the inner planes, as a younger brother may work with an elder one who instructs him and supervises his labors.

Such inner-plane work given to pioneers of one age becomes the established religion for the masses of the succeeding age. Thus, through spiritual evolution or progression, God is constantly revealing wider and larger vistas of His plan for the ultimate destiny of man.

Only those who were able to follow the Master into the high place received the great revelation on this holy Midsummer Day when the very desire currents of the earth were stilled beneath the great outflooding of the White Light of the Christ life.

All of the most important works of the Master bear both an inner and an outer significance. The masses were not ready for the inner meanings of the Sermon on the Mount; they are not even now able to receive it *with the heart.* Only intellectually does the twentieth century man accede to its precepts. The Gospel of Matthew makes it plain that this teaching was not for the multitudes, as the following passages also indicate:

Matthew 7:28-29 — 8:1.

And it came to pass, when Jesus had ended these sayings, the people were astonished at his doctrine: For he taught them as one having authority, and not as the scribes.

When he was come down from the mountain, great multitudes followed him.

"He taught as one having authority, not as the scribes." That is, He taught from experience, not from note, as do those who can merely repeat what others have said.

THE BEATITUDES

Matthew 5:3-12.

1. *Blessed are the poor in spirit: for theirs is the kingdom of heaven.*

Keynote: *Humility,* signifying the Christ power to control all manifestations and phenomena of the earth.

2. *Blessed are they that mourn: for they shall be comforted.*

Keynote: *Comfort.* Mourning pertains only to the present stage of manifestation. Man's eventual elevation to the Christ consciousness will bring that great peace which passeth all understanding.

3. *Blessed are the meek: for they shall inherit the earth.*

Keynote: *Meekness* or *Impersonality,* that complete renunciation of self which is won through *Gethsemane* and which later lifts one to the consciousness of the *Ascension.*

4. *Blessed are they which do hunger and thirst after righteousness: for they shall be filled.*

Keynote: *Putting God first,* the power of the superman or adept.

5. *Blessed are the merciful: for they shall obtain mercy.*

Keynote: *Mercy,* a divine compassion which manifests on all planes in a unity or oneness of all life.

6. *Blessed are the pure in heart: for they shall see God.*

Keynote: *Purity through transmutation,* the Christ within awakened in order to contact the Christ without.

7. *Blessed are the peacemakers: for they shall be called the children of God.*

Keynote: *Harmony,* which is the underlying law of all constructive works of adeptship.

8. *Blessed are they which are persecuted for righteousness' sake: for theirs is the kingdom of heaven.*

Keynote: *Persecution.* Most subtle of all tests, and one passed so gloriously by all the Disciples excepting Judas.

9. *Blessed are ye, when men shall revile you, and persecute you, and say all manner of evil against you falsely, for my sake. Rejoice and be exceeding glad, for great is your reward in heaven: for so persecuted they the prophets which were before you.*

Keynote: *Self-mastery.* Self-control is the keyword given to every disciple of the Christian Mysteries. In the words of Solomon: "Better . . . [is] he that ruleth his spirit than he that taketh a city."

THE BEATITUDES AND THEIR PLANETARY CORRELATIONS

1. *Blessed are the poor in spirit for theirs is the kingdom of heaven.*

Mercury. Humility through the Christed mind.

2. *Blessed are they that mourn: for they shall be comforted.*

Venus. Love is the great antidote for evil. "Perfect love casteth out fear." Faith and Hope are combined in Love.

3. *Blessed are the meek: for they shall inherit the earth.*

Moon. Attracts and increases. The meek are impersonal. "He who loses his life for my sake shall find it."

4. *Blessed are they which do hunger and thirst after righteousness: for they shall be filled.*

Uranus. A divine yearning for the highest. Passion becomes compassion; self-love becomes altruism; the goal is all for one and one for all. The sole object of life is to make the ideal real.

5. *Blessed are the merciful: for they shall obtain mercy.*

Jupiter. Knows only mercy, charity, beneficence. "Whatsoever a man soweth, that shall he also reap." The Jupiterian ray of mercy and compassion attracts to itself benefits of like nature.

6. *Blessed are the pure in heart: for they shall see God.*

Mars. The principal work of Mars is transmutation. The red of the lower nature becomes the pure gold of the higher. The only key to heaven is purity, chastity. Only a life of purity makes it possible for the spiritual centers to flower upon the cross of the body.

7. *Blessed are the peacemakers: for they shall be called the children of God.*

Sun. The Sun is the Christ vibration upon the earth: only as the Sun or Christ is awakened within ourselves will we come into perfect peace.

8. *Blessed are they who are persecuted for righteousness' sake: for theirs is the kingdom of heaven.*

Saturn. The place where the Path becomes narrow like the church steeple. Saturn is the whiplash of sorrow for the neophyte; the thorn-crown becomes the halo of radiance only through Initiation.

9. *Blessed are ye when men shall revile you and persecute you, and shall say all manner of evil against you falsely, for my sake.*

Neptune. Planet of divinity. The higher we aspire the more likely we are to be misunderstood by others.

10. *Rejoice and be exceeding glad; for great is your reward in heaven: for so persecuted they the prophets which were before you.*

The synthesis of the highest qualities of all planets. The attainment of man at the end of the present earth cycle. This path leads to the Great Lord of Compassion. It is here we shall meet Him face to face.

THE LORD'S PRAYER

The Lord's Prayer, or the law of prayer, is the perfect prayer. It contains a sevenfold, a ninefold and a twelvefold meaning.

Matthew 6:9-13.

After this manner therefore pray ye:
Our Father which art in heaven, Hallowed by thy name;
Thy kingdom come. Thy will be done in earth as it is in heaven.
Give us this day our daily bread.
And forgive us our debts, as we forgive our debtors.
And lead us not into temptation, but deliver us from evil: For thine is the kingdom and the power, and the glory forever. Amen.

The Disciples and early Christians used this prayer in the following manner to attract the beneficient down-pouring of the great celestial Hiearchies.

1. *Our Father which art in heaven, Hallowed by thy name:* Invocation of the masculine pole of Spirit, *Will,* through the planet of divinity, Neptune, to the Hierarchy Aries, who gave the first initial impulse of motion.

2. *Thy Kingdom Come:* Invocation of the feminine pole of Spirit, *Wisdom,* through the planet of intuition, Uranus, to the Hierarchy Taurus, who gave the initial impulse of form.

3. *Thy will be done on earth as it is in heaven:* Invocation of the two poles in unison or harmonious *activity,* through Mercury, the planet of wisdom, to the Hierarchy Gemini, who gave the archetype or pattern of the first blending of life with form.

4. *Give us this day our daily* (supernatural) *bread:* Invocation of the feminine pole of Spirit through the Moon, the planet of fecundation, to the Hierarchy Cancer, who awakened the image-forming power in man.

5. *Forgive us our debts:* Invocation of the masculine pole of Spirit through the Sun, the planet of light, to the Hierarchy Leo, the Lords of Flame, who awakened the will power in spirit.

6. *As we forgive our debtors:* Invocation of the biune Powers in unison through Mercury, the planet of wisdom, to the Hierarchey Virgo, who gave, through purity, the pattern of the etheric body.

7. *Lead us not into temptation:* The invocation of the desire nature through Venus, the planet of love, to the Hierarchy Libra, who gave, through love, the pattern of the desire body.

8. *Deliver us from evil:* The invocation of the physical body, through Mars, the planet of action, to the Hierarchy Scorpio, who gave the first archetype of form to evolving man.

9. *Thine is the kingdom:* The invocation of mind through Jupiter, the planet of aspiration, to the Hierarchy Sagittarius, who gave to man the power of mind.

10. *The power and the glory.*

11. *Forever and ever.*

12. *Amen.*

The threefold conclusion forms the invocation of the triune spirit of man to the Hierarchies of Capricorn, Aquarius and Pisces through the planets Saturn, Uranus and Jupiter.

Amen completes the series and records the blending of the four elements of fire, water, air and earth, or the amalgamation of the essence of passion, emotion, mind and body. It points to the perfected man at the end of the present Earth Period.

Instructions in the Transcending of Physical Laws

MIRACLE OF THE LOAVES AND FISHES

The coming of Christ Jesus to humanity inaugurated a new epoch in world evolution.

Freedom may be considered the prime requisite of spiritual and evolutionary development. The various life waves rise in an harmoniously ascending scale consonant with the development of freedom. The plant kingdom possesses a larger measure of freedom than the mineral. In the animal kingdom the power of freedom is increased over the plant. In the human life wave the degree of freedom is greatly increased over that of the animal. As Browning sings:

> *All tended to mankind,*
> *And man produced, all has its end thus far:*
> *But in completed man begins anew*
> *A tendency to God.*

The supreme Master came proclaiming the glories of this greater freedom by word and deed: "Ye shall know the truth and the truth shall make you free." He pointed to the full attainment of Initiate capacity, when the work of the Disciples should equal and even transcend His own: *"Greater* things than these shall ye do," He himself declared.

Perhaps the outstanding demonstration of human freedom as He taught it is found in the setting aside of ordinary physical law and the operation of higher-plane forces. These operations are known to the uninitiated as miracles.

In the performance of these miracles the Christ put into operation certain higher laws of nature, generally unknown, which will in the New Age be as common to our experience as the laws belonging to the physical universe with which we are already familiar.

Each age introduces a new step leading toward ultimate emancipation of the Divine Man made in the image and likeness of God.

From the finite to infinity,
And from man's dust to God's divinity,
Take all in a word: the truth in God's breast,
Lies trace for trace upon ours impressed,
Though He is so bright and we are so dim,
We are made in His image to witness Him.

—*Browning.*

Luke 9:12-17.

And when the day began to wear away, then came the twelve and said unto him, Send the multitude away that they may go into the towns and country round about, and lodge, and get victuals: for we are here in a desert place.

But he said unto them, Give ye them to eat. And they said, We have no more but five loaves and two fishes; except we should go and buy meat for all this people.

For they were about five thousand men. And he said to his disciples. Make them sit down by fifties in a company.

And they did so, and made them all sit down.

Then he took the five loaves and the two fishes, and looking up to heaven, he blessed them, and brake, and gave to the disciples to set before the multitude.

And they did eat, and were all filled; and there was taken up of fragments that remained to them twelve baskets.

The miracles of Christ Jesus, when interpreted esoterically, are found to be in perfect accord with nature's occult or hidden laws, though this is not immediately evident to one whose field of investigation is limited to the phenomenal three-dimensional world. The knowledge of, and power to manipulate, forces governed by higher metaphysical laws constitutes Mastership. Only an Initiate of high attainment can operate the forces by means of which material things can be multiplied.

The body of the earth, when studied clairvoyantly, is found to be of a layer-like formation. Its several strata correspond with layers of forces surrounding the earth, which are reflected in the planetary body. As the candidate progresses along the path of illumination he acquires the ability to investigate these different earth layers at the same time that he is working with their corresponding forces in the outer envelopes of the planet. When he has finished the ninth of the Lesser Mysteries, he has passed through the nine earth layers and is ready to meet the Christ face to face in the very center or heart of the earth, and there know Him as He is. He is then master over all the physical and superphysical laws operating on this planet, and is no longer subject to the limitations of physical existence. He has forged far beyond the present state of human evolution and become a superman. As Matthew says, "The invaders (pioneers) have seized on the kingdom of heaven and taken it by storm."

The Christ, when feeding the multitudes, used the law pertaining to the eighth or atomistic layer of the earth. The forces and powers of this world are reflected in the atomistic stratum of the earth even as objects are reflected in a clear pool. In this sphere the patterns of all created things exist, and one who can control the forces operating here can multiply a thousandfold at will any already existent object. The forces in the atomistic stratum are not creative (that function belongs to a yet higher sphere); they are capable of multiplication only. The occultist must always have a nucleus with which to operate; upon this nucleus he concentrates the feminine, or image building faculty of Spirit, working directly through the fourth or water stratum which is the correlative of the fourth outer envelope of the earth known as the lower mental world, which is the home of the archetypal forces that bring all abstract ideas into form. Through the exertion of the will or the masculine faculty, the physical atoms are marshalled into molds or patterns and the physical nucleus is increased at will. This was the procedure used by the great Master when He multiplied the loaves and fishes..

Mark 8:1-9.

In those days the multitude being very great, and having nothing to eat, Jesus called his disciples unto him and saith to them,

I have compassion on the multitude, because they have now been with me three days, and have nothing to eat;

And if I send them away fasting to their own homes, they will faint by the way; for divers of them came from afar.

And his disciples answered him, From whence can a man satisfy these men with bread here in the wilderness?

And he asked them, How many loaves have ye? And they said, seven.

And he commanded the people to sit down on the ground. And he took the seven loaves, and gave thanks, and brake, and gave to his disciples to set before them; and they did set them before the people.

And they had a few small fishes, and he blessed, and commanded to set them also before them.

So they did eat and were filled; and they took up of the broken meat that was left seven baskets.

And they that had eaten were about four thousand; and he sent them away.

To wield the great creative power here described one must be tested and proved entirely selfless, else there would be havoc in the world. This test the Master passed at the time of the Temptation. The occult power by which the loaves and fishes were multiplied is the same as that by which gold is produced from baser substances, a work understood only by the most advanced.

John 6:4-14.

And the passover, a feast of the Jews, was nigh.

When Jesus then lifted up his eyes and saw a great company come unto him, he saith unto Philip, Whence shall we buy bread, that these may eat? And this he said to prove him, for he himself knew what he would do.

Philip answered him, Two hundred pennyworth of bread is not sufficient for them, that every one of them may take a little.

One of his disciples, Andrew, Simon Peter's brother, saith unto him,

There is a lad here which hath five barley loaves, and two small fishes; but what are they among so many?

And Jesus said, Make the men sit down. Now there was much grass in the place, so the men sat down, in number about five thousand.

And Jesus took the loaves, and when he had given thanks, he distributed to the disciples, and the disciples to them that were set down; and likewise of the fishes as much as they would.

When they were filled, he said unto his disciples, Gather up the fragments that remain, that nothing be lost.

Therefore they gathered them together, and filled twelve baskets with the fragments of the five barley loaves, which remained over and above unto them that had eaten.

Then those men, when they had seen the miracle that Jesus did, said, This is of a truth that prophet that should come into the world.

Although the food produced was used to feed the multitudes, the Master's primary object was to instruct the Disciples in the workings of the law of multiplication. John's account of this incident varies slightly from the record given in the synoptic Gospels. In the latter the miracle is performed by Christ Himself; in John's account the Master endeavored to have the Disciples do the work. He tests both Andrew and Philip, but neither is yet capable of using this law. To do so necessitates the *power of faith* and the understanding of creative mind power, which neither Philip nor Andrew possessed as yet, although these two Discpiles symbolize these faculties in man.

The symbolism of the loaves and fishes was used to designate the work belonging to the Piscean Dispensation with its inner teachings under Virgo, whose symbol is the Madonna, the glorified one, with the sheaf of wheat or manifested powers over the physical earth.

The numbers 2, 7, and 12 are significant in that they are the principal divisions used in the science of the stars when considered astrologically. Their numerical value is also significant in relation to the different steps or degrees of attainment outlined in the four Gospels.

REBIRTH AND CAUSATION

Matthew 11:11-14.

Verily I say unto you, among them that are born of woman there hath not risen a greater than John the Baptist; notwithstanding he that is least in the kingdom of heaven is greater than he.

And from the days of John the Baptist until now the kingdom of heaven suffereth violence, and the violent take it by force.

For all the prophets and the law prophesied until John.

And if ye will receive it, this is Elias, which was for to come.

Matthew 17:1-13.

And after six days Jesus taketh Peter, James, and John, his brother, and bringeth them up into a high mountain apart.

And was transfigured before them: and his face did shine as the sun, and his raiment was white as the light.

And, behold, there appeared unto them Moses and Elias talking with him.

Then answered Peter, and said unto Jesus, Lord, it is good for us to be here: If thou wilt, let us make here three tabernacles; one for thee, and one for Moses, and one for Elias.

While he yet spake, behold, a bright cloud overshadowed them; and behold a voice out of the cloud, which said, This is my beloved Son, in whom I am well pleased; hear ye him.

And when the disciples heard it, they fell on their face, and were sore afraid.

And Jesus came and touched them, and said, Arise, and be not afraid.

And when they had lifted up their eyes they saw no man, save Jesus only.

And as they came down from the mountain, Jesus charged them, saying, Tell the vision to no man, until the Son of Man be risen again from the dead.

And his disciples asked him, saying, Why then say the scribes that Elias must first come?

And Jesus answered and said unto them, Elias truly shall first come, and restore all things.

But I say unto you, That Elias is come already, and they knew him not, but have done unto him whatsoever they listed. Likewise shall also the Son of Man suffer of them.

Then the disciples understood that he spake unto them of John the Baptist.

Matthew 16:13-20.

When Jesus came into the coasts of Caesarea Philippi, he asked his disciples, saying, Whom do men say that I, the Son of Man, am?

And they said, Some say that thou art John the Baptist: some, Elias: and others, Jeremias, or one of the prophets.

He saith unto them, But whom say ye that I am?

And Simon Peter answered and said, Thou art the Christ, the Son of the living God.

And Jesus answered and said unto him, Blessed art thou, Simon Bar-jona: for flesh and blood hath not revealed it unto thee, but my Father which is in heaven.

And I say also unto thee, That thou art Peter, and upon this rock I will build my church; and the gates of hell shall not prevail against it.

And I will give unto thee the keys of the kingdom of heaven; and whatsoever thou shalt bind on earth shall be bound in heaven; and whatsoever thou shalt loose on earth shall be loosed in heaven.

Then charged he his disciples that they should tell no man that he was Jesus the Christ.

In these discourses the Master asserts that John and Elias (Elijah) are one and the same. The ego once known upon earth by the name of Elias had been reborn as John. Rebirth was at this time a generally accepted truth. The people, on seeing the works of Christ Jesus, understood Him to be a re-embodiment of Elias, Jeremiah, or one of the prophets. The subject under discussion was not the truth or falsity of rebirth, but concerned only the identity of the ego that reappeared as Christ Jesus. That the Master Himself took these teachings for granted is indicated by His further question: "And whom do ye say that I am?" Peter's reply is not a refutation of the fact of rebirth, but conveys a knowledge of the deeper truths of the present mission of the Christ, namely, to bring the Christian Mysteries to humanity. Because Peter possessed this knowledge the Christ added, "Upon this rock (the rock of Initiation) will I build my Church."

The Master also elucidates the law of cause and effect in the statement: "Whatsoever you loose upon earth shall be loosed in heaven." Man gains experience upon the earth which he incorporates into spiritual powers in heaven during his sojourn in the inner worlds between earth lives. These added powers become available to him in his next life on earth, there to be further strengthened and enlarged upon by extended experiences in the physical world. In this lies the distinction between the so-called "old soul" who has amalgamated the experiences of many lives and the "young soul" who has passed through fewer such experiences and whose strength and wisdom are correspondingly less. The oftener the ego spends an earth day in this school of experience, the greater the understanding, the deeper the sympathy, the broader the compassion, and the profounder the love nature. At length the time comes when one proclaims with the Christ in His all-embracing understanding: "Judge not lest ye be judged."

The young soul, with its fewer earth-day experiences, is characterized by egotism, a love of self, and a desire to acquire worldly fame, position, and power. He has not yet learned the evanescence of earthly treasures, a fact learned only through sorrow, disillusionment and renunciations. Thus it is that the wise ones affirm: "The gates of Initiation swing wide only through pain."

The first Psalm also becomes understandable only when accepted as a statement of the truth of rebirth.

John 9:1-3.

And as Jesus passed by, he saw a man which was blind from his birth.

And his disciples asked him, saying, Master, who did sin, this man, or his parents, that he was born blind?

Jesus answered, Neither hath this man sinned nor his parents; but that the works of God should be made manifest in him.

In this statement the Christ affirms clearly that the law back of all physical limitation is not punishment, but enlightenment, pointing to the perfect justice of the law of causation which is behind all disease or infirmity of whatever nature. When an ego breaks a law in one life on earth, it (the ego) returns in another life under the limitation which applies directly to the law violated. Through the sorrow and suffering coincident with the limitation, the spirit learns its lesson and the infirmity is removed. Any other form of healing is impermanent. The Christ made this plain when, by the pool of Bethsaida, He healed the man who had been lame for thirty and eight years, saying, "Thou are made whole, go and sin no more, lest a worse thing come upon thee."

An abuse of mental powers reacts as physical disabilities, and physical abuses as mental weaknesses. Through suffering, the spirit comes to realize that the body is the pure and chaste temple of the living God (man's own innate divinity), that this temple must be kept inviolate for the use and development of its own individual spirit.

Such is the teaching on the Law. But through the teaching of the Christ we rise above the Law by the remission of sins. Under the new Christian regime it is no longer necessary for man to be bound by the prolonged operation of the twin laws of rebirth and karma if, awakened to his own inner divinity, he studies his own past causation, learns the lessons it holds for him and, through repentance, reform and restitution, clears away the causative factors. This is the joyous gospel of the

New Age. Having awakened the Christ powers *within* by a life of love, sacrifice and service, man may here and now learn to create a new body, a new environment and a new life in perfect harmony with the promises of the Christ. In this way the inharmonies and discrepancies between the old and the new are reconciled. The laws of causation and karma hold forever true, but the Christian dispensation confers a speedy release from their workings—provided man lives worthily—through the remission of sins.

John proclaimed: "Repent and be baptized for the remission of sins." The word repentance is derived from the Latin, meaning "creeping" or "prostrate," which later came to mean a change of mind as a result of sorrow for conduct that had laid low the spirit. John adds: "Bring forth fruits worthy of repentance." Only thus is the law of consequence nullified. One law may always be superseded by the workings of a higher law. Hence again the wisdom of the maxim: "Humanity moves in circles, the wise ones in spirals."

CONSCIOUS INVISIBLE HELPERSHIP

Mark 4:35-40.

And the same day, when the even was come, he saith unto them, Let us pass over unto the other side.

And when they had sent away the multitude, they took him even as he was in the ship. And there were also with him other little ships.

And there arose a great storm of wind, and the waves beat into the ship, so that it was now full.

And he was in the hinder part of the ship, asleep on a pillow; and they awake him, and say unto him, Master, carest thou not that we perish?

And he arose and rebuked the wind, and said unto the sea, Peace, be still. And the wind ceased, and there was a great calm.

And he said unto them, Why are ye so fearful? How is it that ye have no faith?

Here the Master is teaching the Disciples how to control the elements. He sent the multitudes away, for this work is given only to advanced pupils who have learned how to function consciously on the inner planes. Jesus was in the ship (his own soul body); and there were other little ships (the soul bodies of the Disciples). He was asleep. That is, he was away from them, functioning on still higher planes. Because of His absence they were afraid. *The pupil must learn to work fearlessly and apart from the guidance of the Teacher.* The Christ addressed separately the powers of the winds (the sylphs) and the spirits of the sea (the undines). One who has learned to control these elements, possesses the power to command the nature spirits to do his bidding.

Luke 8:23-25.

But as they sailed he fell asleep; and there came down a storm of wind on the lake; and they were filled with water, and were in jeopardy.

And they came to him, and awoke him, saying, Master, master, we perish. Then he arose and rebuked the wind and the raging of the water; and they ceased, and there was a calm.

And he said unto them, Where is your faith? And they being afraid wondered, saying one to another, What manner of man is this! For he commandeth even the winds and the water, and they obey him.

There are four paths leading to every Temple of Initiation: the paths of (symbolic) Fire, Air, Water, and Earth. Aspirants follow these according to temperament and development. The essences of the experiences of these four paths are all amalgamated in the Mystery Teachings of the Christ. He came as the great unifier of all things.

Matthew 8:18-26.

Now when Jesus saw great multitudes about him, He gave commandment to depart unto the other side.

And a certain scribe came, and said unto him, Master, I will follow thee whithersoever thou goest.

And Jesus said unto him, The foxes have holes, and the birds of the air have nests; but the Son of Man hath not where to lay his head.

And another of his disciples said unto him, Lord, suffer me first to go and bury my father.

But Jesus said unto him, Follow me; and let the dead bury their dead.

And when he was entered into a ship his disciples followed him.

And, behold, there arose a great tempest in the sea, insomuch that the ship was covered with the waves; but he was asleep.

And his disciples came to him, and awoke him, saying, Lord save us; we perish.

And he saith unto them, Why are ye fearful, O ye of little faith? Then he arose and rebuked the winds and the sea; and there was a great calm.

A few verses in the Bible often cover events, experiences, or developments that extend over a long period of time. The supreme test of discipleship is learning to renounce all things of this world for His sake and to make the great surrender of the personal to the universal. Matthew here recounts the failure of the many to do this and their consequent inability to qualify for the deeper teachings. When the Master entered into the ship (His spiritual body) only the Disciples (who had renounced all to follow Him) were able to go with Him and to be instructed in the control of the elements.

John 6:16-21.

And when even was now come, his disciples went down unto the sea.

And entered into a ship, and went over the sea toward Capernaum. And it was now dark, and Jesus was not come to them.

And the sea arose by reason of a great wind that blew.

So when they had rowed about five and twenty or thirty furlongs, they see Jesus walking on the sea, and drawing nigh unto the ship; and they were afraid.

But he saith unto them, It is I; be not afraid.

Then they willingly received him into the ship; and immediately the ship was at the land whither they went.

The Invisible Helper must learn to pass through fire, water, air, and earth on errands of mercy. (Here we refer to the natural, not the symbolic, elements.) He discovers that fire cannot burn, nor water drown the etheric vehicle in which he now functions. He learns the exhilaration of conscious communion with the spirit of these elements; he finds that they are not averse to man's interests but, on the contrary, become his most powerful friends when he learns how to use them aright. This use implies, first of all, complete *self-control.* This is exemplified in the incident connected with the development of Peter.

Walking upon the water represents the mastery of the emotional life, which includes the domination of *fear* and the attainment of the power of *faith*.

Peter's attempt to walk upon the waves, his faltering, and the assistance given him by the Christ, all picture the aspirant's effort to attain this goal. Peter, at this stage of his advancement, had not entirely overcome fear, nor had he developed sufficient faith to retain his poise. It is only the great power of a rational faith that enables one to say: "None of these things move me."

Luke 7:20-23.

When the men were come unto him they said, John the Baptist hath sent us unto thee, saying, Art thou he that should come? Or look we for another?

And in that same hour he cured many of their infirmities and plagues, and of evil spirits; and unto many that were blind he gave sight.

Then Jesus answering, said unto them, Go your way and tell John what things ye have seen and heard; how that the blind see, the lame walk, the lepers are cleansed, the deaf hear, the dead are raised, to the poor the gospel is preached.

And blessed is he whosoever shall not be offended in me.

By their fruits ye shall know them. No sign shall be given, asserted the Christ, but the sign of Jonas (the dove, symbol of the Initiate and the insigne of the Knights of the Holy Grail). The sign of Jonas is the sign of the Initiate whose powers transcend physical laws by calling into operation the higher laws of superphysical planes. The crystallizations of inharmony or *dis-ease* are changed into the rhythmic, harmonious vibrations which can manifest only as new life and health. The limitation of blindness, both physical and spiritual, is effaced by an inflow of the Life that is Light. Gravitation is superseded by levitation. The spirit of inertia is no more. The limitations of the physical world are superseded by the more expansive consciousness of the superphysical world.

"Let there be Light" is the supreme mandate of the Book of Books. The search for Light is the one inescapable responsibility of the disciples of Truth, and an ever-increasing luminosity is the heritage of its ministers.

CHAPTER IV

Crowning Works of the Ministry

The Transfiguration to the Passion

The Rite of Transfiguration

Matthew 17:1-8.

And after six days Jesus taketh Peter, James, and John his brother and bringeth them up into a high mountain apart.

And was transfigured before them; And his face did shine as the sun, and his raiment was white as the light.

And, behold, there appeared unto them Moses and Elias talking with him.

Then answered Peter, and said unto Jesus, Lord, it is good for us to be here; if thou wilt, let us make here three tabernacles; one for thee, and one for Moses, and one for Elias.

While he yet spake, behold, a bright cloud overshadowed them; and behold a voice out of the cloud, which said, This is my beloved Son in whom I am well pleased: hear ye him.

And when the disciples heard it, they fell on their face, and were sore afraid.

Jesus came and touched them, and said, Arise, and be not afraid.

And when they had lifted up their eyes they saw no man, save Jesus only.

The deepest esoteric teachings of the Master began at the time of the Transfiguration. Gradually, as the Disciples were able to bear it, He endeavored to lead them into an understanding of the inner meaning of His mission to the world. In that tremendous and awe-inspiring scene of the Transfiguration, which has been called the Feast and the Victory of Light, He was attended by three of His innermost circle, namely, John, the best loved, which means the most spiritually advanced; James, the first to lay down his life for the cause of the new religion of Christianity; and Peter, the rock, symbolizing the power of faith and works upon which has been builded the Christian religion. These three were now to function amid the glories of the World of Life

Spirit, His own particular realm of unity and harmony. They had learned to raise their vibrations sufficiently high to see Him clothed in His glorious body built of the material of this celestial plane. This is the body John was attempting to describe when he reported that "we beheld his glory, the glory as of the 'only begotten of the Father'."

Peter declared: "We have not followed cunningly devised fables when we made known unto you the power and coming of our Lord Jesus Christ, but were eye witnesses of his majesty." And Luke, who wrote at the dictation of Peter, said, "And as he prayed, the fashion of his countenance was altered, and his raiment was white and glistening." Mark added, "And his raiment became shining, exceeding white as snow, so as no fuller on earth can white them."

Matthew gave the most detailed account of this experience that is to be found in all the Gospels. He no doubt heard these words many times from Peter, James and John after their Teacher had gone from them to return to His home in the World of Life Consciousness. Matthew said: "And he was transfigured before them, and his face did shine as the Sun, and his raiment was white as the light."

The Disciples were lifted to that height in order that they might learn to read from God's Book of Remembrance which is to be found in that plane of being, for therein is a complete record of all that has occurred during the entire Earth Period and an outline of that which shall become manifest in the future.

It was there that they traced the lives of Moses and Elijah, who were embodiments of the same ego. There Christ Jesus taught them to read the imperishable record of His own Ministry and of the decease "which he should accomplish at Jerusalem."

The Transfiguration marked a crisis in His career. After that experience He gave the deepest of His esoteric work to the Disciples, and performed the greatest of His acts for mankind. Following the dazzling glory of the Transfiguration He came down from the Mount to spend His few remaining days upon earth in tender, loving, healing ministries for the sick and sorrowing. The bright heavenly radiance of that which He brought from above offered surcease of woe to those about Him. The lesson to be learned from the Transfiguration is that the only real reason for great spiritual attainment is that we may become more efficient helpers and servers in lowly places. From His great spiritual exaltation, which we can but dimly comprehend at this time, the Master returned to find only the cross awaiting Him.

The Transfiguration represents an actual occurrence wherein a process of transmutation takes place within the body of the Initiate. The essence of powers gained through his lives upon the heart path are blended with the essence of experiences gathered upon the head path, and the union of the two produces a radiant light throughout the body which may be seen by those who have the eyes to see. This amalgamation occurs in the spirit fire or kundalini force within the spinal cord.

This spinal cord is divided into three segments; one portion is worked upon in heart development, another in the head process, and the third in connection with the union of the two. The soul body builded by the mystic is like the whiteness of snow; that of the occultist is golden, tinged with red. The Transfiguration marks the uniting of the two; this union ever occurs at the foot of the cross, or with the liberation of the ego into a larger life or sphere of service. The Christ was transfigured in the presence of the most spiritual of His disciples.

Moses symbolizes the feminine or heart path, which correlates with the Moon, the divine law giver, the measurer of time and regulator of physical events. Elijah represents the masculine or head path, which relates astrologically to the Sun. He is called the prophet of fire and ascends into heaven in a chariot of fire, having accomplished the Initiation by this element.

The voice of God repeats the same blessing given at the Baptism: "This is my beloved Son, in whom I am well pleased." This was the benediction when the Christ accepted the body of Jesus for His three-years' Ministry; it was again the benediction when He prepared, through the Transfiguration, to complete the work of the Crucifixion.

The bodily transfiguration is an actual experience in the life of every high Initiate or Teacher. Buddha says: "On that night in which one attains to the supreme and perfect insight and on the night in which he finally passes away, on these occasions the color of the skin becomes clear and exceedingly bright."

The other world teachers, through a transfiguration, attained unto the Christed consciousness and gained entrance into Christ's own home world. Their earth mission was then complete and they passed on into that high plane. The Christ Spirit had access to this realm at all times and it was there that He went when He departed into the desert, for instance. In the Transfiguration He revealed Himself to those able to see Him as He normally functioned in His own home world, the realm of the Christ Consciousness.

The first three Gospels portray the important preparatory steps in the life of the neophyte which precede the Transfiguration. John begins his Gospel with the Transfiguration, outlining the life of the aspirant after this transmutation has occurred. According to the Gospels of Matthew, Mark and Luke, the Christ prepares His Disciples for His departure between the time of the Transfiguration and the Triumphal Entry into Jerusalem. He endeavors to have them understand the manner of His going and the esoteric reason therefor.

Matthew 20:17-19.

And Jesus going up to Jerusalem took the twelve disciples apart in the way, and said unto them,

Behold, we go up to Jerusalem; and the Son of man shall be betrayed unto the chief priests and unto the scribes, and they shall condemn him to death.

And shall deliver him to mock, and to scourge, and to crucify him; and the third day he shall rise again.

Christ's final instructions deal with the problems of spiritual discipline by which His followers may attain as He has attained. In these essentials He stresses humility and forgiveness as the most important.

Matthew 18:3-9.

And said, Verily I say unto you, Except ye be converted, and become as little children, ye shall not enter into the kingdom of heaven.

Whosoever therefore shall humble himself as this little child, the same is greatest in the kingdom of heaven.

And whoso shall receive one such little child in my name receiveth me.

But whoso shall offend one of these little ones which believe in me, it were better for him that a millstone were hanged about his neck, and that he were drowned in the depths of the sea.

Woe unto the world because of offences! for it must needs be that offences come; but woe to that man by whom the offence cometh!

Wherefore if thy hand or thy foot offend thee, cut them off, and cast them from thee; it is better for thee to enter into life halt or maimed, rather than having two hands or two feet to be cast into everlasting fire.

And if thine eye offend thee, pluck it out, and cast it from thee; it is better for thee to enter into life with one eye, rather than having two eyes to be cast into hell fire.

Following these precepts we find Paul saying: "I determined not to know anything among you save Jesus Christ and him crucified". (I Cor. 2:2)

Mystic Church legends state that the Blessed Lady was also in attendance upon the glories of the Transfiguration. This is borne out by the fact that Mary was higher in attainment than the three chosen for this divine privilege. Since she was the destined teacher of the Christian group after the Ascension, it is natural to presume that she too was permitted to witness the sublime spectacle of the Christ in the height of His earthly glory and, with Peter, James and John, to follow by means of the akashic records the outline of coming events. Thus she would gain a more complete concept of the cosmic meaning of the Christ Ascension and its effect upon human evolution in future generations.

The Keynote of the New Christian Dispensation

The Christ, in these final instructions to His own immediate Disciples, repeatedly emphasized the fact that forgiveness, love, faith and humility are the prime essentials of true discipleship.

Mark 12:30, 31.

And thou shalt love the Lord, thy God with all thy heart, and with all thy soul, and with all thy mind, and with all thy strength; this is the first commandment.

And the second is like, namely this, Thou shalt love thy neighbor as thyself. There is none other commandment greater than these.

Mark 11:22-26.

And Jesus answering saith unto them, Have faith in God.

For verily I say unto you, That whosoever shall say unto this mountain, Be thou removed, and be thou cast into the sea; and shall not doubt in his heart, but shall believe that those things which he saith shall come to pass; he shall have whatsoever he saith.

Therefore I say unto you, What things soever ye desire, when ye pray, believe that ye receive them, and ye shall have them.

And when ye stand praying, forgive, if ye have ought against any: that your Father also which is in heaven may forgive you your trespasses.

But if ye do not forgive, neither will your Father which is in heaven forgive your trespasses.

The aspirant will be able to discover in these words of the Master why ofttimes it seems so difficult to receive an answer to prayer. The fundamental condition necessary for this reception is that attitude of mind which bears love toward all and malice toward none. "As ye pray, forgive, if ye have aught against any." Through the very power of universal love the spirit touches and communes with that Christ life wherein all are one and from which all things manifest.

The Rite of the Anointing

Mark 14:3-9.

And being in Bethany in the house of Simon the leper, as he sat at meat, there came a woman having an alabaster box of ointment of spikenard very precious; and she brake the box and poured it on his head.

And there were some that had indignation within themselves, and said, Why was this waste of ointment made?

For it might have been sold for more than three hundred pence, and have been given to the poor. And they murmured against her.

And Jesus said, Let her alone; why trouble ye her? she hath wrought a good work on me.

For ye have the poor with you always, and whensoever ye will ye may do them good: and me ye have not always.

She hath done what she could: she is come aforehand to anoint my body to the burying.

Verily I say unto you, Wheresoever this gospel shall be preached throughout the whole world, this also that she hath done shall be spoken of for a memorial of her.

Luke 7:36-50.

And one of the Pharisees desired him that he would eat with him. And he went into the Pharisee's house, and sat down to meat.

And, behold, a woman in the city, which was a sinner, when she knew that Jesus sat at meat in the Pharisee's house, brought an alabaster box of ointment.

And stood at his feet behind him weeping, and began to wash his feet with tears, and did wipe them with the hair of her head, and kissed his feet, and anointed them with the ointment.

Now when the Pharisee, who had bidden him saw it, he spake within himself, saying, This man, if he were a prophet, would have known who and what manner of woman this is that toucheth him; for she is a sinner.

And Jesus answering said unto him, Simon, I have somewhat to say unto thee. And he saith, Master, say on.

There was a certain creditor who had two debtors: the one owed five hundred pence, and the other fifty.

And when they had nothing to pay, he frankly forgave them both. Tell me therefore which of them will love him most?

Simon answered and said, I suppose that he, to whom he forgave most. And he said unto him, Thou hast rightly judged.

And he turned to the woman, and said unto Simon, Seest thou this woman? I entered into thine house, thou gavest me no water for my feet: but she hath washed my feet with tears, and wiped them with the hairs of her head.

Thou gavest me no kiss: but this woman since the time I came in hath not ceased to kiss my feet.

My head with oil thou didst not anoint: but this woman hath anointed my feet with ointment.

Wherefore I say unto thee, Her sins, which are many, are forgiven: for she loved much: but to whom little is forgiven, the same loveth little.

And He said unto her, Thy sins are forgiven.

And they that sat at meat with him began to say within themselves, Who is this that forgiveth sins also?

And he said to the woman, Thy faith hath saved thee; go in peace.

John 12:1-8.

Then Jesus six days before the passover, came to Bethany, where Lazarus was which had been dead, whom he raised from the dead.

There they made him a supper; and Martha served; but Lazarus was one of them that sat at the table with him.

Then took Mary a pound of ointment of spikenard, very costly, and anointed the feet of Jesus, and wiped his feet with her hair; and the house was filled with the odour of the ointment.

Then saith one of his disciples, Judas Iscariot, Simon's son, which should betray him,

Why was not this ointment sold for three hundred pence, and given to the poor?

This he said, not that he cared for the poor; but because he was a thief, and had the bag, and bare what was put therein.

Then said Jesus, Let her alone: against the day of my burying hath she kept this."

For the poor always ye have with you; but me ye have not always.

This incident in the life of Christ Jesus is intensely interesting when studied esoterically. Some Bible commentators conclude that the reference in each of the three Gospels is made to the same person, whereas the Mary referred to by John is the sister of Lazarus, and not Mary Magdalene, the woman of sin who was redeemed. Mary, the sister of Lazarus, was one of the foremost of the women disciples. The alabaster vase of ointment symbolizes the dazzling whiteness of the soul body of the mystic, built through love and service and offered in supreme dedication at the feet of the Master. This soul body is formed of the higher ethers which are attracted through love, purity, idealism and selfless service. The hair is a product of the vital body and the understanding reader will recognize that its use by Mary as recorded in the above passage is an allusion to the ethers of the body, or the soul. It was an Oriental custom to thus bathe and anoint the feet of an honored guest. The soul body of a saint emits a fragrance; and when we read that the house was filled with the odor of the ointment, we may know that Mary had reached a high spiritual attainment that was recognized even in the fragrance that emanated from her.

Judas Iscariot, the lower self, always objects to the higher nature dedicating itself to the works of the Christ. "The poor" (those who are not yet ready for this high place in the spiritual life) "ye have always with you, but me ye have not always" (upon the earth functioning in a physical body).

This incident, which is recorded in the Gospels of Mark and Luke, outlines the path of supreme dedication for the aspirant. Every event in the life of the Christ portrays a step on the disciple's path as the Christ is awakened *within* him. In Mark and Luke the woman who performs this service is a sinful or erring one. Esoterically this signifies the feminine pole which is fallen in all mankind. In the Gospel of John, which outlines the pathway to the highest attainment, Mary, who was one of the foremost disciples of the Christ, does the anointing, thus showing that the great transmutation had taken place. Mary is now a high Initiate. The anointing occurs after the raising, or Initiation, of Lazarus, the supreme work done by the Christ upon the earth. It is also significant that this event immediately precedes the Triumphal Entry which is another step in the life of the highly Illumined One.

The anointing with perfumed oil was practiced in Greece as a mark of hospitality.. This service was always performed as a token of honor to some highly favored guest. Throughout both the Old and New Testaments it was used to consecrate priests, prophets and kings, also sacred places and articles of worship. The oil of anointing symbolizes divine wisdom.

It was the custom of the early Christians to anoint the sick with consecrated oil as evidenced in the words of Mark: "And there were some that had indignation within themselves, and said, Why was this waste of ointment made?" (Mark 14:4). Also in the words of James: "Is any sick amoung you? Let him call for the elders of the church; and let them pray over him, anointing him with oil in the name of the Lord" (James 5:14).

A Song of Planetary Phythm

Christ's ministry was now practically completed. These remained only the Passion Week with its deepest esoteric instruction for the Disciples who had qualified themselves to receive it, and the final great work of cleansing and redeeming the earth for the benefit of all mankind.

John was the youngest of the original Twelve and aside from Judas was possibly the only one to escape martyrdom. After the Crucifixion he lived chiefly in Ephesus and there presided over seven churches. Under the Roman Emperor, Domitian, he was accused of using evil magic in his wonderful healings and for this he was banished to Patmos where he received the sublime vision transcribed for us in Revelation.

We discover frequently in early fragments that primitive Christianity was associated with magic and sorcery in the popular mind. This is partially—but not wholly—due to the fact that in the beginning it was almost entirely a Jewish sect. Most of the first Christians were Jews by birth or by adoption. That the popular attitude had some basis in fact is shown in relics discovered in the catacombs of Rome: small golden caskets containing portions of the first chapter of John's Gospel, to be worn as amulets. The circumstance that it is John's chapter on the Logos (Word) which is used as a magic talisman is significant. It indicates that these early Christians understood the tremendous mantramic power contained in John's great song of planetary rhythm. The Tetragrammaton also has been used in magical ceremonials by both Jews and Christians until modern times. It is still important to initiatory work and it is not wholly unknown to the mystic Mason.

The Gospel of John begins with the attainment of the Transfiguration. 'And the Word was made flesh, and dwelt among us, (and we beheld his glory, the glory as of the only begotten of the Father) full of grace and truth" (John 1:14).

After the Transfiguration the great unifying Principle, the Cosmic Christ, is comprehended and realized as the Word made flesh. The first chapter of John is an ecstatic address expressing a realization of the oneness of all life. This necessitates a contact, attained in the Transfiguration, with the realm of superconsciousness.

John 1:1-5.

In the beginning was the Word, and the Word was with God, and the Word was God.

The same was in the beginning with God.

All things were made by him: and without him was not anything made that was made.

In him was life; and the life was the light of men.

And the light shineth in darkness; and the darkness comprehended it not.

John, the great mystic, in a state of high spiritual ecstasy touched the very heart of God, the Feminine or Wisdom Principle of Creation, the Word or Logos. This Logos is the rhythmic or formative power, through and by which all things are brought into manifestation. Every planet sounds its keynote; so too, does every atom. The music of the spheres is a reality. Upon reaching a certain stage of development one is able to hear nature's music, to catch the rhythms by which all things are created, to listen to the symphonies of forests, waters and winds. Such has been the sensitiveness of great musicians and poets.

A yet higher consciousness embraces the music of the planets in their rhythmic dance around the Sun. This was the attainment of Plato.

Rhythm is the basis of all creation. The Word is the formative rhythmic Love Principle, without which was not anything made that was made. Through the unifying Love Principle comes the realization of the onenes of all life. This power was with God in the beginning and was a part of God. The Feminine Attribute voluntarily sacrificed itself by lowering its vibratory rate (the province of the feminine is ever that of loving sacrificial service) in order that the Spirit of God might move upon the Spirit of the Water to create.

Cosmically, this was the first blending of Fire and Water or of the Masculine and Feminine Principles, the Immaculate Conception of the Cosmos, the prototype of the Immaculate Conception in man. The primal manifestation or product of the union was *Light*. In the beginning was God. In Him was Life (the Masculine and Feminine). This Life was the Light of men. It is the proper union of these two Principles that produces the Light of the World and the light *within* man. This is the reason for the early alchemists' repeated use of the symbols of the Sun and Moon. Their work was to discover the proper method of blending the dual Principles, as it involves the secret of turning base metals into gold on every plane of being.

The Gospel of John contains many incidents which deal with the mystery of combining the opposites, Fire and Water, and thus presents a higher phase of spiritual knowledge than do the other Gospels. The secret of blending the Fire and Water Principles is given by the Christ to Nicodemus, as described by John; also to the woman of Samaria. Its power is again demonstrated in the raising of Lazarus.

The work of Initiation is concerned with the awakening of this dual force, its control, and finally its transmutation. The Father aspect (*Power,* Masculine, Fire, Sun) and the Son aspect (*Word,* Feminine, Water, Moon) are within man. Through their proper amalgamation by the activity of the Holy Ghost (*Motion*), Light is born. This is the Light which now shineth in the darkness (materiality) and the darkness comprehendeth it not.

Hermes in his *Book of Pymander* states: "The difference between the form of man and animal is in the latency and activity of *fires*." This vital fire or light (Cosmic Christ emanation) is latent in every atom of the universe. The awakening of this inner fire into dynamic activity produces evolution. Superman will differ from the ordinary man in that he will have awakened, controlled and transmuted this inner fire.

Again we read in the *Book of Pymander*: "Nature being co-mingled with man brought forth a wondrous miracle—the harmonious co-mingling of the essence of seven and her own through fire, or Spirit." Herein lies the mystic code of the Initiate. The entire Gospel of John as an initiatory study follows this mystic code.

In practically every religion, man worships a God of Fire. Jehovah is an all-consuming fire to his devotees. Christ Jesus becomes the Light of the World and the Light of men. The supreme prayer of the mystic Christian must ever be, "Let there be Light."

The Mystic Marriage in Cana of Galilee

John 2:1-11.

And the third day there was a marriage in Cana of Galilee; and the mother of Jesus was there.

And both Jesus was called, and his disciples, to the marriage.

And when they wanted wine, the mother of Jesus saith unto him, They have no wine.

Jesus saith unto her, Woman, what have I to do with thee? mine hour is not yet come.

His mother saith unto the servants, Whatsoever he saith unto you, do it.

And there were set there six water pots of stone, after the manner of the purifying of the Jews, containing two or three firkins apiece.

Jesus saith unto them, Fill the waterpots with water, and they filled them up to the brim.

And he saith unto them, Draw out now and bear unto the governor of the feast. And they bare it.

When the ruler of the feast had tasted the water that was made wine, and knew not whence it was; (but the servants who drew the water knew;) the governor of the feast called the bridegroom.

And saith unto him, Every man at the beginning doth set forth good wine; and when men have well drunk, then that which is worse; but thou hast kept the good wine until now.

This beginning of miracles did Jesus in Cana of Galilee, and manifested forth his glory; and his disciples believed on him.

Bible commentators count the miracle of Christ Jesus at the wedding of Cana as His first because it is given first place in the Gospel of John. The miracle marks the beginning of the deeper work given after the Transfiguration, and the feast marks the time of the great transmutation. Every step toward higher attainment is celebrated by a feast of soul ecstasy. When Matthew was chosen to follow the Master he proclaimed a feast to announce his renunciation of all earthly things. At the Mystic Marriage the glory of white light in the soul of the mystic is united with the ruby splendor in the soul of the occultist; water is transmuted into wine.

The increasing wonder of the Bible is found in the fact that actual physical events are used to conceal profound spiritual truths. Thus it was that the attendance of Christ and the Blessed Lady at the wedding feast in Cana became the opportunity for illustrating the high spiritual process of the mystic marriage within the individual.

The bride in this physical wedding is said to have been related to the family of Joseph and the bridegroom a relative of Mary. The home of the bride was spacious and beautiful, the guest lists large and the entertainment elaborate. It was into this scene of festivity that the Lord Christ chose to introduce one of His most sublime teachings—that of the Mystic Marriage.

There are three principal steps leading to mastership so there were three days of celebration preceding the wedding and on the third day there was a marriage in Cana of Galilee.

Mary, the heart or love power, is the first to say, "There is no wine." The servants represent the lower nature which works under obedience to the Christ within, instructed by the heart: "Whatsoever he saith unto you, do it."

Six is the number of new life. A stone is the body of the Initiate. The Disciples were present; that is, they were being instructed in the art of building that soul body wherein the water of emotion is alchemically transformed into the new wine of Life Eternal.

The Bride and Groom represent two neophytes who are being prepared for the Holy Rite of the Mystic Marriage. During the festivities preceding the wedding, both the Bride and Groom were lifted beyond normal consciousness, and in a transport of spiritual bliss they dedicated themselves to a united life of chaste and holy service, which is the sole purpose of Initiation.

As the Bride and Groom typify the masculine and feminine aspirants working in equality together upon the outer plane, so Christ and Mary represent the harmonious relationship of the masculine and feminine polarities within. Both the presence and work of Mary (the heart) were essential to the transmutation process which must precede the Mystic Marriage Rite.

Astrologically the six pots are Saturn, Jupiter, Mars, Venus, Mercury and the Moon. It is the Sun which, as center and source of all our solar system, works through the planets and transforms all nature into the wine of new life. The running sap is tinged with the colors of the Sun and transformed into the glory of blossoms and fruitage, as the Christ power awakened within the individual produces a new life embellished with noble and inspiring deeds.

The Moon (Mary) produces the water of nature, and the Sun (Christ) gives the wine. Hence, in the Greek Mysteries we find this miracle attributed to Dionysius, and with the same esoteric connotation.

We may also point out another meaning which is not generally observed in this story. The grapevine was an Old Testament symbol for Israel. Turning water into wine is therefore a warning to the people of Israel of Christ's day that God could transform the Gentile nations into Sons of God; that His chosen people are all humanity, not one race alone. In another place Christ states this fact thus: "God can of these stones raise up children to Abraham."

The Initiation of Nicodemus

Nicodemus was a student following the mental path. He seeks Christ "by night" or, in other words, in the darkness of human consciousness or mortal mind. Nicodemus first sought the spiritual light through reasoning about it: "We know thou art a man of God for no one else can do these miracles." As a result of his increasing enlightenment, when the Sanhedrin wished to destroy the Christ, Nicodemus stood forth bravely against them all and championed the despised cause.

The last biblical view of Nicodemus is on the night of the Crucifixion when he brings myrrh and one hundred pounds of aloes to embalm the body of his Lord.

The one hundred pounds of aloes symbolize the unbounded measure of love and service which characterized Nicodemus' life after his great illumination. The myrrh represents both the pain and the sweetness of transmutation. Wise men (Initiates) brought myrrh to the Nativity. Nicodemus, a newly made Initiate or Wise Man, brought myrrh for the Mystic Death Rite.

There is an apocryphal Gospel of Nicodemus which is rich in esotericism. In it he relates an initiatory experience described as the descent of Christ into Hades (purgatorial realms). He saw Christ enter Hades to the chanting of the twenty-fourth Psalm: "Lift up your heads, ye gates, that the King of Glory may come in." He saw Christ overcome the Angel of Death, bind Satan in adamantine chains in the abyss and leave His holy cross there in Hades as a sign of victory, after which He was led by the Archangel Michael to the prophet Jeremiah. Twelve thousand (who had completed their purgation) ascended with Him from the lower regions into Heaven.

What was Nicodemus that he merited this revelation of the descent of Christ into Hades? He was one who had been "born again," as Christ had instructed him.

John 3:3-8.

Jesus answered and said unto him, Verily, verily, I say unto thee, except a man be born again, he cannot see the kingdom of God.

Nicodemus saith unto him, How can a man be born when he is old? Can he enter the second time into his mother's womb, and be born?

Jesus answered, Verily, verily, I say unto thee, Except a man be born of water and of the spirit, he cannot enter into the kingdom of God.

That which is born of the flesh is flesh; and that which is born of the spirit is spirit.

Marvel not that I said unto thee, ye must be born again.

The wind bloweth where it listeth, and thou hearest the sound thereof, but canst not tell whence it cometh and whither it goeth; so is everyone that is born of the spirit.

These verses contain perhaps the most profound teaching given by the Master during His three years' Ministry.

Man's physical body is built through the action and reaction of Fire and Water manipulated by the celestial Hierarchies, particularly the Angels and Archangels. Later in his evolutionary development, through this same action and reaction of Fire and Water, he learns to build for himself a new body of spirit—the living stone of Revelation, with its new name.

Initiatory Processes

The work for humanity done by the Fire and Water Hierarchies:

Aries—Gave the initial power of motion.

Leo—Awakened the Divine Spirit in man and gave the germ of the dense body.

Sagittarius—Gave the link of mind.

Cancer—Awakened the germ of the Christ Spirit.

Scorpio—Originates form.

Pisces—Rules the Virgin Spirits for whom the work of evolution in our solar system is being done.

Preparatory Work for Initiation

Sagittarius—Begins the work of regeneration.

Leo—Its power awakens the esoteric centers as vortices of Light upon the Cross of the Body.

Aries—Awakens the power of the pineal gland and pituitary body.

Cancer—Works with the Christ force (life substance in the body).

Scorpio—Turns generation into regeneration.

Pisces—Represents the egos who work toward the Christing of consciousness.

To be born of water is the natural birth through generation. To be born of Spirit (or Fire) is the new birth through regeneration, or Initiation.

Cancer is said by esoteric astrologers to be the sign through which incoming egos enter the physical world. Cancer is governed by the Moon, the symbol of generation, and represents the birth through water. Cancer is also the exaltation sign of Neptune, the planet of Initiation. Initiation is the birth through Fire.

"The kingdom of heaven is within us," said the Christ. That kingdom belongs to the consciousness of the Initiate, and is not to be found until we are born into the unbroken consciousness of life.

The last verse of the above quoted passage is an accurate description of the ego liberated from the body. It is a life of loving, selfless service that builds the soul body with which to "travel to foreign countries," and which prepares one for the new birth of the Spirit. It was necessary for Nicodemus, as it must always be for every aspirant who seeks this deeper illumination, "to come to the Christ by night."

Jacob Boehme says: "Man sows fire and reaps spirit. Woman sows water and reaps soul." The two together, through interaction, build the body of water in generation. When they learn to work in conjunction, the deathless body, born of Spirit, will be built through regeneration. This is a part of the truth taught by the Master in the verses quoted above.

The Gospel of John contains eleven priceless discourses given by the Master. Nicodemus was one of the Pharisees, a sect composed of strict ritualists. Though a member of the Sanhedrin, Nicodemus, like Joseph of Arimathea, had been attracted to Christ Jesus and became one of His private disciples.

"How can these things be?" asked Nicodemus. Since the Pharisaical religion obscured the spirit beneath certain prescribed rites and ceremonies, Nicodemus found the vast horizon of this new religion at once amazing and captivating. Every spiritual truth begins to crystallize soon after being given; the only hope for spiritual progress, therefore, lies in keeping the mind fluidic to added revelation and the heart awake and active in service.

John 3:16.

For God so loved the world, that he gave his only begotten Son, that whosoever believeth in him should not perish, but have everlasting life.

These words sound the keynote of the universal Gospel; their truth belongs not to the Christian sect alone, but enfolds the entire world in its cosmic meaning. This has been considered the very heart of the Gospel message and the most precious passage in the whole Bible. More than four hundred vernaculars possess these words at the present time. The "only begotten Son" is that Word or Love Principle which, manifesting through the great planetary Christ, becomes the Life and the Light of the World.

Whosoever believeth in Him—not merely by faith alone but in manifestation of His works, for by there fruits they are known—shall have everlasting life (powers transcending those of ordinary humanity) and, through Initiation, enter into the kingdom of Heaven.

Initiatory Instruction to the Woman of Samaria

John 4:7-14.

There cometh a woman of Samaria to draw water; Jesus saith unto her, Give me a drink.

(For his disciples were gone away unto the city to buy meat.)

Then saith the woman of Samaria unto him, How is it that thou, being a Jew, asketh drink of me, which am a woman of Samaria? for the Jews have no dealings with the Samaritans.

Jesus answered and said unto her, If thou knewest the gift of God, and who it is that saith to thee, Give me to drink; thou wouldst have asked of him, and he would have given thee living water.

The woman saith unto him, Sir, thou hast nothing to draw with, and the well is deep: from whence hast thou that living water?

Art thou greater than our father Jacob, which gave us the well, and drank thereof himself, and his children, and his cattle?

Jesus answered and said unto her, Whosoever drinketh of this water shall thirst again:

But whosoever drinketh of the water that I shall give him shall never thirst; but the water that I shall give him shall be in him a well of water springing up into everlasting life.

There was intense hatred between the Jews and the Samaritans so Jewish travelers seldom passed through Samaria. The Christ, by His conversation with the woman of ill repute, opened the land of Samaria to Christianity. Tradition says that the name of this woman was Photina, which in Greek means *light.*

The Samaritans claimed to be the direct descendants of Joseph. They accepted the Pentateuch only as the true Scripture. Mt. Gerizim, where they believed Abraham communed with Melchizedek, was adopted as their chief place of worship, rather than Jerusalem. The Samaritan name for the Saviour was "The Returning One." They declared that Moses would return to the earth and become their spiritual leader. A remnant of these ancient Samaritans continue the faithful observance of their age-old rites on Mt. Gerizim even to this day.

The entire conversation of the Christ with this woman is an endeavor to lift material thought (which belongs to the fallen feminine pole of man's nature, symbolized by the woman of ill repute) to a realization of spiritual truth. The mind is the connecting link between spirit and body; when the mind is spiritualized the fallen feminine nature is lifted, the way of eternal life is found and the parched soul thirsts no more.

A well refers to a deep or hidden truth. Many of the most important incidents in the Bible are connected with wells and with events that occurred in their proximity.

The Christ was reticent about declaring His glory to the multitude, or even to Pilate; but to this lowly woman He asserts that: "I that speak unto thee am he." It is only as the feminine or intuitive principle recognizes the Christ within that the work of this transmutation begins. The waters of eternal life represent the blending of the masculine and feminine powers; they are the waters that were turned into wine at the marriage in

Cana. And again, they stand for the same truth as in the new birth outlined to Nicodemus.

John 7:37-38.

In the last day, that great day of the feast, Jesus stood and cried, saying, If any man thirst, let him come unto me, and drink.

He that believeth on me, as the scripture hath said, out of his belly shall flow rivers of living water.

The masculine pole, or intellect, is symbolized by Nicodemus who inquired: "How can these things be?" The feminine pole, or intuition, is represented by the woman of Samaria who says: "Give me of this water, that I thirst not." Their united powers yield the waters of eternal life which are drawn from the sacred well, the body of the Initiate.

John 4:31-34.

In the meantime His disciples prayed Him, saying, Master eat. But He said unto them, I have meat to eat that ye know not of.

Therefore said the disciples one to another, Hath any man brought Him aught to eat?

Jesus saith unto them, My meat is to do the will of Him that sent me, and to finish His work.

As previously stated, the union of the masculine and feminine polarities constitutes the beginning of the Greater Christian Mysteries. This is the "meat that ye know not of." "My meat is to do the will of Him that sent me." The Disciples could not deflect His attention from spiritual to physical things, for He came to teach these celestial mysteries.

John 7:33-34.

Then said Jesus unto them, Yet a little while am I with you, and then I go unto Him that sent me.

Ye shall seek me and shall not find me; and where I am, thither ye cannot come.

The Master is here pointing to His Passion as pictured even then in the Akashic Records, and marking the commencement of His real mission for humanity and for earth; but they were not yet ready to enter with Him into the high world of the Christed consciousness.

The Testing of Three Pharisees

John 8:1-12.

Jesus went unto the mount of Olives.

And early in the morning he came again into the temple, and all the people came unto him; and he sat down and taught them.

And the scribes and Pharisees brought unto him a woman taken in adultery; and when they had set her in the midst,

They say unto him, Master, this woman was taken in adultery, in the very act.

Now Moses in the law commanded us, that such should be stoned: but what sayest thou?

This they said, tempting him, that they might have to accuse him. But Jesus stooped down, and with his fingers wrote on the ground, as though he heard them not.

So when they continued asking him, he lifted up himself, and said unto them, He that is without sin among you, let him first cast a stone at her.

And again he stooped down, and wrote on the ground.

And they which heard it, being convicted by their own conscience, went out one by one, beginning at the eldest, even unto the last: and Jesus was left alone, and the woman standing in the midst.

When Jesus had lifted up himself, and saw none but the woman, he said unto her, Woman, where are those thine accusers? hath no man condemned thee?

She said, No man, Lord. And Jesus said unto her, Neither do I condemn thee: go, and sin no more.

Then spake Jesus again unto them, saying, I am the light of the world: he that followeth me shall not walk in darkness, but shall have the light of life.

The reason for the inclusion of the above incident in the Gospel of John is found in the words with which it is concluded: "I am the light of the world: he that followeth me shall not walk in darkness, but shall have the light of life."

With the realization of the oneness of all life, all misunderstanding and criticism, all censure and harsh judgment are swept away. In the understanding of the unity of all with God is born the true concept of brotherhood. All are a part of the great whole; every man shares the responsibility of another's failure or sin and is in part accountable for his weakness. Every man's sorrow is our sorrow and every man's joy, our joy. With this consciousness is found a new meaning in His words: "If we walk in the Light as he is in the Light, we have fellowship one with another." This is a realization born of the Christ consciousness, and one who has touched it can never know separateness again.

Professor Caspar Rene Gregory of the University of Leipzig announced that after comparing many old Gospel narratives among the early Christian writings, he discovered on Mt. Athos that the probable mysterious sentences written upon the ground by the Master were:

1. Eldar killed his friend Modor in the wilderness.
2. Hiram cheated Buvan's widow out of her house.
3. Arved's wife was compelled to yield to the power of Meoman.

The three Pharisees named were the most prominent in bringing the erring woman to the Christ. Each in turn slipped away as his name was written by the Christ. The record of the sins of these men written in the sand symbolizes the transitoriness of physical existence, the life wherein all men sin and suffer. Sin in its true concept is ignorance; it is action contrary to cosmic law; it is, etymologically defined, missing the mark. Suffering in consequence of sin is therefore the great enlightener. True wisdom is born of pain, the essence extracted from sorrow. "He that is without sin let him first cast a stone at her."

Filled with the great light of compassion that is born in the realization of the oneness of all, in the tenderness of His loving heart, the Master yearned over these men, who were groping blindly so far away from the true light, with the same infinite pity and compassion which He bestowed upon the erring woman.

Many of the important incidents in the life of the Christ have to do with fallen women. The reason for this is to be found in the fact that every external event bears an inner significance. The first and paramount redemption in man consists in the purification of the lower nature; the dissociation of the mind from the senses and its permanent contact with the spirit. Only in this way is the redemption of the race possible. The work is only possible through a contact with the power of the Christ *within,* which in turn makes possible the communion with the Christ without.

John 10:15.

As the Father knoweth me, even so know I the Father: and I lay down my life for the sheep.

John 10:17.

Therefore doth my Father love me, because I lay down my life, that I might take it again.

John 10:27-30.

My sheep hear my voice, and I know them, and they follow me:

And I give unto them eternal life; and they shall never perish, neither shall any man pluck them out of my hand.

My Father, which gave them me, is greater than all; and no man is able to pluck them out of my Father's hand.

I and my Father are one.

John alone of the Bible writers treats of the works of the Father; these pertain to the religion that will in a future time succeed that of the Christian Dispensation. The Christ earned the privilege of being received into the greater splendor of the works of the Father through the sacrifice He made for the sake of humanity. He verifies this in His words: "Therefore doth my Father love me because I lay down my life." He also avers that the power to lay down His life and to take it up again was received from the Father (the deeper Mysteries belonging to the religion of God the Father). When man is ready to receive this glorious new message of the Father, the world will have passed beyond all creeds, castes and races, and all humanity will be one great brotherhood knowing unity, each for all, under the divine supervision of God the Father.

The return of the Christ will be for the purpose of helping to prepare the world for this new conception. Before that time arrives, the Christ must be accepted as the world Saviour. Such is the teaching of *true* Christianity. "Other sheep I have which are not of this fold; them also I must bring, and they shall hear my voice; and there shall be one fold and one shepherd."

The Rite of Cleansing the Temple

John 2:13-16.

And the Jews' Passover was at hand, and Jesus went up to Jerusalem,

And found in the temple those that sold oxen and sheep and doves, and the changers of money sitting:

And when he had made a scourge of small cords, he drove them all out of the temple, and the sheep, and the oxen; and poured out the changers' money, and overthrew the tables;

And said unto them that sold doves, Take these things hence; make not my Father's house an house of merchandise.

According to the first three Gospels, the cleansing of the Temple occurs late in the Master's Ministry; it is placed after His entry into Jerusalem. In the Gospel of John it is described at the beginning of the Ministry. This final cleansing of the Temple of the body in preparation for its use as a pure and holy channel for the things of the spirit marks a high place in spiritual advancement. John alone mentions the scourge of small cords, referring to a definite process which takes place in the body as the spinal spirit fire is raised to the head.

That this Temple cleansing has an inner as well as an outer significance is shown in the fact that in each of the Gospels it is followed by definite teachings of purity and regeneration. Matthew proceeds with the cursing of the fig tree and the marriage of the king's son; Mark with the vineyard parable; Luke with the story of Zacchaeus; and John with the interview of Nicodemus. Each of these incidents has as its basic note the work of regeneration through purity and chastity.

The external significance of this Temple episode is noted in the fact that the priests received an enormous revenue from those permitted to sell animals in the Temple courts for sacrificial purposes. The deprivation of this revenue augmented their animosity against the great Teacher and led to their concerted efforts in plotting His destruction.

Matthew 21:12-14.

And Jesus went into the temple of God, and cast out all them that sold and bought in the temple, and overthrew the tables of the money changers, and the seats of them that sold doves.

And said unto them, It is written, My house shall be called the house of prayer; but ye have made it a den of thieves.

And the blind and the lame came to him in the temple; and he healed them.

The ejection of the money changers is given an important place in each of the four Gospels, as it represents a most important and necessary event in the life of every aspirant. The Temple is the body which, rightly used, is a house of prayer for the indwelling spirit but which, through the misuse of the sacred life force within for many lives past, has become a den of thieves.

Mark 11:15-16.

And they come to Jerusalem: and Jesus went into the temple, and began to cast out them that sold and bought in the temple, and overthrew the tables of the money-changers, and the seats of them that sold doves;

And would not suffer that any man should carry any vessel through the temple.

When man recognizes his body as the Temple of the indwelling spirit he will keep it pure and undefiled. He will not admit into it such destructive emotions as anger, envy, lust or hatred, knowing that they serve but to defile the holy place.

The education of the youth of the New Age will include a psychology which deals with the power of thought to mold or mar this body-Temple of the spirit, and to the youth will be given the truth that this Temple is the most precious heritage of the spirit.

The Apocrypha states: "Be ye good money changers in that ye know the true from the false, gold from dross, in an understanding of the Scriptures. Ye do, therefore, err, not knowing true things of the Scriptures and for this reason ye are ignorant of the power of God."

Attainment Through Regeneration

(The Story of Zacchaeus)

Luke 17:1-10.

And Jesus entered and passed through Jericho.

And, behold, there was a man named Zacchaeus, which was the chief among the publicans, and he was rich.

And he sought to see Jesus, who he was; and could not for the press, because he was of little stature.

And he ran before, and climbed into a sycamore tree to see him; for he was to pass that way.

And when Jesus came to the place, he looked up, and saw him, and said to him, Zacchaeus, make haste, and come down; for today I must abide at thy house.

And he made haste, and came down; and received him joyfully.

And when they saw it, they all murmured, saying, That he was gone to be guest with a man that is a sinner.

And Zacchaeus stood, and said unto the Lord; Behold, Lord, the half of my goods, I give to the poor; and if I have taken any thing from any man by false accusation, I restore him fourfold.

And Jesus said unto him, This day is salvation come to this house, forasmuch as he also is a son of Abraham.

For the Son of Man is come to seek and to save that which was lost.

If we try to interpret this story literally, we find it to have very little meaning. We even wonder that an episode of such slight significance was included in Luke's narrative. But when we bring to light its spiritual meaning, we find quite another story and one of the most important of all the lessons given to us in the entire Gospel of Luke. From the esoteric standpoint this is not simply the story of a man who climbed a tree in order to see Christ Jesus pass by, and whose guest Christ chose to be for a time. Some no doubt may read into this story a reward of faith in and enthusiasm for the great Master, and that because Zacchaeus possessed these attributes the Master chose him from out the great throng surrounding Him and said that He would be his guest. But there is a much deeper meaning to be found here.

Zacchaeus is taken from the Hebrew name *Zakkay* meaning "the pure." The tree with its rising sap, its leaves, its blossoms and fruitage at the top, has ever been a symbol in all esoteric schools of the ascending spinal spirit fire. Buddha received his enlightenment under the banyan tree; Gurnemanz taught the Grail Knights under a tree; Elijah received his illumination under the juniper tree; and Christ Jesus suffered His great agony for all humanity under the olive tree. All of these stories and many others have the same occult significance: they symbolize the only way by which illumination and liberation, the chief goals of all aspirants, are attained.

By purity, sacrifice and service the aspirant ascends like Zacchaeus to a high place, from which he sees the Master and hears the joyful words of promise: "Today I must abide at thy house."

This story of Zacchaeus is universal in its appeal. Christ Jesus trod the way of the cross for each one of us. His blessed words have been ringing down through the ages: "I am the way, the truth, and the life: no man cometh unto the Father, but by me." And yet man has not understood what He meant. For more than nineteen hundred years we have studied the Bible and still remain blind to its real meaning—namely, that *no one can save us but ourselves.* We must learn that He is indeed the way, the truth, and the life; and at the same time that the way, the truth, and the life are all within ourselves, for we are all Christs in the making.

We must become wholly pure and wholly loving before we can hear Him say, "This day is salvation come to this house" (the purified body), for it is only as we demonstrate purity and love that we may become "a son of Abraham." The story of Abraham is not only the story of the founding of the Jewish race but is the story of the spiritual regeneration of all mankind as well.

Zacchaeus, like Matthew, followed the despised profession of a publican. He lived in the city of Jericho, estimated revenues and collected taxes for the Roman government.

After Zacchaeus became an adherent of Christ, the Master did not bid him renounce all and "follow me" as He had done to Matthew, for not all disciples are called to the teaching ministry but may have another service to perform. Some disciples today, as in the Master's time, must give their all in dedication to the inner life. Others must perform their spiritual work where they find themselves in the world, ennobling their profession and endeavoring to bring spiritual law and order into the affairs of the business world. This seems to have been the task allotted to Zacchaeus as his part in helping to put before mankind the ideals of a Christed regime. It remains an important problem to be dealt with in the New Age, when all business must be centered in the Golden Rule. Nor can it be brought about in any other way than by certain illuminated disciples remaining in the world to serve right where destiny places them.

Inner Realm Teachings

John 14:1-4.

Let not your heart be troubled: ye believe in God, believe also in me.

In my Father's house are many mansions: if it were not so, I would have told you. I go to prepare a place for you.

And if I go and prepare a place for you, I will come again, and receive you unto myself; that where I am, there ye may be also.

And whither I go ye know, and the way ye know.

The many mansions spoken of in this passage are the different realms of the heaven world wherein spirits learn various lessons befitting their development between earth lives. The Master had taught His Disciples the way of attainment unto this high plane. Thomas, Philip and Jude were among those receiving the deeper instructions. He replies to their questions: "I am the way, the truth, and the life: no man cometh unto the Father but by me."

Only as the Christ is awakened within can the aspirant become the true disciple who demonstrates the promise of the Christ: "And whatsoever ye shall ask in my name, that will I do, that the Father may be glorified in the Son. If ye shall ask anything in my name I will do it" (John 14:13, 14). The mystic key which explains why so few have been able to realize this promise is contained in the Master's next words: "If ye love me, keep my commandments." To love the Christ calls for more than lip service; it means keeping His commandments, or *living the life* as He has outlined it in the principal steps of His Ministry. The priceless spiritual compensation to such an one is the fulfillment of that most precious of Christ's loving promises, that whatsoever is asked in His name shall be granted.

John 14:16, 17, 26.

And I will pray the Father, and he shall give you another Comforter, that he may abide with you forever.

Even the Spirit of truth, whom the world cannot receive, because it seeth him not, neither knoweth him: but ye know him; for he dwelleth with you, and shall be in you.

But the Comforter, which is the Holy Ghost, whom the Father will send in my name, He shall teach you all things, and bring all things to your remembrance, whatsoever I have said unto you.

John 15:26.

But when the comforter is come, whom I will send unto you from the Father, even the Spirit of truth, which proceedeth from the Father, He shall testify of me:

The Comforter, explains the Christ, is the Holy Ghost, or the feminine phase of Jehovistic expression. He is the law that has been tempered with love; it is the external concepts that have found inner sanction and the reasoning mind that has become illumined by the light of the heart. The Comforter is the inner guidance which lighteth every man that cometh into the world, that light which so long is obscured by mortal mind but which, when awakened, leads to the fulfillment of all Truth. "He shall teach you all things and bring all things to your remembrance." The soul is the fountain of wisdom, the picture book of past ages. Through the awakened Christ power within, this storehouse of wisdom and understanding becomes accessible and its resources available for daily living.

John 14:18, 19.

I will not leave you comfortless: I will come to you.

Yet a little while, and the world seeth me no more; but ye see me: because I live, ye shall live also.

Material man, bound by the limitation of the physical senses, cannot know the glory of the Christ whose all-enveloping radiance and harmony are discernible to those who have eyes to see and ears to hear; such know always that infinite aura of peace which nothing else can give. "Peace I leave with you, my peace I give unto you: not as the world giveth, give I unto you. Let not your heart be troubled, neither let it be afraid" (John 14:27).

"Abide in me, and I in you" for "without me ye can do nothing." Often the Master reiterates the great truth which is to become fundamental in New Age religion—the Christ must be born within man himself. Let "the Christ be formed in you," says Paul.

John 15:12-15.

This is my commandment, That ye love one another as I have loved you

Greater love hath no man than this, that a man lay down his life for his friends.

Ye are my friends, if ye do whatsoever I command you.

Henceforth I call you not servants; for the servant knoweth not what his lord doeth: but I have called you friends; for all things that I have heard of my Father I have made known unto you.

In this passage we have the greatest of Christ's commandments: to love one another; to love with that love which transfigured the Master's life and caused Him to lay down His life for the world, that He might become the Saviour of all men and the *Planetary Spirit* of the earth. It is this same power of love which has set its seal of glory upon the Gospel of John, so that wherever the Christian Bible is known His message bears the deepest and most potent influence.

John 16:7.

Nevertheless I tell you the truth: It is expedient for you that I go away: for if I go not away the Comforter will not come unto you; but if I depart I will send him unto you.

Christ cleansed the desire strata of the earth so that the desires of man might become purified; in this way He helped prepare for man conditions conducive to higher spiritual development. For the pioneers, His work was the rending of the veil before the Mystery Temple that the deeper Christian Mysteries might be revealed. This Path could only be opened by the Christ through functioning as the *indwelling Planetary Spirit* of the earth, which office He could not assume until after accomplishing the Crucifixion and entering into the very earth itself. The entrance into the deeper Mysteries develops the power of the Christed consciousness, the Comforter to be born within man.

John 16:12-15.

I have yet many things to say unto you, but ye cannot bear them now.

Howbeit when he, the Spirit of truth, is come, he will guide you into all truth: for he shall not speak of himself; but whatsoever he shall hear, that shall he speak: and he will shew you things to come.

He shall glorify me: for he shall receive of mine, and shall shew it unto you.

All things that the Father hath are mine: therefore said I, that he shall take of mine, and shall shew it unto you.

The World of Life Spirit, or of the Christ consciousness, is the realm of divine harmony, unity, eternal life. Therein is contained the complete and permanent record of the Earth Period —its past, present and future development. One who can read its records knows that no secrets may be concealed from him. "He will guide you into all truth," said Christ Jesus; "he will show you many things to come."

John 16:25-28.

These things have I spoken unto you in proverbs: but the time cometh, when I shall no more speak unto you in proverbs, but I shall shew you plainly of the Father.

At that day ye shall ask in my name: and I say not unto you, that I will pray the Father for you:

For the Father himself loveth you, because ye have loved me, and have believed that I came out from God.

I came forth from the Father, and am come into the world: again, I leave the world, and go to the Father.

Through His sacrifice He was uplifted to know the greater glories of the religion of the Father. The Disciples who followed in His way of the cross and martyrdom also were elevated later to this same state of spiritual exaltation. The Christ declares that He will no longer have to conceal the Mysteries beneath words and symbols, for "by their own daily living they will become worthy." He says: "I shall shew you plainly of the Father." Also: "These things I have spoken unto you, that in me ye might have peace. In the world ye shall have tribulation: but be of good cheer; I have overcome the world" (John 16:33).

The Initiate Prayer for the Illumined

The XVII chapter of John's Gospel contains the words of the Master's last prayer upon earth. At this time He had with him only the innermost group of the Disciples who had received the holy teachings embodied in the ceremonial of the Last Supper, and the final teachings contained within the XIV-XVI chapters of John. He concludes this work with prayer for these few who have remained faithful. "I pray for them: I pray not for the world, but for them which thou hast given me; for they are thine" (John 17:9). This last communion closes with a prayer unto the Father in which Christ consigns them to His care and in which He reaches the heights of communion, of at-one-ment: "The Father and I are one." In the beginning of His Ministry He taught them how to pray the universal prayer. His parting instruction pertains to that height of communion wherein the exalted spirit is one with the divine; it is the prayer of the illumined one, the Initiate. It is no longer the prayer of petition, offering or demand, but a wordless, soulful ecstasy which sounds forth in a chant of praise and adoration. It intones a similar keynote to the rhapsody of Paul when proclaiming that: "In him we live, and move, and have our being."

John 17:1-4.

These words spake Jesus, and lifted up his eyes to heaven, and said, Father, the hour is come; glorify thy Son, that thy Son also may glorify thee:

As thou hast given him power over all flesh, that he should give eternal life to as many as thou hast given him.

And this is life eternal, that they might know thee the only true God, and Jesus Christ, whom thou hast sent.

I have glorified thee on the earth: I have finished the work which thou gavest me to do.

The above has reference to the Master's esoteric mission and to His becoming the Planetary Spirit of the earth. Also, it tells of His bringing the new religion to all the world and opening the way of Initiation into the Christian Mysteries for whosoever wills to come.

John 17:5, 24.

And now, O Father, glorify thou me with thine own self with the glory which I had with thee before the world was.

Father, I will that they also, whom thou hast given me, be with me where I am; that they may behold my glory, which thou hast given me: for thou lovedst me before the foundation of the world.

In these verses the Christ refers to His aeonic evolution which began before the creation of the earth. He belongs to the archangelic life wave.

John 17:6-8.

I have manifested thy name unto the men which thou gavest me out of the world: Thine they were, and thou gavest them me; and they kept thy word.

Now they have known that all things whatsoever thou hast given me are of thee.

For I have given unto them the words which thou gavest me; and they have received them, and have known surely that I came out from thee, and they have believed that thou didst send me.

Through first-hand knowledge the esoteric group had learned something of the truth of His work and mission. Throughout this beautiful prayer the Christ is instructing the Disciples how to surround themselves with an aura of protection.

John 17:15-17.

I pray not that thou shouldest take them out of the world, but that thou shouldest keep them from the evil.

They are not of the world, even as I am not of the world.

Sanctify them through thy truth: thy word is truth.

Christ sent His Disciples forth to demonstrate His teachings, for in them His precepts had become living powers; this is true discipleship. "As thou hast sent me into the world, even so have I also sent them into the world" (John 17:18).

Christ came to point the way to first hand knowledge not only to His immediate Disciples, but to all the world. "Neither pray I for these alone, but for them also which shall believe on me through their word; that they all may be one; as thou, Father, art in me, and I in thee, that they also may be one in us: that the world may believe that thou hast sent me" (John 17:20, 21).

Whosoever knocketh, to him it shall be opened. Whosoever thirsteth, he shall be filled. Each aspirant to Christian discipleship must live the life, that he may know the doctrine. Every spirit is potentially divine; every ego, a Christ in the making.

John 17:25, 26.

O righteous Father, the world hath not known thee: but I have known thee, and these have known that thou hast sent me.

And I have declared unto them thy name, and will declare it: that the love wherewith thou hast loved me may be in them, and I in them.

To achieve that perfect communion voiced in the above a complete submergence of self is necessary, as instanced in the life of the Christ. The manifestation of the Father in man means the spiritualizing of the mind; the manifestation of the Christ, or son, in man means the illumination of the life with the power of the heart or Love Principle by way of the Comforter, the Holy Ghost, which works within both. One in whom this has been accomplished partakes at will of the mystic bread and wine, and performs the love works of a Christed one amid the sufferings of the world. In him the Holy Trinity manifests as a living power in a renewed body (a new mind and heart) and in a transformed consciousness. This is the goal of the Christian religion and was demonstrated by the Disciples at Pentecost, when they realized something of that for which the Christ prayed to the Father: "that the love wherewith thou hast loved me may be in them, and I in them."

HANDWRITING ON THE WALL OF TIME

Legends that Usher in the New Dispensation

Matthew 24—*Mark* 13—*Luke* 21

No one can fail to observe that many of the signs herein described are now in evidence upon the earth. Another decade will produce the manifestation of many of them, as the great travail increases that will only "be shortened for the elect's sake."

In the light of the hidden wisdom, the Holy Land becomes the focal center of spiritual vibrations released upon the earth. Palestine was prepared by Initiates for the mission of Christ Jesus vast cycles of time preceding His coming. Their work is still being carried on through the channels of various Initiatory Temples. The spiritual currents are being concentrated for such purpose by the Master Jesus and the Disciples from their center in the spiritual realms above the city of Jerusalem, in preparation for the rebuilding of that New Earth which must presage the second coming of the Christ.

There are numerous references to this higher Jerusalem. Peter in his revelation says: "We have created the upper Jerusalem above the waters which are above the Third Heaven, hanging directly over the lower Jerusalem." And Paul in Galatians 4:25, 26 writes: "Now this Agar is Mt. Sinai in Arabia and answereth to Jerusalem that now is, and is in bondage with her children. But Jerusalem which is above is free, which is the mother of us all."

These truths were familiar to the early Christian communities, hence the custom of praying with faces turned toward Jerusalem.

From the occult viewpoint the most important event of the World War was bringing Palestine again under the banner of Christ. The coming travail which will be world-wide in scope and intensity, will center again in the Holy Land. It will be here that the final conflict, the great battle of Armageddon, will take place. This conflict will mean the final overcoming of the powers of destruction and the definite ushering in of the New Day, the New Order of Angels and of men.

Matthew, Mark and Luke describe the chaotic world condition into which humanity is now entering. The knell of the final destruction which leads toward the light of the New Day is given in Luke 21:20: "And when ye shall see Jerusalem compassed with armies, then know that the desolation thereof is nigh."

Reading in the Memory of Nature, the Christ showed His most advanced Disciples, Peter, James, John and Andrew, the signs that accompany the closing days of the present age. Chaos and confusion, both in the workings of nature and in the life of man, must herald such a great disintegration.

Many shall come proclaiming themselves the great Teacher, and promising deliverance from this chaotic condition. The teachings of the Bible are clear and definite on this subject. The Christ will never return to earth again in a physical body. A sufficient number must qualify to meet Him in the air of the New Earth, and such will behold Him coming in the clouds with great power and glory.

This generation (age, earth-day) shall not pass until these things are fulfilled. The present earth shall pass away (with the end of material manifestation) but the words of the Christ are the precepts of eternal Law. The Christ taught the eternal progression of the spirit through and beyond all time and space. Not even the Angels or Archangels, of whom the Christ is chief, may know the time of His return; for that depends solely upon the progress of man. Man's failure to keep pace with the evolution prescribed for him by the Lords of Destiny evoked the first coming of this great Being Who offered Himself as the Lord and Saviour of the world. The time of His second coming waits the awakening of the Christ powers within man himself and their demonstration outwardly.

The esoteric truth concerning the Christ and His mission, a clearer understanding of what it is that man must do to speed His return, is the gospel that must first be published among all nations. The Christ came as the Redeemer of the world. He belongs to no one nation, race, or creed. His mission is universal and in Him was realized that for which all previous Teachers labored: "what I say unto you I say unto all, Watch."

CHAPTER V

Culmination of the Ministry:

The Passiontide

The exalted initiatory work undertaken through the week of the Passion was inaugurated on the Saturday preceding the Triumphal Entry with the Initiation Rite of Lazarus. Due to the upward course of man's evolution, the ancient phases of Initiation, together with certain aspects of the Jehovistic religion, were passing away. The Christ came "to make all things new." The forces which He released with His coming were necessary to save humanity from losing its way in a materialism which was destined to become darker and denser for many centuries that lay ahead. But in the orderly processes of growth, the new takes over and incorporates the values that have been created in the old. Thus, in the initiatory Rite of Lazarus both the processes that prevailed in the old rituals and those that were now being instigated in the new were combined, the result being the birth of the new Christian Mysteries. This event, therefore, marked the beginning of the Holy Easter Mysteries, or the deeper spiritual teachings upon which was founded the early Christian Church.

The great power possessed by the early Church—power to heal and to perform miracles—was derived from its knowledge of these Mysteries. Later, as worldly interests encroached more and more upon the Church and materialistic thinking darkened increasingly the consciousness of man, the Church lost contact with its original source of power and fell into relative impotency, a condition that has prevailed for centuries past and which continues into our own time. Not until the truths of Initiation are recovered by the Church can it again come into the power that will enable it to lead mankind in effecting the regeneration required to qualify it for establishing a Christed order on this earth. There have been always some, both in and out of the Church, who have retained the inner light and conserved for humanity the wisdom of the initiatory teachings. These we know as the illustrious saints whose lives and works have glorified the pages of history in centuries past and present.

For example, in the ancient rites of Egypt and Babylon, rites derived originally from Atlantis, the candidate for Initiation was taken out of his physical body by the supervising Teacher. During a three and a half day period on the inner planes the active desire centers of the applicant made their impress on the centers of his etheric body, these two vehicles having been withdrawn simultaneously for this purpose. Thus a supernormal condition induced by an Initiate Teacher was necessary to achieve this result. With the coming of the Christ this condition was altered, making it possible for man to attain to his development in normal waking conditions which had hitherto been possible only in an abnormal state and with specially supervised conditions under higher guidance. Awakening from the trance state, the neophyte of the pre-Christian Initiations was hailed as one risen from the dead. He was truly "new born," having acquired supernormal faculties and powers which had hitherto been beyond his experience.

Materialistic thinking and sensual living tend to interlock the etheric and desire bodies so closely as to make Initiation extremely difficult, if not impossible. Such was the general condition of humanity at the time of the coming of Christ Jesus. His work was to set man free from this barrier to higher spiritual attainment. The beginning of this accomplishment is produced by means of concentration and meditation to which is added the nightly exercise of retrospection, all of which formed a part of the teachings of the early Church. In concentration the masculine pole of spirit, or the will, is primarily active; in meditation, the feminine pole, or imagination, is the dominant factor. By means of such exercises the centers of the desire body can be impressed upon the etheric without dissociating the latter from the physical body. At the present time, due to the prevailing materiality, the difficulty in severing the two vehicles in the way of pre-Christian times is so great as to be likely to prove disastrous. Insanity and even death would too often be the result.

The most highly advanced of all the followers of Christ was chosen to receive the new form of Christian Initiation, This was the disciple best beloved of the Master whose initiatory name was Lazarus. The name Lazarus means "whom God assists." It was the high status of his devolpment that enabled him to respond to the initiatory summons: "Lazarus come forth."

It was the bridging of the Old and the New that took place in the raising of Lazarus which brought such great rejoicing to the people when Christ Jesus made His triumphal entry into Jerusalem on Palm Sunday, the day following the Initiation of Lazarus.

"Come forth! Loose him and let him go." These mystic words bear the message of the spiritual advancement that came to Lazarus. But they were not agreeable to the Pharisees and chief priests who were not accepting Christ Jesus as their Messiah since He was performing rites in the open that they had held to be kept secret. They resented whatever did not conform to the established religious practices. Hence the persecution of the Christ and His followers. Fearing that the raising of Lazarus would so increase His popularity as to cause Him to become great enough to jeopardize Temple interests, they began on this same night to plot His destruction. The passage from the Old Dispensation into the fresh revelations of the New did not come without placing Christ Jesus on the Cross and the sacrificial blood of the countless Christian Martyrs that followed.

John 11:47-53

Then gathered the chief priests and the Pharisees a council, and said, What do we? for this man doeth many miracles.

If we let him thus alone, all men will believe on him: and the Romans shall come and take away both our place and nation.

And one of them, named Caiaphas, being the high priest that same year, said unto them, Ye know nothing at all,

Nor consider that it is expedient for us, that one man should die for the people, and that the whole nation perish not.

And this spake he not of himself: but being high priest that year, he prophesied that Jesus should die for that nation;

And not for that nation only, but that also he should gather together in one the children of God that were scattered abroad.

Then from that day forth they took counsel together for to put him to death.

This was man's reaction to the heritage of eternal life and light which the great Teacher brought to earth. And though thousands of years have passed, only the few have as yet any true conception of what this eternal life really is, or the process that leads to its realizaion.

THE PASSIONTIDE

The Rite of the Triumphal Entry

Mark 11:1-9.

And when they came nigh to Jerusalem, unto Bethphage and Bethany, at the mount of Olives, he sendeth forth two of his disciples.

And saith unto them, Go your way into the village over against you: and as soon as ye be entered into it, ye shall find a colt tied, whereon never man sat; loose him, and bring him.

And if any man say unto you, Why do ye this? say ye that the Lord hath need of him; and straightway he will send him hither.

And they went their way, and found the colt tied by the door without in a place where two ways met; and they loosed him.

And certain of them that stood there said unto them, What do ye, loosing the colt?

And they said unto them even as Jesus had commanded; and they let them go.

And they brought the colt to Jesus, and cast their garments on him, and he sat upon him.

And many spread their garments in the way: and others cut down branches off the trees, and strawed them in the way.

And they that went before, and they that followed, cried, saying, Hosanna; Blessed is he that cometh in the name of the Lord:

John 12:12-17.

On the next day much people that were come to the feast, when they heard that Jesus was coming to Jerusalem,

Took branches of palm trees, and went forth to meet him, and cried, Hosanna: Blessed is the King of Israel that cometh in the name of the Lord.

And Jesus, when he had found a young ass, sat thereon; as it is written,

Fear not, daughter of Sion: behold, thy King cometh, sitting on an ass's colt.

These things understood not his disciples at the first; but when Jesus was glorified, then remembered they that these things were written of him, and that they had done these things unto him.

The people therefore that was with him when he called Lazarus out of his grave, and raised him from the dead, bare record.

One-third of the Gospels is devoted to the death and the Resurrection of Christ Jesus. Holy Week, the last week that He remained among men, constitutes the most important part of His work upon earth. The Triumphal Entry, which is celebrated in the Church as Palm Sunday, begins this eventful week, every step of which is fraught with mystic meaning for the aspirant to the higher life.

As Christ did not belong to the human life wave, He had no earth causation to liquidate, and consequently He was able to cover the entire Path of Initiation for our Earth Period in the three years of His ministry. Man requires many life cycles for such attainment, the length of time depending upon his development and the degree to which he spiritualizes the human will and awakens the power of love that is within.

As we have pointed out so frequently, the important events in the life of the Christ have their parallels in other religions and in the lives of other Teachers of cosmic truths. In the Mysteries of Eleusis, the Triumphal Entry had its correspondence in the joyous procession led by the victorious neophyte who had become an Initiate. Of Buddha it is recorded: "With the solemn entry of Buddha, the people swept the pathway, the gods strewed flowers on the road and branches of the coral tree; the men bore branches of all manner of trees, and men and gods shouted 'All hail'." In the Egyptian Mystery processionals a picture was carried of the new king driving his chariot and waving palm branches to the plaudits of the assembled multitude.

The Triumphal Entry, therefore, is symbolic of a high spiritual illumination attained through Initiation, and has been so considered throughout the ages. The ass signifies a bearer of peace; the palm, honor and victory. Palms were planted around the Holy of Holies.

To the wisdom of the ancient teachings, as given in the Lunar Mysteries, the Christ added a new note. He asked for a colt whereupon man never sat: *Loose him and bring him.* He commissioned the Disciples to do this, as He was instructing them in the deeper Mysteries belonging to the new Christian religion. *The Lord* (law) *hath need of him.* Spiritual evolution always follows a spiral path. Man outgrows old forms of spiritual understanding just as he does obsolete modes of transportation and crude means of physical illumination.

Jesus was set upon the colt, only after the Disciples had placed their garments (works, fruitage of their labors) thereon. He was the ideal whom they were attempting to emulate. And as He went they spread their clothes in the way. Bethphage means "a house of dates" and Bethany, "house of figs," "fecundity or growth through the multiplying of fruits." As the Disciples visioned the new earth and the new race, when the more profound Christian teachings would be understood and manifested, they began to rejoice and praise God for all the mighty works they had seen. The king, one who attains in the name of cosmic law, is always heralded by Angel songs, that same joyous caroling that was heard on Holy Night: *Peace on earth and glory in the highest.* This peace was brought to the earth for the solace of all mankind by the King of Peace. Blessed indeed are those who find and walk in His way.

The Initiations brought to earth by the Christ are the very life-blood of humanity's future; they *are* the future. If these were withdrawn, man's spiritual evolution would cease and the very stones would cry out for the life urge that would depart therewith. The Christ wept over the city of Jerusalem because it was so enmeshed in materiality and external forms and ceremonials. The Temple devotees, the priests, who should have been the first to accept and aid in the furtherance of His work, were the most active and hostile in their denunciation and persecution of Him. History repeats itself. It is the prevailing established form of religion that is strongest in opposition to any new or advanced teaching. Yet, since the love and wisdom of God are infinite, so, too, are His continued and progressive revelations of Himself.

The two most advanced of the Disciples, Peter and John, found the colt (wisdom) tied without in a place where two paths meet. These two paths, the way of knowledge and works and the way of faith and vision, meet at the cross of liberation from the body. This was demonstrated by the Christ. The blending of the powers produced on the two ways—the path of the head and the path of the heart—produces the superman, the Adept.

This is the work of the Christian Mysteries, and the ceremonial of the Triumphal Entry symbolizes the entrance into these higher truths. That this work is difficult of attainment is shown by the fact that Palm Sunday (the ideal) prcedes the sorrows of Holy Week. But that this ideal will be ultimately accomplished is assured in the glorious consummation of Holy Week, the Resurrection Morn or Easter. Easter symbolizes not only the Christ as the Way-Shower teaching man the way immortality through His resurrection from the grave—or liberation from the body through Initiation—but also signifies his eventual liberation from the wheel of birth and death upon the physical plane. Advanced souls, however, are still free to return as teachers and helpers of the race if they choose. This is the inspiring goal of the Christian religion. It heralds the return of both the Master Jesus and the Christ in the active preparation of turning the kingdom over to God the Father.

Astrologically this work refers to the cycles of the Sun's passage through the paired zodiacal signs of Capricorn-Cancer and Sagittarius-Gemini.

Every event enacted in the life of Christ during the Passiontide represents some phase of Initiation into the Christian Mysteries. The Triumphal Entry typifies the joys of the Path as Calvary symbolizes its sorrows.

The culminating work of discipleship is that of being able to become en rapport with the Teacher at any moment and in any place. This ability was demonstrated perfectly by Mary all during the days of the Passiontide. Her continuous prayer at this time was that she might know in its totality all the suffering of her Lord. By means of her high and mystical attunement with Christ, Mary was able to receive and amalgamate within her own pure soul the tremendous powers emanating from the various initiatory experiences represented by the events which transpired in the life of the Master during the Passiontide, thus tremendously accelerating her own spiritual progress.

Although she remained in the house of Lazarus in Bethany, in this mystical attunement Mary both visioned and shared in the joyful and the sorrowful events of the Triumphal Entry. She noted, in contrast to the general rejoicing and plaudits of the multitude, the sorrowful though majestic demeanor of the Master as He gazed sadly out over beloved Jerusalem, His understanding heart heavy with foreknowledge of the anguish of centuries ahead because the people would repudiate their Lord Christ.

The First Three Days of the Passiontide

Lazarus and his sisters, Mary and Martha, were among the innermost circles of Christ. The first three days of the Passiontide were spent in their home. Here His closest followers were assembled for a few final, precious days of instruction and communion with their beloved Teacher. In the interval between Sunday of the Triumphal Entry and Holy Thursday, to Mary the Saviour imparted many of the Mysteries of His coming and the processes of the Atonement.

To the disciples who were ready to receive it, Christ revealed the processes of mystic transmutation whereby the Mother Mary would become a part of His suffering and travail, and also something of the glorious recompense of glory to be hers in the heights of the Easter Vigil.

The deeper teachings given during these days to Mary and Martha are beautifully portrayed in the allegory of the supper prepared for the Master in the home of Lazarus as described by John in the twelfth chapter of his Gospel. Although Martha was being prepared through service for the higher exaltation of consciousness termed Initiation, the text makes plain that she was not ready to partake fully of the great spiritual feast. Lazarus, the recently initiated one, sat at the Master's table and partook freely with Him of the Waters of Eternal Life and of that Bread which, when a man learns to partake of it, shall free him from ever hungering again.

Mary, further advanced than Martha, stood at the very entrance to the Temple of Light, as evidenced by her dedicatory ceremonial of anointing the feet of the Master.

On the second day of the Passiontide the Master instructed other men and women disciples in advanced work preparatory to the glorious Resurrection Rite.

On the third day Judas succumbed to the temptation of the priests. Judas typifies the lower, instinctive nature; the priests, the human or mortal. When these two forces are paramount, the Christ or spiritual nature is always betrayed and, in turn, their own self-destruction is inevitable as instanced by Judas' tragic end.

The Sublime Rite of the Eucharist

The origin of the ceremonial of the Last Supper is lost in antiquity. Its observance may be traced through the earliest of the Mystery Schools. The Persians celebrated the Festival of the Eucharist, a Greek word meaning "thanksgiving" or Love Feast. Upon receiving the initiatory Mithraic rites, certain words were spoken and the neophyte partook of bread and water. This was also one of the important customs connected with the Eleusinian Mysteries in Greece. These Mysteries were built around Ceres, the goddess of grain, and Bacchus, the god of wine. Wheat was considered the most valuable of all plants given to man; it was a love gift from the gods of Venus. Bacchus was the god of true spiritual ecstasy obtainable only through direct communion with the Divine Lover. From the Temple comes the mystic utterance: "Love grows cold without Bread and Wine."

The Mithraic sacrament included three large vases filled with white wine. Before the enchanted gaze of the candidate these changed into blood-red, purple, and azure blue. One who has touched the inner Mysteries knows that this transformation belongs to the work of the high Initiate. Bread and wine signify that spirit must enter into and transform matter; that divinity is awakened within through the quickening processes of Initiation.

The Old Testament conceals the secrets of the New while the New Testament reveals the inner teachings of the Old. Melchizedek, the mysterious priest of Salem, in his consecration of Abraham, gave to the new Aryan peoples the ideal symbolized by the Feast of Bread and Wine. Canaan became Palestine; Salem, the city of Jerusalem. And here the Christ consecrated His Disciples through the conjoined powers signified by the bread and wine, the Christ Himself being *a priest forever after the Order of Melchizedek.*

The degree of sanctity with which the Last Supper is observed varies according to the development of the peoples to whom it is given. Regeneration is typified by seed and grape. The vineyard, throughout ancient symbology, is mankind: the vine is life; the fruits, the essence of experience. The king and a son of the king partake of the wine from above, through which is born wisdom and understanding.

The early Christians celebrated the Holy Supper nightly, and mighty works were done through the spiritual influences generated in these assemblies. The bread consecrated in these sacred feasts was so imbued with spiritual power that it could be taken out among the sick and used as a means for restoring them to health.

Origen says: "If thou wilt go up with Christ to celebrate the Passover, He will give to thee that bread of benediction, His own body, and will vouchsafe to thee His own blood."

St. Ambrose of Milan describes the spiritual status of one who partakes worthily of this sacred feast thus: "Purer than any solar ray should be that hand; the mouth filled with spiritual fire, the tongue purpled with that glorious blood."

This mystic ceremonial was divided into three separate steps or degrees, to each of which participants were admitted according to development. Only two, Peter and John, were ready to receive the deepest work.

The first part consisted of a prayer of general thanksgiving and ended with a seraphic hymn in which the participants were joined by many invisible hosts (visible alone to those who have eyes to see). The second part included the consecration of the elements by invoking the power of the Holy Spirit. Not so many were eligible for the advanced work of this second degree as for the first. In the third part the consecrated elements were taken out and distributed among the sick and the imprisoned to aid in their healing and redemption.

Ignatius, a disciple of John, referred to this consecrated bread as the medicine of immortality. Tertullian explained the breaking of this sacred bread as a symbol of multiplication of the power of the Divine Word, that Word which the Master proclaimed as being spirit and life—which truth the early Christians so gloriously demonstrated in their lives and works.

Through the Bible study of the present Piscean era, the reign of orthodox Christianity, the sacrifice of the Holy Supper has been merely an external concept held in commemoration of that last evening the Saviour was with His Own. The New Age Bible study seeks to reveal the inner workings of this sacred ceremonial so that modern disciples of mystic Christianity may again manifest the powers possessed by those holy men and women who sat at His feet and learned to follow in His steps. The New Age demands a revitalized Christianity capable of demonstrating the truths taught by the Master and made manifest among the first Disciples. Nothing less than this will satisfy. Reason demands an answer for the truths which the heart has always sanctioned.

Matthew 26:17-30.

Now the first day of the feast of unleavened bread the disciples came to Jesus, saying unto him, Where wilt thou that we prepare for thee to eat the passover?

And he said, Go into the city to such a man, and say unto him, The Master saith, My time is at hand; I will keep the passover at thy house with my disciples.

And the disciples did as Jesus had appointed them; and they made ready the passover.

Now when the even was come, he sat down with the twelve.

And as they did eat, he said, Verily I say unto you, that one of you shall betray me.

And they were exceeding sorrowful, and began every one of them to say unto him, Lord, Is it I?

And he answered and said, He that dippeth his hand with me in the dish, the same shall betray me.

The Son of man goeth as it is written of him: but woe unto that man by whom the Son of man is betrayed! It had been good for that man if he had not been born.

Then Judas, which betrayed him, answered and said, Master, is it I? He said unto him, Thou hast said.

And as they were eating, Jesus took bread, and blessed it, and brake it, and gave it to the disciples, and said, Take, eat; this is my body.

And he took the cup and gave thanks, and gave it to them, saying, Drink ye all of it;

For this is my blood of the new testament, which is shed for many for the remission of sins.

But I say unto you, I will not drink henceforth of this fruit of the vine, until that day when I drink it new with you in my Father's kingdom.

And when they had sung an hymn, they went out into the mount of Olives.

Matthew, the Gospel of Dedication to the Path, contains only the outline of work symbolized by the Last Supper. The more definite steps of accomplishment are described in the Gospels of Mark and Luke.

"Take, eat, this is My body." These were not mere empty words spoken as the bread was eaten. As previously stated, only those partook who were able to infuse into the elements a spiritual power and only holy men were able to do this.

The "blood of the new testament which is shed for the remission of sins" refers to the spiritual development offered to humanity in the new and deeper Christian Initiations. It is the law of love superseding that of the earlier dispensation which was under the law of consequence, or karma, decreeing an eye for an eye and a tooth for a tooth. Through repentance and reform this law of cause and effect may be surmounted here and now. The Master knew that the ideals He inculcated in the pioneers of the Piscean Age would not be accepted and demonstrated fully by humanity until the time of His return when He would drink the new wine (the enlarged powers of the spirit) in a New Age with a new and regenerated race.

Mark's account of the Last Supper states that all of the Disciples drank of it, meaning thereby that they all qualified for the deeper spiritual works.

In the original text the word used to describe the upper room designated by Christ Jesus is the same as the word used to describe the inn in Bethlehem wherein was no room for the Holy Birth.

The secret of the betrayal was known only by the Christ, Judas, Peter and John. The powers of faith and love always effect a transformation of the lower nature. "He then having received the sop went immediately out; and it was night."

Mark 14:17-21.

And in the evening he cometh with the twelve.

And as they sat and did eat, Jesus said, Verily I say unto you, One of you which eateth with me shall betray me.

And they began to be sorrowful, and to say unto him one by one, Is it I? and another said, Is it I?

And he answered and said unto them, It is one of the twelve, that dippeth with me in the dish.

The Son of man indeed goeth, as it is written of him: but woe to that man by whom the Son of man is betrayed! good were it for that man if he had never been born.

The ceremony of the Last Supper represents the complete transmutation of the lower nature into the higher; consequently,

Judas, the lower, could not remain. *It is one of the twelve that dippeth with me in the dish.* The awakened Christ within works upon mortal man and uses this redeemed power in building the new golden chalice of the soul. Chapters XIV to XVII of John's Gospel contain the most profound spiritual work given the Disciples. This work was revealed at the conclusion of the Holy Supper, *after the disappearance of Judas,* and is recorded only in John.

Christ sent Peter, who represents the faith which has become a dynamic quality in life, and John, who represents the power of love, into *the city,* or a new state of consciousness. The man with the pitcher of water, whom they were destined to meet, is the androgynous man of the Aquarian Age. The *guest chamber* is the new body that each must build through the spiritual attainment termed Initiation. The *upper room,* all furnished and prepared, symbolizes the organs in the head awakened through the transmutation of the life force. Only through these different steps mentioned in the Bible can we make ready for Him to enter and celebrate the Holy Supper within our own bodies..

These truths also have their outer significance. The *upper room* is said to have been the home of Mary, the mother of the writer of the Gospel of Mark, namely, John Mark. Here the risen Lord met with His Disciples, and later in this holy place they experienced the sacred mystery of Pentecost.

When the hour was come, refers to about 6 p. m. "The early evening stars were visible, and the threefold blast of the silver trumpet from the temple mount announced to all waiting Jerusalem that the Pascha had again begun."

"With desire I have desired," is a Hebrew expression meaning, "I have desired earnestly." Christ used this because He knew they could not partake of the Last Supper until they had made themselves worthy. This was no mere outward ceremonial of eating bread and drinking wine, but consisted of the deepest esoteric work in preparation for the inner Mysteries.

St. Dionysius, the first bishop of Athens, said that the sacrament was divided into three parts: first, Purification; second, Initiation; third, Accomplishment or Perfection. He also states that part of the ceremony pertained to the acquiring of deeper sight. These esoteric sacraments were open to the faithful only, and no spectators were allowed at the communions.

The apocryphal Acts of Thomas relate that a young man had committed murder. He came to partake of the Eucharist, but as he did so both his hands became paralyzed and he was unable to raise them to his mouth. The observance of this sacrament possessed much greater spiritual potency in Bible times than at present, due to the greater spiritual attainment both of those who administered the rite and those who took part in it. The celebrants of that early Christian period were Initiates; they were holy men and women, or such as were consciously preparing for Initiation. The early Christian Fathers state that demons, obsessing entities, were exorcised through the power of the Holy Supper.

"Take this, and divide it among yourselves." This points to preparatory work toward the ultimate establishment of an order of true brotherhood and fellowship.

Wine represents the masculine or head principle; bread the feminine or heart principle within man. Christ was teaching them to build the Philosopher's Stone within themselves. The body is the workshop of the spirit, and contains all the elements necessary to produce the *elixir vitae*. The Philosopher's Stone is not exterior to the body; the alchemist himself becomes that stone.

We must learn to make the cup within ourselves. It must be constantly filled with the waters of eternal life. When the disciple is able to drink in full understanding from this cup, which includes also the act of its replenishment, his love of and desire for the personal life are finished. He has found the entrance to a new and larger life that is immortal and eternal.

As has been previously stated many times throughout these New Age Bible Interpretations, the Christ came to bring the teachings of complete equality between man and woman. The privileges accorded His women disciples depended not upon their sex but upon their spiritual attainment.

The Mystic Christian knows that upon that Holy Thursday night, the great Master, in the final dispensation of His Grace and the concluding hours of His earth ministry, bestowed upon the most worthy of His followers the sublime powers of the Eucharist. Women were not excluded from this holy Rite. The women's table was presided over by the most blessed of women, the divine Mary. Much of the Revelation given to John as He rested upon the Master's heart, concerned the exaltation of the feminine and its relation to woman in general and to the holy Mary in particular. There are veiled references to these truths given in some of the church legends and it is only as the veil of secrecy is withdrawn that woman can assume her rightful place in the life and work of the Lord Christ.

THE RITE OF THE FOOT WASHING

John 13:4-17.

He riseth from supper, and laid aside his garments; and took a towel, and girded himself.

After that he poureth water into a basin, and began to wash the disciples' feet, and to wipe them with the towel wherewith he was girded.

Then cometh he to Simon Peter: and Peter saith unto him, Lord, dost thou wash my feet?

Jesus answered and said unto him, What I do thou knowest not now; but thou shalt know hereafter.

Peter saith unto him, Thou shalt never wash my feet. Jesus answered him, If I wash thee not, thou hast no part with me.

Simon Peter saith unto him, Lord, not my feet only, but also my hands and my head.

Jesus saith to him, He that is washed needeth not save to wash his feet, but is clean every whit: and ye are clean, but not all.

For he knew who should betray him; therefore said he, Ye are not all clean.

So after he had washed their feet, and had taken his garments, and was set down again, he said unto them, Know ye what I have done to you?

Ye call me Master and Lord: and ye say well; for so I am.

If I then, your Lord and Master, have washed your feet; ye also ought to wash one another's feet.

For I have given you an example, that ye should do as I have done to you.

Verily, verily, I say unto you, The servant is not greater than his lord; neither is he that is sent greater than he that sent him.

If ye know these things, happy are ye if ye do them.

Luke 9:48.

And he said unto them, Whosoever shall receive this child in my name receiveth me; and whosoever shall receive me receiveth him that sent me; for he that is least among you all, the same shall be great.

Matthew 23:23, 25, 27.

Woe unto you, scribes and Pharisees, hypocrites; for ye pay tithe of mint and anise and cummin, and have omitted the weightier matters of the law, judgment, mercy and faith. These ought ye to have done, and not to leave the other undone.

Woe unto you, scribes and Pharisees, hypocrites; for ye make clean the outside if the cup and of the platter, but within they are full of extortion and excess.

Woe unto you, scribes and Pharisees, hypocrites; for ye are like unto whited sepulchres, which indeed appear beautiful outward, but are within full of dead men's bones, and of all uncleanness.

The two words which encompass the entire life and work of the Master are love and humility. Nowhere in the Hebrew or any other oriental Scripture is there a more touching representation of these qualities than in the story of the Foot Washing as it is told in the New Testament of Christ. Throughout the Gospels the Master warns against the sins which stand, as it were, in contrast to the divine virtues of love and humility; and His denunciations of hypocrisy and pride, the contraries of love and humility, are particularly scathing. It is only in the Gospel of John, however, that the Rite of the Foot Washing occurs, the most humble of the Master's deeds, for it was not a miracle such as had excited the admiration of the multitude and the awed respect of the Disciples. It was a simple, domestic act which anyone could perform and which carried with it no halo of fame or extrinsic reward.

According to oriental custom, the feet were clad only in sandals. It was the duty of servants to perform this menial service for guests, pouring water on the feet as they were held over a basin, and drying them with a towel. The Disciples had made no effort toward thus serving the Christ, nor yet one another. They were occupied instead in disputations among themselves as to "which of them was accounted to be the greatest." When the Master observed their selfish personal ambitions He gently and lovingly took upon Himself the lowly task of performing this service for them. "What I do, thou knowest not now, but thou shalt know hereafter."

This simple deed has emphasized humility as the most essential requisite for aspirants to Christian attainment. "I have given you an example that ye should do as I have done unto you."

The Philosopher's Stone, that celestial body which Paul describes in the fifth chapter of II Corinthians, that body which becomes either as a diamond or a ruby stone, depending on the type of development, is not built when courting the adulation of throngs or seeking positions of prominence. The lofty spiritual development of the Christ lifted Him to the heights of the Transfiguration, and His love for humility caused Him to take upon Himself the form of a servant and to be fashioned in the likeness of man.

Thomas ā Kempis says in his incomparable manual of devotion, *The Imitation of Christ:* "He is truly great who hath great love. He is truly great that is little in himself and that maketh no account of any height of honor. He is truly wise that accounteth all earthly things as dung, that he may win Christ. And he is truly learned, that doeth the will of God, and forsaketh his own will."

John's is the only Gospel in which the denial of Peter is foretold. The other three simply record the fact after its occurrence. At the conclusion of the Last Supper at which He had given His Disciples His deepest esoteric instruction, the Master had but one more word for them, and that was love.

John 13:34, 35.

A new commandment I give unto you, That ye love one another; as I have loved you, that ye also love one another.

By this shall all men know that ye are my disciples, if ye have love one to another.

This commandment is as applicable to the present age as when spoken by the Lord of Love. Just so long as there are wars and rumors of wars, so long as man hates his fellowman and seeks revenge for wrongs, we are Christians in little more than profession and aspiration, for we are still in that attitude of mind or state of consciousness which belongs to the Jehovistic regime and the external law of the Ten Commandments. Christians are followers of that Way which is set forth in the Sermon on the Mount. Not until we begin to live these precepts are we truly Christians; before that we are merely aspirants to the Christian ideal.

After the inner lesson given to the Disciples through the Triumphal Entry, the Master again emphasized the importance of love as the supreme power.

The Testing of Peter

Mark 12:30, 31.

And thou shalt love the Lord thy God with all thy heart, and with all thy soul, and with all thy mind, and with all thy strength: this is the first commandment.

And the second is like, namely this, Thou shalt love thy neighbor as thyself. There is none other commandment greater than these.

John 13:36-38.

Simon Peter said unto him, Lord, whither goest thou? Jesus answered him, Whither I go, thou canst not follow me now; but thou shalt follow me afterwards.

Peter said unto him, Lord, why cannot I follow thee now? I will lay down my life for thy sake.

Jesus answered him, Wilt thou lay down thy life for my sake? Verily, verily, I say unto thee, The cock shall not crow, till thou hast denied me thrice.

Let him that standeth take heed lest he fall. Peter in this phase of development emphasizes the difficulty encountered by the aspirant in the cultivation of the *power of faith* which is unalterable. He had yet to become the perfected rock of Faith upon which the Church is builded.

The complete dedication of life is required, whether it be by a total renunciation of the physical body or laying it down as a *living* sacrifice. There can be no half-way measures in the working of spiritual law: hence the narrowness of the path and the few that are chosen. "I will lay down my life for thy sake." This avowal immediately brings its subtle tests and they are always threefold, as in the case of Peter. "And the Lord said, Simon, Simon, behold, Satan hath desired to have you, that he may sift you as wheat" (Luke 22:31). And most familiar also are the sorrowful words of the Teacher: Verily, verily, I say unto thee, thou wilt deny me thrice.

Peter was destined to learn the full meaning of the Agony Rite in the Garden. After his triple denial of the Master he returned in abject contrition to the Garden, there to face his own Gethsemane which was the conquest of Peter.

There, in that highly charged area, strengthened and encouraged by the ministering aid of Angels, this earnest and sincere Disciple by means of repentance and added purification lifted himself in consciousness to that exalted place where he would be further prepared and sustained for the higher illumination which he was to receive in that mystic interval between the Resurrection and the Ascension.

The Agony Rite in the Garden

Mark 14-26-38.

And when they had sung a hymn, they went out into the mount of Olives.

And Jesus saith unto them, All ye shall be offended because of me this night: for it is written, I will smite the shepherd, and the sheep shall be scattered.

But after that I am risen, I will go before you into Galilee.

But Peter said unto him, Although all shall be offended, yet will not I.

And Jesus saith unto him, Verily I say unto thee, That this day, even in this night, before the cock crow twice, thou shalt deny me thrice.

But he spake the more vehemently, If I should die with thee I will not deny thee in any wise. Likewise also said they all.

And they came to a place which was named Gethsemane: and he saith to his disciples, Sit ye here, while I shall pray.

And he taketh with him Peter and James and John, and began to be sore amazed, and to be very heavy;

And saith unto them, My soul is exceeding sorrowful unto death: tarry ye here, and watch.

And he went forward a little, and fell on the ground, and prayed that, if it were possible, the hour might pass from him.

And he said, Abba, Father, all things are possible unto thee; take away this cup from me: nevertheless not what I will, but what thou wilt.

And he cometh, and findeth them sleeping, and saith unto Peter Simon, sleepest thou? couldest not thou watch one hour?

Watch ye and pray, lest ye enter into temptation. The spirit truly is ready but the flesh is weak.

To the sincere neophyte, Gethsemane becomes a familiar place, watered with tears for suffering, sorrowing humanity. He too, becomes a man of sorrow and acquainted with grief, for whoever goes forward upon the way toward high spiritual attainment becomes increasingly responsive to the hurts of all living things about him and feels their suffering as his very own.

Finding the Garden of Sorrows is a very necessary step upon. the path, for it is pain only that unbars the gates of glory. "Before the feet can stand in the presence of the Masters, they must be washed in the blood of the heart."

The lesson of Gethsemane is learning to stand alone and to say, "Not my will but Thine be done." Many times we must follow Christ Jesus to drink of the cup of sorrow upon that lonely mount until this lesson has been learned. We must drain the cup to the very dregs, until by the cumulative pain which well nigh bursts the heart, we die to the personal self and live that we may give ourselves unreservedly and completely for healing and helping the world. When one learns to do this, by a sort of divine alchemy all passion becomes changed into compassion and into a divine understanding whose very power enables one to soothe and to heal. We can no longer blame others, judge harshly, criticize, or hate. We ask only that we may become a living sacrifice upon the altar of humanity, expecting no favors, no gratitude, not even understanding from those who are nearest and dearest to us. Our only desire is to live that we may serve. This is an extremely high ideal of attainment, but it is one which all must find before the final liberation from Gethsemane.

After the Supper, Christ Jesus and the Eleven passed through one of the open gates of the city, crossed the Kedron and ascended the steep slope of the Mount of Olives. Taking with Him Peter, James, and John, He asked the other Disciples to remain beneath the trees. The three who accompanied Him had been with Him at the raising of the daughter of Jairus, and had witnessed the Transfiguration. Peter and John had made the preparation for the Triumphal Entry and also for the Last Supper. These events have reference to certain spiritual developments of the Disciples.

The phrases "greatly amazed" and "sorely troubled" mean, in Greek, an awful isolation, a mental agony. At the time of the Temptation, Christ was tempted through pleasure and power. In Gethsemane He was tempted through pain and sorrow. The neophyte who learns to follow Him must pass through these same tests, their severity depending upon his own particular state of development. The higher we ascend, the harder become the tests. Very true it is that whom God loveth, He chasteneth.

Christ Jesus was endeavoring to have Peter, James, and John leave their bodies and follow Him into the World of Life Spirit, there to read the heavenly records and to understand the esoteric meaning of His mission, that they might know that His great Passion and death were not the end, but only the beginning of His work. But they failed Him. They betrayed the Christ within themselves, as well as the great Master, for they were yet so engrossed in the material, still so given to disputing about the high places they should receive in the New Kingdom, that they were unable to follow Him; "they were asleep" to these high spiritual truths. Christ Jesus knew now that the path must be trod alone. Humanity must remain yet for a time in darkness as to the real meaning of His work. He must continue to be misunderstood and betrayed, even by His own best-beloved, until the very end. The Disciples never fully understood the inner meaning of His work until that blessed day of illumination which we know as Pentecost.

The testing of Christ was threefold: The Temptation in the Wilderness, Gethsemane, and the Crucifixion. Of these, the agony of Gethsemane was likewise threefold: The failure of the beloved Disciples, the betrayal by Judas, and the realization that the cup must be drained to the last drop in misunderstanding and loneliness.

Judas had been made the treasurer of the band. His personal ambitions were thwarted by Christ Jesus' refusal to lead an army against Rome. He had expected the Master to proclaim Himself king and that he, Judas, should receive a high place among officials. As the Christ gave deeper and more spiritual truths, Judas became more hopelessly confused. Having no understanding of the deeper work, his confusions turned into baffled rage and hatred, culminating in the betrayal.

The powers of Christ, of John and of Judas, all represent powers within ourselves. It is for us to transmute the force of Judas into that of John and so awaken the divinity of the Christ within. We may well ponder the axiom of the ancient Greeks: "Man, know thyself."

Matthew 26:42-56.

He went away again the second time, and prayed, saying, "O my Father, if this cup may not pass away from me, except I drink it, thy will be done."

And he came and found them asleep again: for their eyes were heavy.

And he left them, and went away again, and prayed the third time, saying the same words.

Then cometh he to his disciples, and saith unto them, "Sleep on now, and take your rest: behold the hour is at hand, and the Son of man is betrayed into the hands of sinners.

Rise, let us be going: behold, he is at hand that doth betray me."

And while he yet spake, lo, Judas, one of the twelve, came, and with him a great multitude with swords and staves, from the chief priests and elders of the people.

Now he that betrayed him gave them a sign, saying, "Whomsoever I shall kiss, that same is he: hold him fast."

And forthwith he came to Jesus, and said, "Hail, Master;" and kissed him.

And Jesus said unto him, "Friend, wherefore art thou come?" Then came they, and laid hands on Jesus, and took him.

And behold, one of them which were with Jesus stretched out his hand, and drew his sword, and struck a servant of the high priest's, and smote off his ear.

Then Jesus said unto him, Put up again thy sword into his place: for all they that take the sword shall perish with the sword.

Thinkest thou that I cannot now pray to my Father, and he shall presently give me more than twelve legions of angels?

But how then shall the scriptures be fulfilled, that thus it must be?"

In that same hour said Jesus to the multitude, "Are ye come out as against a thief with swords and staves for to take me? I sat daily with you teaching in the temple, and ye laid no hold on me."

But all this was done, that the scriptures of the prophets might be fulfilled. Then all the disciples forsook Him, and fled.

Gethsemane is formed of two words, *gath*, "a press"; also "bitterness"; and *shemen*, "oil," "understanding," "wisdom." The cross must ever precede the crown; true wisdom is born of pain.

Three times did the Christ return to find the Disciples sleeping. They were unable to reach the exaltation of spirit that He knew. The betrayal of the Christ within man is threefold and comes through the weakness of the flesh, the strength of the desire nature, and the lack of spiritual power to know the constant, abiding communion of the "I am" within.

The Christ healed the ear of Malchus, servant of the high priest, by the use of the powerful life forces emanating from His own home world where all is life and love and harmony. The Christ transmitted the radiations from the high sphere to such a degree that to merely stand in His presence was to receive them.

The Master could have summoned legions of Angels and Archangels to His side, for He is Lord of them all, but He remained true to that vow which is always taken by one who would wield the powers of the Initiate: Every aid for others; nothing for self.

Luke 22:39-45.

And he came out, and went, as he was wont, to the mount of Olives; and his disciples also followed him.

And when he was at the place, he said unto them, Pray that ye enter not into temptation.

And he was withdrawn from them about a stone's cast, and kneeled down, and prayed.

Saying, Father, if thou be willing, remove this cup from me: nevertheless not my will, but thine, be done.

And there appeared an angel unto him from heaven, strengthening Him.

And being in an agony he prayed more earnestly: and his sweat was as it were great drops of blood falling down to the ground.

And when he rose up from prayer, and was come to his disciples, he found them sleeping for sorrow.

The Disciples were sleeping from sorrow. They were sorrowful because they were not yet able to reach that high place wherein the Master was endeavoring to lead them.

"His sweat was, as it were, great drops of blood falling to the ground." One of the never-ending wonders of the Bible is that deep occult truths are concealed within a few words. The Transfiguration depicts the transformation effected through the power of spirit; Gethsemane is this same power in its effect upon the body. The blood is "a most peculiar essence" and is the medium for the operations of the spirit in the body. The blood of the most advanced of the new race will be a gaseous light-substance. Its development depends upon the manifestation of love, harmony, unity and fellowship among men. John was looking far into the future when he stated: "If we walk in the light as He is in the light, we have fellowship one with another." The coming of the Light is dependent upon the manifestation of brotherhood and fellowship. The generation and concentration of power through the association of man with man and nation with nation in harmony of thought, unity of purpose, each for all and none for self, would establish a rhythm within the body of the earth that would bring about such transformations that the new heaven and the new earth would be brought into manifestation here and now. The Christ was instructing His Disciples in the inner workings of these powers of the spirit.

Upon *man himself* depends the realization of the light of that glad, new day, when the earth and its humanity shall know the holy joys of Resurrection time. Without the Crucifixion the wondrous mission of the Christ would have remained unfulfilled. The Gospels all make mention of this fact.

Matthew 26:54.

But how then shall the scriptures be fulfilled, that thus it must be?

Mark 14:49.

I was daily with you in the temple teaching, and ye took me not: but the scriptures must be fulfilled.

Luke 22:42, 43.

Saying, Father, if thou be willing remove this cup from me: nevertheless not my will, but thine be done.

And there appeared an angel unto him from heaven, strengthening him.

John 18:11.

Then said Jesus unto Peter, Put up thy sword into the sheath: the cup which my Father hath given me, shall I not drink it?

Each of the Gospels represents a different phase of spiritual development; therefore, many of the statements generally considered contradictory are found to be simply varied treatments of identical truths. Both Matthew and Mark state that all the Disciples fled when the Christ was imprisoned. The Christ Himself says: "Sleep on now and take your rest, behold the hour is at hand when the Son of man is betrayed into the hands of sinners."

Since the Disciples represent attributes of the soul to be awakened within man, at a certain stage they are asleep and unable to aid in the liberation of the imprisoned Christ.

Luke states that Peter, the power of faith, followed Him afar off.

John 18:15-18.

And Simon Peter followed Jesus, and so did another disciple; that disciple was known unto the high priest, and went in with Jesus into the palace of the high priest.

But Peter stood at the door without. Then went out that other disciple, who was known unto the high priest, and spake unto her that kept the door, and brought in Peter.

Then saith the damsel, that kept the door, unto Peter, Art not thou also one of this man's disciples? He saith, I am not.

And the servants and officers stood there, who had made a fire of coals; for it was cold: and they warmed themselves: and Peter stood with them, and warmed himself.

Peter and John are faith and love, the two wings of the spirit without which the Resurrection could not take place. Love leads the way. Faith wavers for a time without the door; that is, it remains an intellectual concept only. Such faith will never remove mountains. Before it can do this, it must, in company with love, be *brought within,* there to become a working magnetic power in consciousness. The damsel, spiritual intuition which always stands guard at the door, tempts the newly awakened light of faith. Often the Christ within is denied, while light and sustenance are sought among the outer or purely mental faculties, the officers and servants.

The Christ, in foretelling the betrayals of Peter and of Judas, was describing the failures and weakness of every aspirant who endeavors to walk the way of true Christian discipleship.

Gethsemane

The Agony Rite in the garden may well be termed the Rite of Transmutation. Christ's agony was caused by His effort to attune His vibration, that of a luminous Archangel, to the limiting confinement of the earth that He might become its indwelling planetary Spirit. When He opened Himself to the earth rhythm all the powerful and sinister currents of evil that abound in the world swept over Him. He not only felt their crushing weight but saw, in kaleidoscopic vision, their origin and purpose. Lust, anger and bitterness seared Him like flames while greed, selfishness and hatred bore down upon Him as leaden weights. The sorrow and anguish and suffering caused by man's wrongdoing wounded Him to the very depths of His loving and compassionate heart.

The limit of agony even an Archangel can know was brought about as pictures of the future passed before His vision and He saw how few of humanity's vast multitudes would recognize the meaning of His coming or the real significance of His purpose. He watched with profoundest sorrow as the dark veil of materialism blinded the modern world; then its consequent failure of discernment, its restlessness and fear. The blindness and ignorance of the masses as to His mission, the crystallization and ever-narrowing concept of those avenues which were formerly dedicated channels to His service, brought His Agony Rite to its culmination in the prayer: *Let this cup pass from me: nevertheless not as I will.*

Gethsemane was not on the Mount of Olives by chance. It was there because the mount marks the most highly charged of earth's areas. What the Christ accomplished in that highly charged Garden beneath the over-shadowing wings of Angels and Archangels was of profound significance for all mankind. It was the time when the whole program of planetary evolution received an added and powerful impulse destined to carry it further upon the ever-ascending spiral.

To this Mount of Olives, vibrant with spiritual power, John the Beloved, and Mary, the Holy Madonna, made frequent pilgrimages when they no longer knew the Master's physical presence. This was a favorite retreat for meditation and prayer and it was to this place that she often called the disciples for instruction. The area was particularly vibrant during the processes of transmutation, for it was here that the gates of heaven opened for these holy men and women and communion with the Celestial Hosts became more readily accessible.

The Betrayal by Judas Iscariot

Matthew 26:14-16.

Then one of the twelve, called Judas Iscariot, went unto the chief priests,

And said unto them, What will ye give me, and I will deliver him unto you? And they covenanted with him for thirty pieces of silver.

And from that time he sought opportunity to betray him.

Luke 22:1-6.

Now the feast of unleavened bread drew nigh, which is called the Passover.

And the chief priests and scribes sought how they might kill him; for they feared the people.

Then entered Satan into Judas surnamed Iscariot, being of the number of the twelve.

And he went his way, and communed with the chief priests and captains, how he might betray him unto them.

And they were glad, and covenanted to give him money.

And he promised, and sought opportunity to betray him unto them in the absence of the multitude.

Only Matthew and Luke mention the betrayal by Judas, the lower nature, which ever seeks to sell the higher, Christ within, to the priests or material power. The never ceasing wonder of the Bible is that its every incident finds a complete parallel in consciousness at whatever level we wish to place it. It holds for all degrees from the birth of the Christ in the mind of man up to the birth of the new spiritual body of the Initiate, and the still higher attainment when the great Initiator is followed into the Temple of Light that is His own home world. The Bible is indeed the spiritual textbook of the world.

The betrayal was preceded by the Last Supper, the occasion for the highest spiritual teaching imparted by the Master.

The lowest and the highest, the gamut of human accomplishment, is encompassed in one chapter of this Book of Books. Judas, of the tribe of Judah (Leo), signifies the heart when linked to the lower sense life; the Christ, the supreme symbol of Leo, is this same heart power at one with the Spirit.

Matthew's is the Gospel of the Dedication. It is the only Gospel in which the thirty pieces of silver are mentioned. Silver is a feminine metal belonging to the Moon, and the number three is the complete dedication of the threefold aspect of man to evil symbolized in the character of Judas Iscariot, even as the gifts of the Three Wise Men signify the consecration of this same threefold aspect to the higher nature or the Christ. It is the divine plan that Judas, or the lower nature in man, shall eventually destroy or redeem itself and thereafter be supplanted by Matthias, the higher self. The key to this transmutation is given in Zachariah:

Zechariah 11:8, 12-15.

Three shepherds also I cut off in one month; and my soul loathed them, and their soul abhorred me.

And I said unto them, If ye think good, give me my price; and if not, forbear. So they weighed for my price thirty pieces of silver.

And the Lord said unto me, Cast it unto the potter; a goodly price that I was priced at of them. And I took the thirty pieces of silver and cast them to the potter in the house of the Lord.

Then I cut asunder mine other staff, even bands, that I might break the brotherhood between Judah and Israel.

And the Lord said unto me, Take unto thee yet the instruments of a foolish shepherd.

The three shepherds who are abhorred signify the threefold aspect previously referred to when manifesting on the sense plane. The price, thirty pieces of silver, must always be cast in the house of the Lord (law) through the purification of the body in regeneration. Until this transmutation has been accomplished man always bears the instruments of a foolish shepherd.

I am the good shepherd and know my sheep and am known of them are the words of the Great Shepherd and He proved His words by laying down His life that all men, through Him, might find the Way to Life Eternal.

Matthew 26:56.

But all this was done that the scripture of the prophets might be fulfilled. Then all the disciples forsook him, and fled.

All the Disciples fled, even Peter, James and John. In severe trials when the path narrows to a point like a church steeple and we see only a cross at the end, faith, love and even hope may desert us unless the Christ is awakened within. The soul must learn to find its strength within; no human solace can be depended upon. This applies to great crises in human life as well as when the neophyte is worthy to attain to Initiation.

Mark 14:51, 52.

And there followed him a certain young man, having a linen cloth cast about his naked body; and the young men laid hold on him.

And he left the linen cloth, and fled from them naked.

Historically this young man is said to have been Mark himself. Esoterically these two verses outline the path of discipleship. In the lesser degrees of Eleusis the neophyte wore a white garment; in the greater rites he was unclothed (resurrection into new life or larger life). The Christ left His linen clothes in the tomb where they were discovered by Peter and John.

The garments represent the final debt of causation to be liquidated. The men that laid hold on the young man represent the opponents of Christ, the higher nature; they are the subtle tests and temptations of the world and carnal man. The youth won liberation through overcoming the lesser nature, and fled naked away, having been born again on another plane of consciousness and manifestation.

THE TRIALS

First Trial Before Annas

As the Master suffered in Gethsemane, there were heard the uproar and cries of an approaching throng which broke the awed stillness of the Garden wherein had occurred His great conflict with sorrow. The glimmering of many lights threw strange and weird shadows upon the olive trees that had witnessed His last mighty ordeal and final submission. The soldiers of the Sanhedrin approached, accompanied by Judas who gave the traitorous kiss. The Christ met this with an infinite compassion and love transcending anything the world has ever known as He spoke gently to Judas and called him "friend." Here is the perfect ideal for humanity to follow. They were no idle words He pronounced to those gathered about Him on the Mount on a certain summer day: *Love your enemies, bless them that curse you, do good to them that hate you, and pray for them which despitefully use you.* He taught them the secret of a great vibratory power which man must learn to build within himself if he would become a Christed one—the power of love which is beneficent and triumphs over all enmity.

While the Sanhedrin was being assembled at midnight, Annas endeavored by subtle questioning to cause Christ Jesus to convict Himself. The charges which they held against Him were, first, His words concerning the destruction of the Temple, which they interpreted to mean the material Temple in Jerusalem, and second, His affirmation that He was the Messiah. Though Annas found no reason for His condemnation, he bound Him and sent Him to the high priest, Caiaphas.

Between the preliminary examination by Annas and the first trial of Caiaphas, Christ Jesus witnessed His betrayal by Peter. Again the *Rock* man became the *Water* man. As the Christ was being led away from the apartments of Annas to those of Caiaphas, He heard the third denial.

The trials of the neophyte are in proportion to his spiritual status. The farther one advances upon the Path, the more subtle and far-reaching become his testings. None could compare in severity with those undergone by Christ Jesus for no one possesses His spiritual strength and power.

Matthew 27:3-5.

Then Judas, which had betrayed him, when he saw that he was condemned, repented himself, and brought again the thirty pieces of silver to the chief priests and elders,

Saying, I have sinned in that I have betrayed the innocent blood. And they said, What is that to us? see thou to that.

And he cast down the pieces of silver in the temple, and departed, and went and hanged himself.

Between the trials by Caiaphas and Pilate, Judas threw the thirty pieces of silver at the feet of the priests and went out and hanged himself. Evil always destroys itself. Wrongdoing can only bring its own reaction in greater evil. This is an immutable law of all nature and finds a perfect correspondence in the lives of the Disciples. Judas died in shame and disgrace; Peter repented of his terrible failure and became the stepping stone, the rock or foundation stone of the new religion. Temptation is one of the greatest factors in soul growth. Libra, the balance, suspended between Virgo and Scorpio, spirit and flesh respectively, is aptly called the trial gate. The discrimination exercised by the disciple as he stands in this place reveals to the Wise Ones the position to which he has attained in his spiritual progress.

Luke 22:59-62.

And about the space of one hour after another confidently affirmed, saying, Of a truth this fellow also was with him: for he is a Galilean.

And Peter said, Man, I know not what thou sayest. And immediately, while he yet spake, the cock crew.

And the Lord turned, and looked upon Peter. And Peter remembered the word of the Lord, how he had said unto him, Before the cock crow, thou shalt deny me thrice.

And Peter went out, and wept bitterly.

The greatest failure often becomes the most important stepping stone toward higher attainment. After the denial Peter returned to the Garden of Gethsemane, the crucible of pain and tears wherein base metal is transmuted into pure gold. From the Garden Peter came forth purified, redeemed. Long previously the beloved Master had said to Peter, *Thou art clean, but not all clean.* Through deep humiliation and intense sorrow the final cleansing was accomplished. But tradition tells us that Peter never lost the memory of this experience. Wonderful and glorious as were his after-works in the name of Christ Jesus and for the glory of His kingdom upon earth, his eyes were never without the glimmer of tears.

Second Trial Before Caiaphas

Caiaphas, high priest in the time of Christ Jesus, was a son-in-law of Annas. Annas was a Sadducean aristocrat. His immense wealth was derived in part from Temple traffic. He was responsible chiefly for the Temple becoming a "den of robbers." This accounted for his intense animosity against Christ Jesus and his determination to bring about His destruction.

Caiaphas was appointed high priest by Valerius Gratius, predecessor of Pilate, in A.D. 25, and was deposed about A.D. 36. Caiaphas as ruling high priest was president of the Sanhedrin at the trial of the Master.

A legal assemblage could not be held before sunrise; but as many had come together through curiosity, it was decided to hold an informal meeting immediately. Many witnesses gave conflicting testimony. Finally two were found who swore that they had heard Christ's words concerning the destruction of the Temple. Caiaphas asked, "Art thou the Christ?" When the latter replied, "I am," Caiaphas rent his fine linen vestment in token of blasphemy, and the Sanhedrin condemned the Nazarene to a blasphemer's death. The judges then departed for a few hours' rest and refreshment, leaving the Christ in care of the Temple guards.

At that time anyone under sentence of death was subject to the sport and mockery of the soldiers, so the gentle Nazarene was left to their mercies. To pass the time between trials, they blindfolded and beat Him. They struck Him in the face and, as a crowning indignity, spat upon Him. They wounded those blessed hands which had been used only to help and to heal. They bruised that tender face which had shone upon the earth with the reflected light of heaven. With one word, one gesture, He could have been free, His torturers helpless at His feet. There was never such an example of calmness in adversity, such poise and peace in a hostile environment, such self-restraint and self-control under the most provocative circumstances.

The Sanhedrin was composed of seventy members and the high priest. A verdict required a unanimous vote. The regular trial, held after sunrise, was merely routine and the sentence of death for blasphemy was pronounced quickly. Both Nicodemus and Joseph of Arimathea were private disciples of the Master and protested the verdict. It is said that no less than twenty-seven irregularities occurred in the trial, any one of which could have annulled the sentence of death. Esoterically, we understand how and why the death sentence was not refuted and why the Crucifixion had to take place. It was a necessary step toward the Christ becoming the indwelling planetary spirit of the Earth.

The cowardice and treachery of Pilate may be compared with that of Peter and Judas. He realized that the rulers and priests were envious of His great powers. "For he knew that for envy they had delivered Him" (Matthew 27:18).

The wife of Pilate, Claudia Precula, was a devotee of the new Christian sect. Among the first fruits of true esotericism is a consciousness that continues unbroken through the waking and the sleeping states, and which serves in greater freedom during the night hours when it is apart from the body. Although popularly confused with the dream state, the night-consciousness is far from being a mere fantasy of the subconsciousness.

Matthew 27:19.

When he (Pilate) was set down on the judgment seat his wife sent unto him, saying, Have nothing to do with this just man: for I have suffered many things this day in a dream because of him.

Due to the excitement in the city, the Roman procurator, who resided in Cesarea, came to Jerusalem at the time of the Passover, attended by a large number of soldiers, and took up his residence in the citadel of Antonia. For the trial of Christ Jesus, Pilate was conducted by Caiaphas to the Praetorium, presumably the hall of the castle of Antonia. "And the servants and the officers stood there, who had made a fire of coals; for it was cold; and they warmed themselves; and Peter stood with them and warmed himself" (John 18:18).

The members of the Sanhedrin might not enter the Praetorium else they would be defiled and forbidden to partake of the Passover; therefore Christ was taken alone before Pilate by the Roman guards.

Mark 15:1-13.

And straightway in the morning the chief priests held a consultation with the elders and scribes and the whole council, and bound Jesus, and carried him away, and delivered him to Pilate.

And Pilate asked him, Art thou King of the Jews? And he answering said unto him, Thou sayest it.

And the chief priests accused him of many things: but he answered nothing.

And Pilate asked him again, saying, Answerest thou nothing? behold how many things they witness against thee.

But Jesus yet answered nothing; so that Pilate marvelled.

Now at that feast he released unto them one prisoner, whomsoever they desired.

And there was one named Barabbas, which lay bound with them that had insurrection with him, who had committed murder in the insurrection.

And the multitude crying aloud began to desire him to do as he had ever done unto them.

But Pilate answered them, saying, Will ye that I release unto you the King of the Jews?

For he knew that the chief priests had delivered him for envy.

But the chief priests moved the people, that he should rather release Barabbas unto them.

And Pilate answered and said again unto them, What will ye then that I shall do unto him whom ye call the King of the Jews?

And they cried out again, Crucify him.

In the public festivals of Greece and Rome it was customary to release to the people one prisoner of their own choice. This custom was introduced into Jerusalem by the Romans. Barabbas had been a leader of an insurrection against the Romans, and was, therefore, considered a hero among the people. In the ancient Babylonian initiatory rites, a malefactor, representing the declining sun, was put to death after various cruelties had been perpetrated upon him, and another malefactor was given his freedom. A version of this same custom was preserved among the Hebrews. In their rites the sacrificial victim was a goat which was slain upon the altar, while another was loaded by imprecation with the sins of the people and sent free into the desert.

Matthew 27:24-26.

When Pilate saw that he could prevail nothing, but that rather a tumult was made, he took water, and washed his hands before the multitude, saying, I am innocent of the blood of this just person: see ye to it.

Then answered all the people, and said, His blood be on us, and on our children.

Then released he Barabbas unto them: and when he had scourged Jesus, he delivered him to be crucified.

At the equinoctial feast in Spring, as celebrated in both Babylon and Persia, there was a triumphant processional led by a condemned prisoner dressed as a king. At the end of the processional the prisoner was shorn of his fine raiment, scourged and crucified. Philo, in describing this ceremony as it was observed in Alexandria, gives the condemned criminal's name as Karobas.

Matthew 27:27-31.

Then the soldiers of the governor took Jesus into the common hall, and gathered unto him the whole band of soldiers.

And they stripped him, and put on him a scarlet robe.

And when they had platted a crown of thorns, they put it upon his head, and a reed in his right hand: and they bowed the knee before him, and mocked him, saying, Hail, King of the Jews.

And they spit upon him and took the reed, and smote him on the head.

And after they had mocked him, they took the robe off from him, and put his own raiment upon him, and led him away to crucify him.

This has been a mystic formula of Initiation throughout all ages, and it still is.

John 19:13-16.

When Pilate therefore heard that saying, he brought Jesus forth, and sat down in the judgment seat in a place that is called the Pavement, but in Hebrew, Gabbatha.

And it was the preparation of the passover, and about the sixth hour; and he saith unto the Jews, Behold, your King.

But they cried out, Away with him, away with him, crucify him. Pilate saith unto them, Shall I crucify your King? The chief priests answered, We have no king but Caesar.

Then delivered he him, therefore, unto them to be crucified. And they took Jesus, and led him away..

Gabbatha means "a pavement laid with stones." Hiram Abiff was laying plans upon this same pavement when he was attacked by three ruffians and murdered. The three ruffians, in the life of Christ Jesus, are Annas, Caiaphas and Judas.

The four different paths of Initiation are concealed within the trials of the Christ. Following are the correlations:

Annas—Earth	Pilate—Water
Caiaphas—Fire	Herod—Air

The preparatory steps for these Four Gates are concealed within the works of Peter (water) and Judas (fire), and the blending of these two by the Christ on the cross.

Third Trial Before Pilate

The Sanhedrin voted for the death of Christ Jesus, but it had no power to carry out its decree unless sanctioned by the Roman government. Pilate was the fifth of seven procurators or governors in the Roman province of Judea; he ruled from 26 to 36 A.D. A man of inferior birth and culture, hostile to and suspicious of the Jews, he regarded their manners and customs with great contempt.

The Jews knew that the Roman governor would condemn no man to death for blasphemy, so they charged the Christ with sedition and with making a false claim to royal power—which was considered treason against Rome. Their gross materialism could not comprehend that Christ desired no earthly throne and that His was not a physical kingdom.

Pilate, to excuse himself, sent Christ Jesus to Herod, who was in Jerusalem at the time. Disappointed and chagrined because the Teacher refused to answer his questions or perform miracles for him, Herod mocked the prisoner and returned Him to Pilate.

Pilate's weaknesses were those that cause so many to fall—indecision and a cowardly fear to take a stand for right against the opinion of the majority. When Pilate saw that a mob was forming he feared that violence would follow, with the result that Rome would judge him adversely for inefficiency and inability to maintain order. He therefore "took water, and washed his hands before the multitude," a symbolic act and one which many a Christian neophyte performs every day. Everyone who does this under similar circumstances is leaving the Christ within himself to be scourged and crucified by his own lower nature.

Trials must constantly beset the path of the neophyte, for it is only as he is tested and tried that his strength is determined.

Many times and in many lives we must stand trial before we prove our worthiness for Initiation. How do we face the trials designed to serve as stepping stones toward a higher goal? Do we meet them with the hypocrisy and treachery of a Judas, with the indecision and cowardice of a Pilate, or with the infinite compassion and forgiveness of the Christ?

The Latin Gospel of Nicodemus, or the Acts of Pilate, record many interesting events in the Master's later life. Among these is the following: "And Pilate, having called the officer, saith to him, 'Let Jesus be brought with gentleness.' The officers went out and having recognized Him, worshipped Him, and taking a scarf in his hand spread it on the ground and said to Him, 'Lord, walk here and come in for the governor calleth Thee!'

"And when Jesus entered and the standard bearers holding the standards, the tops of the standards bowed down and worshipped Jesus. And when the people saw the manner of the standards, how they bowed down and worshipped Jesus, they cried out exceedingly against the standard bearers. Pilate said: 'Do ye not marvel how the banners bowed down and worshipped Jesus?' The governor called the standard bearers and said to them, Why did ye so? They said to Pilate: 'We are Greeks and wait upon the Gods, how could we worship Him? But as we were holding the banners, they bowed down themselves and worshipped Him.'

"Pilate said to the people: 'Choose ye strong and powerful men, and let them hold the standards and let us see if they bow down of themselves.' Pilate said to the officer: 'Take Him out of the praetorium and bring Him in again in what manner thou wilt.' And Jesus and the officer went out of the praetorium. Pilate called those who held the banners and saith to them: 'I have sworn by the salvation of Caesar that if the standards do not bow down when Jesus entereth I will cut off your heads.'

"And the governor gave the order the second time that Jesus should come in. And the officer did the same as before, and earnestly entreated Jesus to tread upon his scarf. And He trod upon it and came in. And as He entered the standards bowed down again and worshipped Jesus."

In the letter of Pilate to Herod, he details incidents of the Resurrection. "Now when Procla, my wife, heard that Jesus was risen and had appeared in Galilee, she took with her Longius, the centurion, and twelve soldiers, the same that had watched at the sepulchre, and went to greet the face of Christ, as if to a great spectacle, and saw Him with His disciples."

After his conversion Pilate was sent for by Caesar in Rome. Caesar questioned him and then commanded Albius, a captain, to cut off Pilate's head as Pilate had commanded the execution of the Christ. An Angel of the Lord came and received the head. When Procla, Pilate's wife, saw the Angel "she, being filled with joy, forthwith gave up the ghost and was buried with her husband."

The following excerpts are taken from a letter supposedly addressed by Herod to Pontius Pilate, the governor of Jerusalem. This letter is taken from a Greek manuscript belonging to the fifth century.

"As my daughter, Herodias, who is dear to me, was playing upon a pool of water, which had ice upon it, it broke under her and all her body went down and her head was cut off and remained upon the surface of the ice. And behold, her mother is holding her head upon her knees in her lap and my whole house is in great sorrow.

"It is certain that because of the many evil things done by me to John the Baptist and because I mocked the Christ, behold! I receive the reward of righteousness. The judgments of God are righteous and every man receives according to his thought. But since thou wast worthy to see that God-man, therefore it becometh you to pray for me. My son, Azbonius, also is in the agony of the hour of death. I, too, am in great affliction because I have the dropsy and am in great distress and all because I persecuted the introducer of Baptism by water, which was John. Therefore, my brother, the judgments of God are righteous."

The Way to Calvary

The principal obstacles on the Path are represented in the trials before Annas or mortal mind, the trial before Caiaphas or worldly ambition and before Pilate, typifying weakness and vacillation of mind when required to stand for Truth at the risk of endangering personal position and prestige.

As the supreme wayshower for all mankind, no aspect of the Path was omitted from this pattern-life.

The scourging symbolizes the pain and discomfort which accompany the awakening of certain centers lying along the spine within the body of the aspirant. The crown of thorns has a similar significance as it refers specifically to certain areas in the head.

Three times the Lord Christ fell beneath the weight of the cross. That which He enacted physically is representative of corresponding moral failures to which humanity is prone to succumb as it learns to walk the spiral way leading toward the Light. Man falls beneath the weight which veils of matter have placed upon his spirit; also he falls because of his earth-bent desires; yet again by reason of the worldly glamor to which his spiritually unillumined mind succumbs. Three pitfalls on the Path come from the weakness of the physical, the power of desire and the darkness of the human mind.

As Christ ascended Calvary He was met three times by bands of holy women. These represent the activity of the divine feminine (love-wisdom) principle that works for purification of the physical and desire bodies and spiritualization of the mind.

By means of her mystical at-one-ment with Christ, Mary continued to both vision and feel His every experience throughout the Passiontide. Mary and the other holy women remained in the Jerusalem house of Mary, the mother of Mark, during all this momentous time.

Mary, in perfect attunement with Christ, knew with Him all the agony of the Garden. The Cosmic Scroll of Time was unwound for her also in those dark hours. Realizing the Master's sorrow for the blindness and ingratitude of mankind, she knew the pain and grief that gripped His great compassionate heart.

Again, Mary was one with Him throughout the injustice of the trials and the cruelty and inhumaneness of the Calvary journey. No anger or resentment touched her pure heart. During these dark hours it was the perpetrators of the most foul crimes who were the recipients of her most ardent intercessory prayers. Humanity's debt of karmic retribution for its reception of earth's supreme Messenger has been tremendously lessened by the loving, sacrificial service of this great compassionate one who continues to labor with man to alleviate the karmic effects of this terrible deed.

In the Revelations of St. Bridget of Sweden, the Blessed Lady is quoted as saying: "His suffering became my suffering because

THE NEW CHRISTED MAN

His heart was mine. . . . So in a certain sense my Son and I redeemed the world with one heart."

The Master made reference to this heavy debt of causation incurred by mankind as he pondered over Jerusalem's rejection of His ministry: "O, Jerusalem, Jerusalem, thou that killest the prophets, and stonest them which are sent unto thee, how often would I have gathered thy children together, even as a hen gathereth her chickens under her wings, and ye would not!" (Matt. 23:37).

And again, when foretelling troubles that were to come as a result of man's departure from spiritual law: "For behold, the days are coming, in the which they shall say, Blessed are the barren, and the wombs that never bare, and the paps which never gave suck. Then shall they begin to say to the mountains, Fall upon us;; and to the hills, Cover us. For if they do these things in a green tree, what shall be done in the dry?" (Luke 23:29-31).

The Rite of the Crucifixion

"Father, forgive them; for they know not what they do."
Luke 23:34

The two paths of development, the mystic and the occult, converge at Gethsemane where the candidate for Initiation is weighted with sorrow that flowers into compassion—the compassion which weeps above Jerusalem and breathes in gentle tones of infinite understanding beneath the heavy burden of the cross, "Daughters of Jerusalem, weep not for me, but weep for yourselves, and for your children." And again, after three hours of agony on the cross, He voices that immortal prayer, "Father forgive them; for they know not what they do."

In the Crucifixion we stand before one of the holy mysteries which must ever remain sealed to the profane. The sacredness of its meaning can only be touched upon briefly. *Its true, inner purpose can only be revealed to those who seek and find the light within themselves, the flame of the great Christ love which passeth all understanding.*

When Barabbas was released, Christ Jesus was scourged and heaped with indignity and abuse. His garments were torn off, *and a certain cloak was put upon Him.* A crown of thorns was woven, placed upon His head, and crushed down into His temples. This phase of the stigmata is produced visibly in the mystic through intense concentration upon the Passion of our Lord. In the occultist the same is produced *invisibly* through certain exercises received by those who have made themselves worthy by living the life. The spiritual currents generated in the vital body of such a person are so powerful that the body is literally *scourged* by them, particularly in the region of the head where the pain of the Crown of Thorns is produced; also in the palms of the hands, the arches of the feet, and the side.

In Matthew, the Gospel of Dedication, the *robe of scarlet* is the symbol of service through purification. (Many artists portray the Christ in a robe of red).

"They placed a reed in his right hand." The reed or wand is the insignia of Initiate power gained through lifting the spinal spirit fire. The reed was placed in His *right* hand, signifying the positive path of development. The crown of thorns represents the pain produced in the head as the cranial nerves are revivified by the ascending spirit fire force.

Mark 15:17-20.

And they clothed him with purple, and platted a crown of thorns, and put it about his head,

And began to salute him, Hail, King of the Jews!

And they smote him on the head with a reed, and did spit upon him, and bowing their knees worshipped him.

And when they had mocked him, they took off the purple from him, and put his own clothes on him, and led him out to crucify him.

The Gospels of Mark and John outline a further development. The Master is robed in purple, the kingly color. Purple is a combination of red and blue. (Red, the lower nature, purified through service; blue, the reflection of spirit.)

The ascent of the awakened currents to the head is described in the words: "They smote him on the head with a reed."

Luke 23:11, 12.

And Herod with his men of war set him at nought, and mocked him, and arrayed him in a gorgeous robe, and sent him again to Pilate.

And the same day Pilate and Herod were made friends together: for before they were at enmity between themselves.

The Hebrew royal dress was white; the *gorgeous robe* refers to the White Light of pure spirit. Herod represents the carnal or lower man, the fleshly appetites; Pilate, the material or concrete mind. Through the power of spirit these two opposing forces are redeemed and united in greater manifestations of spiritual power.

Only the Gospels of Matthew and Mark mention the reed and crown of thorns. These are early manifestations of the inner work produced within this wonderful temple of the indwelling spirit, the physical body, as the process of liberation begins.

The sublime Christ on the cross is the perfect symbol in every detail of the future attainment of all humanity.

There have been, altogether, sixteen crucified World Saviours, whose lives reveal the mystic meanings of Initiation. Orpheus says, "They pierced my hands and my feet."

Matthew 27:33-37.

And when they were come unto a place called Golgotha, that is to say, a place of a skull.

They gave him vinegar to drink mingled with gall: and when he had tasted thereof, he would not drink.

And they crucified him, and parted his garments, casting lots: that it might be fulfilled which was spoken by the prophet, They parted my garments among them, and upon my vesture did they cast lots.

And sitting down, they watched him there;

And set up over his head his accusation written, THIS IS JESUS THE KING OF THE JEWS.

Golgotha, the place of the crucifixion, is an Aramaic word, meaning "the place of the skull." The word has the same meaning as the Greek word *kranion,* which the Latin Vulgate translates as *Calvaria,* or Calvary.

Professor Drews in his *Christ Myths* states: "Golgotha was a hill outside Jerusalem where, in pre-Christian days, was held an initiatory ritual sacred to Adonis." This was a ritual drama in which crucifixion, death and burial took place. Afterwards, through the lamentation of women, the victim was produced alive to the people. The fundamental principles of spiritual progression or evolution have ever been the same. Upon these principles all religions have been founded.

Luke 23:26-28.

And as they led him away, they laid hold upon one Simon, a Cyrenian, coming out of the country, and on him they laid the cross, that he might bear it after Jesus.

And there followed him a great company of people, and of women, which also bewailed and lamented him.

But Jesus turning unto them said, Daughters of Jerusalem, weep not for me, but weep for yourselves, and your children.

Mark 15:40, 41.

There were also women looking on afar off: among whom was Mary Magdalene, and Mary the mother of James the less and of Joses, and Salome;

(Who also, when he was in Galilee, followed him, and ministered unto him;) and many other women which came up with him unto Jerusalem.

It is only as students of esoteric Christianity that we discover the unifying principle that binds the religions of the world together and places them all, in ever-ascending steps, at the feet of the Christ. Every world Teacher has been a high Initiate and every religion holds some phase of Initiation as its highest goal. They each lead to the throne of the Christ, whose mission it was to bring the spiritual power of the Greater Mysteries to the world.

Josephus says that punishment by crucifixion was introduced into Palestine during the reign of Alexander Jannaeus, 104-74 B. C., and that many Pharisees were put to death in this way. It was the common form of capital punishment during the early Christian era. Many of the disciples and followers of Christ Jesus were martyred in this manner.

In primitive times every incident connected with crucifixion was designed to prolong and increase the agony of the victim. The upright stake of the cross was placed on the ground, and the *cruciarius,* as he was called, was stripped of his clothing, laid on his back on the stake and the transverse beam thrust under his shoulders. The arms and feet were stretched out and tied by ropes or nailed to the cross, which was then set up. Thus the victim was left to linger through death, which might come through loss of blood or exposure, fever or hunger. The slowly dying *cruciarius* was exposed to the heat of day and the chill of night. The rabble who gathered around were at liberty to abuse the victim in any way it desired. Besides being subjected to beatings and having missiles thrown at him, the agonized victim was also often attacked during the night by wild beasts. We learn that Andrew was protected from an attack of this kind by a shaft of light from heaven which frightened the beasts away.

It was customary to place a board at the head of the cross bearing a statement of the victim's crime. That all might understand the inscription placed upon the cross of Christ Jesus, it was written in three languages: Greek, the language of culture; Latin, the language of power; and Hebrew, the language of religion. The one in Latin read: *"Iesus Nazarenus Rex Iudaeorum"* abbreviated as *"I. N. R. I."* Esoterically deciphered in Hebrew, "I am" (I) symbolizes water; "Nour" (N), fire; "Ruach" (R), air or spirit; and "Iabeshah" (I), earth. Alchemically they symbolize salt (I am and Iabeshah); sulphur (Nour); mercury (Ruach). "Ruach" also symbolizes the sublimated essence of spiritual power, Azoth. Herein lies the secret of the meaning of the Crucifixion which shows us why each one must *individually* follow Christ upon the path which leads *unto this place,* unto Golgotha, the place of the skull.

Jesus Nazarenus Rex Judaeorum therefore contains a great mystic formula. Christ Jesus was the type of perfection for the entire human race, so it was essential that the letters I. N. R. I. be placed above the cross and in several languages. This is not the Path for a single race or creed but for all mankind.

I. N. R. I, *Igne Natura Renovatur Integra* is also an old Rosicrucian motto meaning "Nature renovated by fire; matter renovated by spirit".

Every detail of the story of the Crucifixion is fraught with mystic meaning. The *two thieves* who were crucified with Him, the *seamless tunic* for which lots were cast, the *piercing* with the *lance,* and the issue of *blood and water* from His side, *the seven last words,* and the *burial* in the *new tomb* cut in the *solid rock* in the *garden* facing *Golgotha,* are all details worthy of deep and earnest meditation for they will yield much light upon the subject of Initiation that may be found in no other way.

Mark 15:27-32

And with him they crucify two thieves; the one on his right hand, and the other on his left.

And the scripture was fulfilled, which saith, And he was numbered with the transgressors.

And they that passed by railed on him, wagging their heads, and saying, Ah, thou that destroyest the temple, and buildest it in three days,

Save thyself, and come down from the cross.

Likewise also the chief priests mocking said among themselves with the scribes, He saved others; himself he can not save.

Let Christ the King of Israel descend now from the cross, that we may see and believe. And they that were crucified with his reviled him.

The two thieves represent the physical and the desire bodies, the weakness of the flesh and the strength of the desires. It is at this stage of development that the spirit is ever crucified upon the cross of sorrow, pain and remorse. In the Gospels of Matthew and Mark, both thieves are unrepentant. "And they that were crucified with him reviled him." In the Gospel of Luke one thief accepts Him and receives the promise of Paradise with Him.

The unrepentant thief signifies the physical or lower nature which must be overcome; the thief who accepts Him and receives the promise of entrance into Paradise represents the accomplishment of purification.

In pre-Christian days a "king's son" was the *cruciarius* and two evil doers were sacrificed on either side of him. The process of purification is always the same. A similar processs is concealed within the story of Joseph in relation to the butcher and the baker, one of whom forgot Joseph while the other remembered him and secured his liberation from prison.

The *stigmata* in hands, feet, and head are in the same relative positions to each other as are the points of the five pointed star. The *five nails* are the five senses which bind the spirit to the cross of the physical body. Plato declares: "Each pleasure and pain is a sort of nail which rivets soul to body." The spirit is bound most closely to form through the five senses and here the power of the spirit fire must be most potent. The drawing of the nails from these points results in the Five Sacred Wounds.

The *scourging* is caused by the creative fire mounting upward through the threefold spinal cord. After this ascending process has been in progress for a time, Neptune lights the spinal spirit fire. This fire vibrates the pineal and pituitary glands in the head, and as the vibratory action strikes the frontal sinus, it awakens to life the cranial nerves, or crown of thorns. Later the crown of thorns becomes a halo of light, and the scarlet robe is changed for one of royal purple.

John 19:19-21

And Pilate wrote a title, and put it on the cross. And the writing was, Jesus of Nazareth the King of the Jews.

This title then read many of the Jews: for the place where Jesus was crucified was nigh to the city: and it was written in Hebrew, and Greek, and Latin.

Then said the chief priests of the Jews to Pilate, Write not, The King of the Jews; but that he said, I am King of the Jews.

John states that the above words were written by Pilate who, despite the requests of the priests, refused to change them. They refer to the process of illumining the lower mind. When illumination is accomplished, the spirit within will always proclaim that Christ is King.

Matthew 27:45-48.

Now from the sixth hour there was darkness over all the land unto the ninth hour.

And about the ninth hour Jesus cried with a loud voice, saying, Eli, Eli, lama sabachthani? that is to say, My God, my God, why hast thou forsaken me?

Some of them that stood there, when they heard that, said, This man calleth for Elias.

And straightway one of them ran, and took a sponge, and filled it with vinegar, and put it on a reed, and gave him to drink.

Day began with the sunrise at 6 a.m. Christ Jesus was placed on the cross at the third hour, or 9 a.m. At the sixth hour, or high noon, the earth was darkened. At the ninth hour, or 3 p.m., came the liberation.

As the Christ Spirit was liberated from the body of Jesus and passed into the center of the earth His great Soul Light flooded the entire earth with a surpassing brilliance, so intense that the sunlight itself seemed to darken in comparison.

Every sacrifice bears its spiritual compensation. Every man who dies on the field of battle for something he counts to be greater than himself, is reborn on a higher level of attainment. The evolutionary status of the ego is advanced when the blood, which is its direct vehicle, is cleansed of impurities through flowing from the body at death. Every ego, during its vast cycles of earth pilgrimage, knows at least one life where the spirit passes out as the blood flows.

The Christ, by His sacrifice on the cross, was lifted into the great Initiations belonging to the kingdom of the Father. It was His ecstasy of spirit which Matthew and Mark record in the words: "My God, My God, how hast thou glorified me!"—a passage mistranslated: "Why hast thou forsaken me?"

John 19:23, 24.

Then the soldiers, when they had crucified Jesus, took his garments, and made four parts, to every soldier a part; and also his coat: now the coat was without seam, woven from the top throughout.

They said therefore among themselves, Let us not rend it, but cast lots for it, whose it shall be: that the scripture might be fulfilled, which saith, They parted my raiment among them, and for my vesture they did cast lots. These things therefore the soldiers did.

All Initiates possess a body of light, the seamless tunic of John. Plutarch writes of Osiris: "That vestment of Osiris has no shadow nor variation, but is one simple image of light."

It was the custom to divide the garments of a crucified person among the soldiers who were the executioners. The cloth was divided into four parts, symbolizing the four elements, Fire, Air, Water and Earth, the sublimated essence of which forms the seamless tunic or the new body of light. The first three Gospels describe how lots were cast for the parted garments, these parts being representative of the regenerative process. Only John records the completion of the seamless tunic.

The Seven Last Words

The concluding ceremonial or consecration of the Mysteries was always a sacred formula uttered to show that the rites were complete.

Each of the Seven Words contains a key to the powers of one of the seven worlds, and rightly used or reverberated gives access to that plane of consciousness or realm of manifestation to which it is correlated.

The First Word is recorded by Luke: *Father forgive them for they know not what they do.* This was uttered as the nail-pierced body was lifted into place on the cross, and indicates that the esoteric reason for His crucifixion had not dawned on the humanity of His day—nor has it even to this, our own day. The First Word correlates with the highest realm of consciousness, World of Divine Spirit, home world of God the Father. It possesses the power that lifts above all personal hurts, reaching a state wherein all thought of *me* or *mine* is lost in God's universal love and life.

The Second Word is recorded in Luke: *Today thou shalt be with Me in Paradise.* The word *Paradise* comes from the Persian and means "the king's garden." Through the lifting of the fallen feminine pole of spirit, the ego no longer knows the dual consciousness of good and evil. Eden is regained; the kingdom of heaven is found within. One capable of functioning in the soul body gains entrance into the new Eden. This ability is acquired by work done in the higher etheric realm.

The Third Word is given by John: *Woman, behold thy son; John, behold thy mother.* This incident is recorded only in the Gospel of John and deals with the last esoteric work concerning polarity. It was given to the most advanced disciples, Mary the Virgin and John the best-beloved. This step represents the final and complete transmutation of desire. It marks the stage where passion has become compassion, and self has been lost in selflessness. The Word opens the realms of soul life, soul light and soul power.

The Fourth Word from the Cross is found in Matthew and Mark: *My God, my God, how hast thou glorified me!* The darkness of mortal or concrete mind is vanquished in the radiant white light of the spirit.

The Fifth Word is given by John: *"I thirst."* This Word correlates the inner Mysteries of the physical earth and the dense body of man.

The women of Jerusalem prepared a drink composed of wine and myrrh for condemned prisoners. In the account of the crucifixion written by Petronius, chief centurion of Pilate, it is stated that the drink was offered to Christ Jesus by Judith, the sister of Judas, who, moved by His sufferings, bribed the executioners to help Him. This drink symbolizes the sorrow (bitterness) of the Path of the Cross. Some artists portray this cup of vinegar as the same cup held by the Angel in Gethsemane.

The names of Judas and Judith are made up of *Jud,* the root; *as,* the masculine suffix and *ith* the feminine. Judas (the lower nature) hanged himself; Judith (the awakened or higher nature manifesting love and compassion) offered a drink to the Christ. It is only when the lower nature is redeemed in all mankind that it will be able to quench the thirst of the Christ.

I was an hungered, and ye gave me meat: I was thirsty and ye gave me drink. . . . Inasmuch as ye have done it unto one of the least of these my brethren, ye have done it unto me.

The Sixth Word is found in Luke: *Father, into thy hands I commend my spirit.* This Word refers to the powers of Abstract Thought or God Consciousness. Through His great sacrifice the Christ lifted Himself to this high realm.

The Seventh Word is recorded by John alone: *It is finished.* This is the triumphant cry of every victorious Initiate.

Christ *alone* ascends to the throne of the Father. The Greater or Solar Initiations focus in the homeland of the Christ, or the plane of universal consciousness.

Matthew 27:51.

And behold, the veil of the temple was rent in twain from the top to the bottom; and the earth did quake, and the rocks rent.

The earthquake was caused by a change in the atomic vibration of the earth as the Christ Spirit began functioning within the planetary body. The vibratory rate of every particle of the earth's envelopes was accelerated and its substance lightened.

The great veil which hung before the Holy of Holies within the Temple, and which was so heavily embroidered in gold, silver, and precious stones that three hundred priests were required to lift it, was rent asunder. The veil before the Temple of Initiation had been both literally and figuratively rent in twain so as to open the way henceforth for whosoever wills.

John 19:31-34.

The Jews therefore, because it was the preparation, that the bodies should not remain upon the cross on the sabbath day, (for that sabbath day was an high day,) besought Pilate that their legs might be broken, and that they might be taken away.

Then came the soldiers, and brake the legs of the first, and of the other which was crucified with him.

But when they came to Jesus, and saw that he was dead already, they brake not his legs:

But one of the soldiers with a spear pierced his side, and forthwith came there out blood and water.

Caiaphas and the high priests, bitter in their hatred of the Christ, were still pursuing Him and, fearful lest the Sabbath should be profaned by the Crucifixion, they asked the soldiers to break the legs and so hasten death. This was a cruelty practiced only upon the lowest and vilest of criminals.

Piercing the side with a Sacred Lance is an ancient initiatory custom and refers to a certain process which takes place within the body of the candidate before he can be released from the cross of the physical body. Mystically, the issue of blood and water is the evidence that the candidate is ready "to travel in foreign countries and receive the wages of a Master." This incident is noted only in the Gospel of John which, as previously stated, portrays the most advanced work of spiritual illumination.

Luke 24:47.

And that repentance and remission of sins should be preached in his name among all nations, beginning at Jerusalem.

Tradition states that the name of the centurion was Longius; also, that he was so impressed with Christ Jesus that he accepted the new religion, became a bishop of Cappadocia and later died a martyr's death.

The Burial Rite

Luke 23:50-53.

And, behold, there was a man named Joseph, a counsellor; and he was a good man, and a just;

(The same had not consented to the counsel and deed of them;) he was of Arimathea, a city of the Jews: who also himself waited for the Kingdom of God.

This man went unto Pilate; and begged the body of Jesus.

And he took it down, and wrapped it in linen, and laid it in a sepulchre that was hewn in stone, wherein never man before was laid.

The intention was to bury the Sacred Body beside Judas in ground purchased with the thirty pieces of silver. Joseph of Arimathea, assisted by Nicodemus, (both private disciples of the Master) obtained the body by permission of Pilate and anointed it with a hundred pounds of aloes and myrrh—the bitter and the sweet, reminiscent of cross and crown, Gethsemane and Transfiguration, Crucifixion and Resurrection: the path of tears transformed into the path of love.

Joseph of Arimathea, like Nicodemus, was a prominent and influential resident of Jerusalem. The fact that he was a member of the Sanhedrin did not render him immune to the fury of persecution visited on all who were known to be associated with the crucified Nazarene.

Joseph narrates in his Gospel: "After I had begged the body of the Master, the Jews in their hatred and fury shut me up in prison. During the fifth hour of the night, Christ Jesus appeared unto me. With Him there was a great light and there was a fragrance as of Paradise about Him. I found myself out of prison and we were going toward Galilee. The body of the Master seemed altogether made of light. He was surrounded and ministered unto by Angels. I remained with them for three days then I no longer saw them, and was in my own home." Thus this worthy disciple gives an intimation, as do so many of the others, of some of the glories belonging to Initiation into the Christian Mysteries.

The apocryphal history of Joseph of Arimathea tells us that later, accompanied by other Christian Initiates—among them Mary Magdalene—he set sail across the Mediterranean and carried the torch of the great new spiritual light first into Gaul (France) and then into Britain where he founded the Abbey of Glastonbury, the first seat of the Christian Mysteries to be established in the western world. These first emissaries from the Holy Land spoke and taught in Greek, the language of Hellenistic culture which at that time dominated civilization although Rome held the political power. It has been said that when the pure spirit of Hellenism was dying in its own native land it still flourished in Gaul where there were a number of centers of Greek learning. Much remains to be discovered of this pristine Christianity planted in a Hellenistic culture in the western world. Overlaid with Latinism, it has become buried from sight, but it may well be that many old legends are traceable to this source.

The new tomb wherein man never was laid, is the new Path of Initiation opened by the coming of the Christ. Hewn in stone is the deathless body of the Initiate, the new *petra* or rock upon which the New Age religion is founded.

Matthew 27:60, 61, 66.

And laid it in his own new tomb, which he had hewn out in the rock: and he rolled a great stone to the door of the sepulchre, and departed.

And there was Mary Magdalene, and the other Mary, sitting over against the sepulchre.

So they went, and made the sepulchre sure, sealing the stone, and setting a watch.

The great stone which seals the sepulchre and which must be rolled away before the Resurrection takes place is the force or weight of desire. Man must divest himself of this weight so as to be free and, in the words of Paul, be "as a strong man to run a race." The watch that is set is the aura that serves as a constant protection. This the neophyte learns to build by love and service and the prayer that continues "without ceasing." The Gospels of Luke and John do not mention these earlier processes.

Mary Magdalene, the lower feminine, and Mary, the mother of Jesus, the higher, are beside the tomb, because the possibility of the Resurrection depends on the lifting of the fallen feminine pole of the spirit. The inner comprehension of the Crucifixion is intimately connected with the esoteric significance of the blood. Eliphas Levi describes the blood as vitalized light, a splendid occult description of this strange and powerful life essence.

"Verily I say unto you, unless ye eat the flesh of the Son of man and drink his blood, ye have no life in you." These words of the Teacher can only be properly understood through an esoteric study of the blood. As the blood flowed on Calvary the Christ Spirit passed into the earth, cleansing and purifying the desire envelope of the planet and opening the way for the building of new and finer race bodies.

One of the chief works undertaken by the indwelling Christ was the gradual eradication of egotism or separativeness which commenced with the first race body in Lemuria, when the evolution of self-consciousness had its beginnings. This cleansing and regenerating process could not be accomplished except that Christ become an indwelling Presence. It was possible only by superseding the regime of law with a religion of love.

In an esoteric study of the life of Christ Jesus there are seven important events which have to do with the flowing of blood:

1. *The Circumcision*—Called the Rite of Purification.
2. *The Agony on the Garden*—Beginning of the blending.
3. *The Scourging*—Ascent of the fire currents.
4. *The Crowning with Thorns*—Awakening of cranial nerves.
5. *Carrying the Cross*—Transmutation through pain.
6. *Crucifixion*—Liberation from cross of the body.
7. *The Lance-pierced Side*—The blending consummated.

The Mystery of the Cross

The Path of the Cross symbolizes the path of the kundalini fire as it rises from the base of the spine to the head. The Christ signifies the ego, the spirit within man whose ultimate destiny is to become a Christed one. The Fourteen Stations or Steps of the Cross represent not alone so many events in the life of the Master, but symbolize also the steps or stations of development in every man. Only the New Age Religion will bring to light the full significance of the Grecian Mystery Temple inscription: "Man, know thyself."

Truly every mystery of the universe is to be found within the body of man, the microcosm. The Fourteen Stations of the Cross represent in man the seven positive and the seven negative latent powers of the sympathetic nervous ganglia. The preliminary steps deal with the conservation and lifting of the sacred creative force within the body. After a time the Neptunian spirit fire begins to play upon this creative life force. This effects a blending of the Fire and Water, the passional and emotional principles within man. This is the great crucifixion when ofttimes for a period the physical body is broken, so that it may be replaced by a new, finer and more tenuous body. Jesus represents the sacred life force and the Christ the spirit fire.

The sympathetic nervous system consists of a series of nerve centers extending on each side of the spinal column from the head to the coccyx; they follow the Way of the Cross. In this system are seven principal glands, or centers of latent spiritual force. They correspond to the seven sense centers of the desire body. The path of the ascending spirit fire along these centers corresponds to the fourteen Stations of the Cross. The current of fire force flows between these centers. In one who "lives the life" the currents are powerfully augmented in strength and force; the blood rarifies, the body becomes luminous with a strange lustre that impresses all who see it, as though it were enveloped in a robe of light.

1. Christ Jesus condemned to death.—*Dedication to Initiation.*
2. Christ Jesus takes up His cross.—*Path of Initiation.*
3. Christ Jesus falls the first time.—*Symbolic of human frailty.*
4. Christ Jesus meets His mother.—*Ideal of the Exalted Feminine.*
5. Simon helps carry the cross.—*Simon's Dedication to Discipleship.*
6. Veronica wipes the face of Christ Jesus.—*Transmutation of Feminine.*
7. Christ Jesus falls the second time.—*Symbolic of failure through desire.*
8. Christ Jesus speaks to weeping women.—*Sorrow for degradation of feminine.*
9. Christ Jesus falls the third time.—*Symbolic of material mind.*
10. Christ Jesus is stripped of His garments.—*Renunciations.*
11. Christ Jesus is nailed to the cross.—*Development of Stigmata.*
12. Christ Jesus dies on the cross.—*Initiation Consummated.*
13. Christ Jesus is taken from the cross.—*Liberation from the body.*
14. Christ Jesus is laid in the tomb.—*Path of further Initiation.*

Each fall immediately follows a meeting with women. The Gnostic Mysteries assert that *the saving blood is feminine.*

All occult philosophy is based upon the fall and the redemption of the feminine principle in man. The Eve of Genesis becomes the Sun-clothed Woman of Revelation. The Christ came to open the new way to this attainment by the power of His cleansing blood.

The stations or steps of the cross as connected with Initiation are celebrated in the etheric temple above the city of Jerusalem by the Master Jesus and His disciples at the four holy festivals of the year, namely, the Solstices and the Equinoxes.

"If ye would be my disciple, ye must take up your cross and follow me," said the Christ. There is no other way. It is only as the aspirant begins the ascent that leads to Golgotha that the spiritual centers awaken, and the roses, or lotuses blossom upon the cross.

The powers awakened through the seven centers of the sympathetic nervous system develop through the work of the Nine Lesser, or Lunar Mysteries. They are:

1. Clairvoyance
2. Clairaudience
3. Telepathy
4. Prophecy
5. Healing
6. Projection of consciousness
7. Liberation from the cross of the body

The nails are identified in the body as follows: Hands, feet, liver, pineal gland, and pituitary body.

The powers awakened through the five centers of the cerebro-spinal system develop through the work of the Four Greater, or Solar (Christian) Mysteries. They are:

1. Christ consciousness
2. Instantaneous healing
3. Polarity
4. Creative word
5. Projection to other planets

The nails: Sex, heart, larynx, and the knees.

To be able to enter more completely into the mysteries of the Crucifixion, it is essential that some consideration be given to the extensive symbolism contained in a study of the cross.

Mabel Collins writes: "In the psychic world the disciples endure the crucifixion and suffering with the entire human race, as the Christ Himself still suffers." Also: "The Litanies of the Crucifixion deal with the formulae of the Christ Initiations as outlined in the Gospels. When the disciple finds this key, he learns to find and study this same path of Initiation in the world about him, in the changing seasons and in the stars."

The symbol of the cross has been discovered in all parts of the world. Its observance by the human race is universal. The

Hermetic cross with its four arms pointing to the four cardinal points was in use thousands of years ago.

In the Egyptian Temple of Philae there is a picture of a new Initiate. Standing before him is the figure of Mercury pouring a stream of the water of a new life upon his head. The water is interlaced in the shape of a cross. In ancient Peru, the Caduceus was called the Mercury-Heaven-Cross.

The symbol of Venus, which is the same as the sacred cross of Egypt and which was carried by the Pharaohs, was called the Crux-ansata or Sign of Life.

Madame Blavatsky states: "The cross may be traced back into unfathomable Archaic Ages. Its mystery deepens rather than clears. We find it engraven on rocks in Easter Island, in Central and South America, in Mexico among the Aztecs. Everywhere this symbol is found to be connected with the spiritual mysteries."

There is an occult truth underlying the necessity for the universal symbolism of the cross. It is the representation of the androgynous life throughout all nature. It represents both the masculine and feminine in opposition and in equilibrium. The androgynous in opposition depicts present conditions of mankind; in equilibrium, man's future development.

The cross is the symbol of man's progress and its changing form always indicates his next step forward. The division of the sexes and the fall of man are set forth in the form of the cross. As this fall is the common heritage of all men, so the cross bears a universal aspect. The figure of the Christ upon the cross has been the object of adoration during the Piscean or Church Dispensation because it represents the great Spirit whose Crucifixion became necessary because of the fall of man. With man's ultimate redemption accomplished, the cross will no longer represent the status of humanity, and will therefore be replaced by two upright columns (| |). Man will no longer know the cross of opposition, but will realize the two columns of equilibrium. This attainment is shadowed forth in the Jachin and Boaz of Solomon's Temple, also in Revelation wherein John writes: "He that overcometh I will make a pillar in the temple of my God and he shall go no more out."

The way of attainment that is outlined for all men is to be found in the structure of church buildings. The edifice represents the human body, the habitation of spirit, with its three divisions, the head, the body and the limbs. It has the large assembly room where the people congregate, the partition for the choir (the few) and the pulpit for the priest alone.

"Many are called, but few are chosen." The way is opened to come and partake of the waters of life freely. Few heed the call of the higher life, and of these few only the rare soul succeeds in lifting the veil and passing into the Holy of Holies, there to minister before the altar of conscious helpership beyond the veil of flesh.

The steeple of the church surmounted by the cross symbolizes the straight path that leads ever upward and grows so narrow that finally there remains nothing but the cross. It is then that Liberation is near. If the aspirant continues persistent and faithful, the great goal is won. With the gladsome cry of the Master, *"It is finished,"* the victorious one is free! He is now released into wider realms for a larger life of love and service.

Holy Saturday

The culminating event on Holy Saturday occurred at the midnight hour with the observance of the profoundly esoteric Baptismal Rite. This had to do with the Second Degree or the Rite of Illumination. Those who aspired to pass into the inner sanctuary of this Degree began a rigorous preparation under the Teacher's care at the beginning of Lent and were known as "those who are being illuminated." A number of the holy men and women prominently mentioned in the Gospels passed this Degree on Saturday night and were thus enabled to greet the Sun of that momentous Easter dawn as new-born brothers of the risen Christ. These included the women to whom Christ appeared in that early dawning.

Water has a special affinity for etheric substance; hence, when the etheric body of a candidate for Initiation has been sufficiently sensitized by pure and holy living, the immersion of the body in water tends to loosen the normally firm bond that holds the etheric and physical bodies together. When a separation between the two is effected, and the centers in the vital or etheric body are awakened, consciousness is opened to the inner planes and the soul encounters transcendental experiences which leave a lasting impress upon the future life. To undergo the Baptismal Rite unprepared would be to invite a condition fraught with danger since the influx of spiritual power accompanying the Baptism, while bringing Illumination to the duly prepared, will carry destruction to vehicles not properly cleansed and qualified.

Certain centers in the invisible bodies of man are especially susceptible to the spiritual influence accompanying the Baptismal Rite. When the administrator of this ceremony is sufficiently advanced, he will direct his inner vision to these centers and condition the work in accordance with the aspirant's development. It was John the Baptist's possession of this ability that revealed to him the exalted status of Jesus and caused him to feel his great unworthiness to baptize a Soul already so illumined. The invocation used by the early Christians at the Baptismal Ceremony were words of music to the eager, expectant devotee: "Open your eyes and ears and draw in the sweet savor of eternal life."

The Resurrection or Easter Rite

John 20:1-18.

The first day of the week cometh Mary Magdalene early, when it was yet dark, unto the sepulchre, and seeth the stone taken away from the sepulchre.

Then she runneth, and cometh to Simon Peter, and to the other disciple, whom Jesus loved, and saith unto them, They have taken away the Lord out of the sepulchre, and we know not where they have laid him.

Peter therefore went forth, and that other disciple, and came to the sepulchre.

So they ran both together: and the other disciple did outrun Peter, and came first to the sepulchre.

And he, stooping down, and looking in, saw the linen clothes lying; yet went he not in.

Then cometh Simon Peter following him, and went into the sepulchre, and seeth the linen clothes lie.

And the napkin, that was about his head, not lying with the linen clothes, but wrapped together in a place by itself.

Then went in also that other disciple, which came first to the sepulchre, and he saw, and believed.

For as yet they knew not the scripture, that he must rise again from the dead.

Then the disciples went away again unto their home.

But Mary stood without at the sepulchre weeping: and as she wept, she stooped down, and looked into the sepulchre,

And seeth two angels in white sitting, the one at the head, and the other at the feet, where the body of Jesus had lain.

And they say unto her, Woman, why weepest thou? She saith unto them, Because they have taken away my Lord, and I know not where they have laid him.

And when she had thus said, she turned herself back, and saw Jesus standing, and knew not that it was Jesus.

Jesus saith unto her, Woman, why weepest thou? whom seekest thou? She, supposing him to be the gardener, saith unto him, Sir, if thou have borne him hence, tell me where thou hast laid him, and I will take him away.

Jesus saith unto her, Mary. She turned herself, and saith unto him, Rabboni; which is to say, Master.

Jesus saith unto her, Touch me not; for I am not yet ascended to my Father: but go to my brethren, and say unto them, I ascend unto my Father, and your Father; and to my God, and your God.

Mary Magdalene came and told the disciples that she had seen the Lord, and that he had spoken these things unto her.

The body of Christ Jesus remained in the tomb through Friday night, the whole of Saturday, and part of Sunday. The student of mystic Christianity understands that the three days refer to the process of Initiation. During the three Creative Days comprising the Saturn, Sun and Moon Revolutions of the Earth Period, and the cosmic nights between, the Creative Hierarchies worked in the Great Deep perfecting the inner parts of man and the planet. The earth emerged from its watery stage of development in middle Atlantis. Men in reviewing this time through Initiation are said to be three days in the tomb or darkness, and on the fourth day at sunrise to be reborn into the light of a new day.

The story of the Descent into Hell is found in most pre-Christian religions, perhaps the oldest story in preservation being the Babylonian, known as the "Descent of Ishtar." In ancient Greek and Roman literature we find numerous descents into Hades, perhaps the most familiar being those of Hercules, Dionysus and Persephone. These legends all contain the story of Initiation; consequently the steps of progress must be similar. Buddha descended into Hades to preach to mortals there. It is interesting to note that each of these saviours or heroes descended into the underworld to aid or rescue some one else. *Here we find the key which alone unlocks the door of Initiation.*

The Empty Tomb

The empty tomb has been the cause of much speculation among exoteric or orthodox Christians. Its meaning, however, becomes plain when studied esoterically. The atoms of the body of Jesus, pure and holy as He was vibrated at a much slower rate than the vibratory forces of the Christ Spirit. Consequently, frequent acceleration of the atoms of Jesus' body had to take place during the three-year Ministry. This acceleration of the vibration of the atoms would have shattered the physical body of Jesus had not the powerful will of the Master, assisted by the skill of the Essenes, held it together. Had the atoms of the body been asleep, as those in the bodies of ordinary humanity, it would have required a long time for the physical form to disintegrate after it had been vacated by the Christ; but in the case of Jesus the atoms had become so highly charged with life that they quickly found their full freedom so soon as the integrating Christ Spirit left the physical body at the time of the Crucifixion. When we learn to make and to keep our bodies fully alive, we shall not change atoms or bodies so often, nor will the work of disintegration be so long a process as at the present time.

No trace was ever found of the bodies of Moses, Pythagoras, or Appollonius of Tyana. Buddha's death is described as "that utter passing away in which nothing whatever remains behind,"

The stone that was rolled away from Jesus' sepulchre was a great circular rock moving in a groove like a mill stone which, when rolled over the entrance, closed it like a door. The Romans sealed it by drawing cords in front of it, the cords being fastened on each side of the tomb by wax or clay so the authorities would know if the tomb had been entered. Such a stone would require several men to move it.

The stone rolled away means esoterically the complete overcoming of materiality and all obstacles that prevent attainment of that complete self-mastery which opens the way of Initiation. This overcoming is always accomplished through the resurrection of the Christ power within man himself.

The earthquake recorded as having occurred when Christ Jesus arose from the tomb was caused by the change of atomic vibrations in the earth as the great Sun Spirit freed Himself from its confines. The same phenomenon took place for the same reason when He entered the earth at the time of His Crucifixion.

Among the characters described in the New Testament, Saul of Tarsus and Mary Magdalene are foremost examples of what may be accomplished through redemption. Truly the greatest sinner may become the greatest saint.

The first day of the week instead of the seventh is now held sacred in commemoration of the resurrection of Christ Jesus. The seventh day is Saturn's day, a day of law, form and ceremonial worship. The Resurrection ushered in a new regime of spirituality, the dawn of love which supersedes law. Hence the first day of the week, the Sun's day, is sacred to the Christian world.

In the Ritual of the Empty Tomb, the Christ as the Way-Shower for all mankind demonstrated to His followers the final and most difficult work to be accomplished on this physical earth. That work is the transmutation of matter into spirit. When this has been learned, man will have gained mastery over sickness, age and death. In esoteric terminology, this attainment comes with the Initiation belonging to Earth, the densest of the four elements. It is the last of the Four Great Initiations. When the light of this sublime illumination has been spread abroad, altars will be erected to the Christ in our physical laboratories as well as in our churches. The *spirit* behind and within matter will have been recognized.

With the Earth Initiation comes liberation from the wheel of birth and death. The necessity for reincarnation is over because earth's lessons have been learned. Man's spirit is henceforth free to pursue its further development in other and higher spheres, or to remain with humanity in order to help man mount the sooner to the level to which it has attained. Such are the Graduates of humanity, the Masters of Wisdom and our Elder Brothers of Compassion.

Peter, too, passed through the Ritual of the Mystic Death on this Easter Morning preparatory to attaining the Degree of Mastership. Together with Mary and John he came to the empty tomb, and according to the Gospel record Peter alone entered it, the other two remaining outside. This incident translated symbolically points to the fact that the other two had previously undergone the experience of entering the "tomb" and arising triumphantly therefrom. Hence they were assisting Peter to pass into the exalted glory of the consciousness which was theirs.

Through the processes of Initiation mortality puts on immortality. This is its all-inclusive end and aim. To the consciousness of the Initiate, life and death are but different aspects of the spirit's progressive unfoldment. Realizing this, the burial ceremonial among the early Christians was a glorious rite. Life was its theme. Leaves of ivy and laurel were placed in the casket and a complete text of the Gospels laid over the heart. Palms and olive branches were carried by those attending and the procession to the grave was marked, not by mourning and lamentation, but by the sound of glad hosannas. In keeping with this spirit was their garb which was not in the darkness of the grave but in the brightness of the light that greets the soul upon its birth into the realms of spirit. Early Christian graves were cross-shaped in recognition of the fact that the body of mortality which is laid aside is the cross of matter from which the soul is liberated in death, as it is the body from which the spirit rises free when attaining to the light of Initiation.

During the interval between the Crucifixion and the Resurrection (Friday evening until Sunday morning) the Christ Spirit was active within the earth planet, as previously described. "He descended into hell." Such is the credal phrase for His entrance into the lower astral or desire sphere of this earth, whereunto He went to bring His gospel to discarnate souls still in the realm of darkness. Thus the Christ came to minister not only to incarnate humanity but also to its discarnate members. Moreover, His mission extends to the redemption of the fallen Lucifer Spirits, whose place of activity is the Desire World, and also all the other kingdoms of life on earth who suffer evolutionary retardation because of the "fall" of man, their elder brother. This is the all-inclusive cosmic aspect of His redemptive work.

In the early morning hours of the first Easter, several women came to the empty tomb besides the blessed Mother Mary and Mary of Magdala. These included the Virgin Mother's sister; also Mary, the mother of James and Jude; Salome and Joanna, the wife of Herod's steward, Chuza. These women were all there in preparation for entering into the Mystic Death and experiencing the illumination that follows upon passing through the Rite of the Resurrection. The two Angels that they saw guarding the open grave represent the purified desire body and the luminous etheric body of the ready candidate. That even greater attainment was awaiting these women appears from the words the Master addressed to them when He bade them "Go on into Galilee and I will meet you there." According to the Zohar, "The complete resurrection will begin in Galilee. The resurrection of bodies," it goes on to say, "will be as the uprising of flowers. There will be no more need of eating and drinking for we shall all be nourished by the Glory of the Shekinah."

The Essenes, who so reverently preserved the knowledge of the Easter Mysteries, continued throughout the years of their group activity to keep the night hours of Holy Saturday and the sunrise hours of Easter sacred with prayers and hymns of praise.

The Mystic Sunrise Rite

The Rite of the Resurrection is the rite of the impersonal life. In the experiences of the mystic death the disciple becomes aware of the illusions of matter and the limitations of finite life. The Resurrection consciousness brings the realization of the oneness of all life with God. The stone of separation has been rolled away. Henceforth one who has passed into this sublime experience knows that no ill can affect a part without hurting the whole, and that no good can come to the one without at the same time benefiting all.

One who comes to know the glory of the Resurrection can never again wound or kill even his younger brothers of the animal kingdom, for they, too, are living expressions of the same divine life that lives and moves and has its being in man. In the Resurrection consciousness the passion of the unregenerate desire body is transformed into the compassion of the all-embracing spirit. The newly awakened is bathed in the golden refulgence of the risen Christ and becomes one with Him in the realization that death has been merged into the victory of eternal life.

Meditation upon the transcendent experience of the Resurrection Rite brings a deeper understanding of and reverence for the inner significance of that salutation with which the esoteric Christians greeted each other in the early radiance of the mystic Easter Dawn, in the light of their own illumination: "The Christ is our Light."

In later years the night of Holy Saturday and the morning of Easter Sunday were times of Initiation for those advanced souls whose life and works are mentioned in the Gospels. And there must have been many others not so mentioned for in the words of John's Gospel, "many other signs therefore did Jesus in the presence of the disciples which are not written in this book." Still later, St. Gregory wrote a beautiful hymn describing the Holy Mary's dedication at the mystic sunrise, and early legends declare that it was to her that the risen Master made His first appearance.

Matthew 28:1-6.

In the end of the sabbath, as it began to dawn toward the first day of the week, came Mary Magdalene and the other Mary to see the sepulchre.

And behold, there was a great earthquake: for the angel of the Lord descended from heaven, and came and rolled back the stone from the door, and sat upon it.

His countenance was like lightning, and his raiment white as snow:

And for fear of him the keepers did shake, and became as dead men.

And the angel answered and said unto the woman, Fear not ye: for I know that ye seek Jesus, which was crucified.

He is not here: for he is risen, as he said. Come, see the place where the Lord lay.

Matthew records the appearance of the Angel of the Lord (law) to the two Marys. Mary represents the formative or mother principle in nature, and as the Holy Virgin is adored as the mother of God by one of Christendom's largest religious bodies. Universal Essence manifests as spirit and matter, the two poles of Being. From the time that God as Spirit, the positive masculine aspect, externalized Himself in nature or matter, the negative or feminine pole, the purpose of spiritual evolution has been to sublimate or redeem that manifestation, or the externalized "fallen" feminine. The Holy Mary is a personalized expression of this uplifted principle.

One of the outstanding features of the New Age reading of the Bible is the universality of its appeal. To every aspirant in whom the Christ Within is resurrected, the same Angel of the

Lord (law) is waiting to proclaim the glorious tidings: "He is not here, for he is risen."

Matthew 28:9.

And as they went to tell his disciples, behold, Jesus met them, saying, All Hail. And they came and held him by the feet, and worshipped him.

After the resurrection into the new life and consciousness of the spirit comes the meeting face to face. This is that most holy time of which Paul sings: "No longer through a glass darkly, but face to face."

THE INITIATION OF MARY OF MAGDALA

John 20:11-18.

But Mary stood without at the sepulchre weeping: and as she wept, she stooped down, and looked into the sepulchre,

And seeth two angels in white sitting, the one at the head, and the other at the feet, where the body of Jesus had lain.

And they say unto her, Woman, why weepest thou? She saith unto them, Because they have taken away my Lord, and I know not where they have laid him.

And when she had thus said, she turned herself back, and saw Jesus standing, and knew not that it was Jesus.

Jesus saith unto her, Woman, why weepest thou? whom seekest thou? She, supposing him to be he gardener, saith unto him, Sir, if thou have borne him hence, tell me where thou hast laiid him, and I will take him away.

Jesus saith unto her, Mary. She turned herself, and saith unto him, Rabboni; which is to say, Master.

Jesus saiith unto her, Touch me not; for I am not yet ascended to my Father: but go to my brethren, and say unto them, I ascend unto my Father, and your Father; and to my God, and your God.

Mary Magdalene came and told the disciples that she had seen the Lord, and that he had spoken these things unto her.

In the Gospel of John, only Mary Magdalene, the fallen one, is recorded as communing with the Christ. The Virgin Mary represents the attainment of this redeemed force in man and the perfect type of woman who shall inhabit the earth at the time of the return of the Christ. Mary Magdalene represents this principle in the process of transmutation. Astrologically the two may be described by the signs Virgo and Scorpio. These two signs, once united, are now separated, and Libra, the Scales or Balance, is placed between. Eventually, when man has learned to know only good, the balance will no longer be necessary. Then the reunion will occur, and Virgo and Scorpio will again be one. (Esoterically this is the reason for both these signs being feminine.)

Rabboni is a term of deepest reverence, meaning *most exalted Master.* So great was its distinction that it was applied to but seven of the most noted rabbis.

The word "touch" is used here in the sense of intimate contact. No longer was the same kind of communion possible between Master and disciples as when He lived on earth in a physical body. Now His desire was that He should no more descend to them but that they should ascend to Him and function with Him in His own realm. "I go to prepare a place for you, that where I am, there ye may be also."

The fact that Mary of Magdala was able to see and commune with her Lord as He functioned in His Life Spirit body bespeaks her exalted degree of Initiateship at this time.

In her sublimely exalted state, Mary Magdalene touched the realm of Christed realization which is possible under the supervision of a Teacher. Hence, before this elevation of awareness had occurred Mary did not recognize her Master in this resplendent spiritual Being. It was only as He assisted her to gradually lift her consciousness to the levels whereon He now functioned that she was able to recognize Him in all His transcendent glory. It was then that she sank to her knees and addressed Him as "Rabonni," meaning most high Master.

The three Marys who occupy so prominent a place in the life of the Master bear an interesting astrological significance. They typify the three great feminine signs of the Zodiac, Taurus, Cancer and Virgo. Mary Magdalene represents Taurus, the redemption of the sense life through love; Mary, the sister of Lazarus and the beautiful mystic, is the intuitive, imaginative sign of Cancer; Mary, the Madonna, is her own sign of Virgo, spiritual love flowing out in service and sacrifice and the symbol of the Immaculate Conception.

Mark 16:1-7.

And when the sabbath was past, Mary Magdalene, and Mary the mother of James, and Salome, had bought sweet spices, that they might come and anoint him.

And very early in the morning the first day of the week, they came unto the sepulchre at the rising of the sun.

And they said among themselves, Who shall roll us away the stone from the door of the sepulchre?

And when they looked, they saw that the stone was rolled away: for is was very great.

And entering into the sepulchre, they saw a young man sitting on the right side, clothed in a long white garment; and they were affrighted.

And he saith unto them, Be not affrighted: Ye seek Jesus of Nazareth, which was crucified: he is risen; he is not here: behold the place where they laid him.

But go your way, tell his disciples and Peter that he goeth before you into Galilee: there shall ye see him, as he said unto you.

When superficial students of Scripture deny that there is an Initiation for women in the Christian Mysteries it is necessary to point out to them the peculiar esoteric significance of certain incidents in which women disciples figure in the Bible story. It is by no means difficult to show that concealed within the Gospel allegory of the redemption of mankind generally there is also a formula for the Illumination of egos in feminine embodiment particularly; for conditions in the material world bear more heavily upon them than upon egos in masculine embodiment.

We have taught repeatedly that there is a true polarity in the human spirit; that the ego is biune, both masculine and feminine, but that these polarities are known in spirit as Powers, not organs. Spiritual work requires that the two poles of spirit function harmoniously together, not sacrificing one to the other since both are essential to the creative process. This fact is reflected in our mundane sphere in the equality of the sexes. Such is the esoteric interpretation of Christ's appearance to the Eleven as recorded in all four Gospels. Eleven (11) is the number of equilibrium. The Master's appearances were made not only to the *eleven* Disciples (Judas, the lower man, was missing), but also to a group of women disciples who partook of spiritual joys equally with the men.

Luke refers to Mary, Mary Magdalene and Joanna, the wife of Chuza, the steward of Herod. Mark makes reference to Mary, the mother of James, Mary Magdalene and Salome. a grand niece of Herod Antipas. Matthew mentions Mary and Mary Magdalene; John names Mary Magdalene only. Matthew and Mark describe one Angel at the tomb—the great ideal shadowed forth by the Lord (law). Luke and John make mention of two Angels—the attainment of proper functioning of the two poles of spirit which lifts mind and heart away from the consciousness of the Tree of Good and Evil, and brings to light the Tree of Life, the new and extended powers of consciousness. This means a revelation to the soul of the mystic, joys of its own individual resurrection morn.

Luke 24:1-10.

Now upon the first day of the week, very early in the morning, they came unto the sepulchre, bringing the spices which they had prepared, and certain others with them.

And they found the stone rolled away from the sepulchre.

And they entered in, and found not the body of the Lord Jesus.

And it came to pass, as they were much perplexed thereabout, behold, two men stood by them in shining garments:

And as they were afraid, and bowed down their faces to the earth, they said unto them, Why seek ye the living among the dead?

He is not here, but is risen: remember how he spake unto you when he was yet in Galilee,

Saying, the Son of man must be delivered into the hands of sinful men, and be crucified, and the third day rise again.

And they remembered his words,

And returned from the sepulchre, and told all these things unto the eleven, and to all the rest.

It was Mary Magdalene, and Joanna, and Mary the mother of James, and other women that were with them, which told these things unto the apostles.

In the stupendous glory of the vigil of the Mystic Sunrise, Mary attained unto the highest culmination of pure soul ecstasy. By her powers of Initiate-vision she had witnessed all the inner plane experiences of Christ during the "Interval of Waiting," that is, the time between the Crucifixion on Friday and the sunrise of the Resurrection Morn.

It was in the flood-tide glory of the Mystic Sunrise that, the inner-plane mission of Christ accomplished, He returned for His final days upon earth with the chosen Disciples. Upon witnessing the wondrous transformation of Mary when the new Sun arose, her profound joy and her exaltation of consciousness, John and the holy women, realized that the blessed Master was again upon the earth with men. Their transcendent experiences of the Easter Day were soon to confirm this knowledge.

Such a Sabbath Day had never dawned upon the world before. All things wore a look of outward quiet in Jerusalem. An intense calm followed the excitement of those strange scenes on Golgotha. Crowds of silent worshippers filled the court of the Temple for the sacrificial service exactly as they had done for so many hundreds of years before.

But how different the scene in the inner realms! What gladsome hosannahs were being sung by the angelic hosts! They were able to perceive waves of dazzling light and their cleansing and purifying influence on the dark ad murky strata of the Desire World, opening the way of a new redemption for all the world.

Easter Afternoon

In the Gospel of Luke is recorded the memorable walk to Emmaus. Cleophas, the father of James and Jude, and another of the Disciples were walking to the little suburban village of Jerusalem when the Master suddenly appeared and accompanied them into their home, where He blessed their evening meal. But it was not until He broke the bread for them that they recognized His true identity. In the ceremonial of the Last Supper they had seen Him pour His radiant life force into the bread until it became a luminous magnet of healing power. By this same sign it was that He now broke their bread, whereupon they knew that He who was among them was none other than the risen Christ Himself. While they had not reached the development that enabled them to recognize Him at their first encounter on the road, it indicated no mean attainment for them to merit coming thus intimately into His presence and to recognize Him at all on the level from which He now functioned. Immediately the Christed One had disappeared from their sight, they hastened to Jerusalem to proclaim the joyous news of His appearance.

Easter Evening

On Easter evening the Disciples that had been most intimately associated with the Master met again in the Upper Room which was still vibrant with the power released there on the eve of the Holy Supper. And as they there received the two from Emmaus and listened eagerly to their joyous report, lo He Himself stood in the midst of them and said, "Peace be unto you. See my hands and feet," said He further, "that it is I myself."

This is but a cryptic fragment of what then occurred. The Master was then imparting to His Disciples instructions pertaining to "pulling the nails" from the hands and feet at points where the etheric body is tied, as it were, to the physical body. There are also other points where the two bodies are similarly linked, but it is those in the hands and feet that are the most difficult to sever. Hence the pain, and the "Sacred Wounds" in the language of the Church.

Thomas was not among the company. But on the following or Octave Sunday in that same Upper Room, Thomas, the doubter, was bidden by the Christ, who again appeared, to place his hands in "the print of the nails." Doing so "he believed;" that is, he came into firsthand knowledge of truths that opened for him the door to Initiation.

Easter Monday

On Easter Monday the Master appeared again to His most advanced Disciples at the sea of Tiberias. In the company were Peter, James, John, Nathaniel and Phillip. Peter, around whom this incident chiefly revolves, announced his intention to go fishing. Thereupon his companions joined him and, stepping into a boat, they put out to sea. During the night they caught nothing. In the morning they saw Jesus standing on the beach. Addressing them He said, "Cast your net on the right side of the boat and ye shall find." They did so and the catch was great. When Peter learned from John that it was the Lord who stood before them, he cast himself into the sea and drew the net full of fishes to the land.

This incident is recorded in the twenty-first chapter of St. John, the most esoteric of all the Gospel records as it is written by the Master's closest and most beloved Disciple. The experience here described is altogether spiritual and occurred on the inner planes. The sea symbolizes the etheric realms and the boat the soul body in which man functions in that realm. Fish is a symbol of the hidden mysteries or esoteric truth. The number of fishes caught, which is given as 153, gives the numerological value of nine or the number of man's evaluation, indicating that humanity as a whole will be caught up or saved when the Cosmic Christ is universally acknowledged as the World Saviour.

Peter, together with those who were with him, was here being taught by the Master how "to throw the nets on the right side of the boat"—or, in other words, how to attune himself to the positive or right-hand currents of the earth. These currents are under the control of Mercury, God of Wisdom, whereas the negative or left-hand currents come under the direction of Mars, ruler of the emotions, That man has not yet well learned how to "cast the net on the right side" is amply demonstrated by the discords and upheavals through which the world is now passing.

In order to attune life to the positive earth currents it is necessary to unite the right and the left-hand currents or the forces of head and heart, respectively. This was part of Peter's instruction as he jumped into the sea and came to Jesus. He was learning to walk in the Way that He taught. Peter furthermore demonstrated his readiness for added instruction when he "went up and drew the net to land."

We read that when the Disciples reached the shore they saw a fire on which were laid bread and fish. This is the spinal spirit fire that must be ablaze with light before a candidate can receive and assimilate the fish or esoteric truths that have to do with the Great Transmutation. The bread represents the powers of the pure body temple of a Christed one.

After the Master had broken the fast with His Disciples He asked of Peter, "Lovest thou me?" "Yea, Lord," was the emphatic reply. Thrice the Lord repeated the question and thrice Peter gave like answer. To these affirmations the Christ enjoined him to feed His sheep.

In this incident is outlined the Three Degrees of the Christian Mysteries, all of which Peter had now passed successfully. He had, therefore, earned the privilege or attained to the powers that enabled him to "feed the sheep," become a teacher of men, and, in fact, the very rock of Initiation upon which the Church was founded. That the Church has lost the power it had when first established is due to its having forsaken the Teachings of the Mysteries. Only when these are again restored will the mystic powers wielded by the early Church be regained.

Other disciples of Christ there were who did not attain to the sublime Degree of Mastership until the outpouring of the spirit forty days later at Pentecost. Then added numbers became clothed with the powers of the Mastership Degree which enabled them, in the words of St. Mark's Gospel, to cast out demons "in my name."

". . . they shall speak with many tongues;

"They shall take up serpents; and if they drink any deadly thing, it shall not hurt them; they shall lay hands on the sick, and they shall recover."

Since the first great outpouring of the pentecostal fires humanity has drifted far into the world of materiality wherein the powers of the spirit have become less and less manifest. But from their long "burial" they are due to experience a universal resurrection in the New Day that is now dawning. Another time of "miracles" is at hand; a second Pentecost is near. From the urn of Aquarius there is being poured out on all the earth a new fire from the heavens, which is destined to awaken humanity to new spiritual realizations and to create the conditions that will make it possible for the Christ Spirit to return fully to the consciousness of men even as He manifested to those near Him in Palestine in the days of His first coming.

The Resurrection of Christ is not primarily an historical event for mere ecclesiastical commemoration. It is a recurring cosmic festival. It is an annual spiritual as well as physical upsurge of life for man's present experience and upliftment. Only as that experience is inwardly appropriated can man enter into the realization of the transcendent significance of the Holy Easter Mysteries.

CHAPTER VI

The Mystic Interval between the Resurrection and the Ascension

The Risen Christ

The Christ appeared thirteen times to His Disciples during the forty days between the Resurrection and the Ascension. These were not visions nor were they mere social visits, but on each occasion He demonstrated occult principles which He had previously taught them, and also instructed them in yet deeper mystic truths.

The Apocrypha state that the first appearance was to the Virgin Mary. The remaining twelve appearances were to the following:

1. Mary Magdalene, as related by John.
2. The three Marys.
3. Peter at the tomb.
4. The Two on the way to Emmaus.
5. The Disciples in the upper room.
6. Again a week later in the upper room to the Eleven.
7. The Seven Disciples fishing on the sea of Galilee.
8. The Disciples. (Matthew 28:16-20).
9. The Five Hundred in Galilee.
10. James (1 Corinthians 15:7).
11. Joseph of Aramathea.
12. Paul (1 Corinthians 15:8).

These appearances offer interesting esoteric studies. Some of them were in an etheric body; others in a physical body. (A Master's vital body is so strongly magnetic that it can attract physical atoms readily and easily.)

Until the silver cord, which connects the vital and physical bodies, is severed after death, the etheric body possesses the power of attracting dense or physical atoms, a fact which explains why the life-like form of one who has just passed over in death is so frequently seen by near relatives or friends of the departed spirit. The power of etheric manifestation is strong enough during this period to become thus visible to others, and for this manifestation distance offers no hindrance, for to the etheric body distance is almost non-existent. After the severance of the silver-cord, however, the vital body no longer possesses this attractive power; the image vanishes, and the body is dissolved. The Christ possessed a soul body not subject to dissolution; consequently He was able to enter the upper room through closed doors and there attract sufficient atoms to form a physical body, and dissolve it at will when leaving. Physical walls are no barrier to the etheric vehicle.

"All power is given unto me in heaven and in earth." This was Christ's first utterance to the assembled Disciples after the Resurrection. By this He meant that He had now, through the sacrifice on Golgotha, become the indwelling Planetary Earth Spirit, and that all earth evolution was under His direct guidance.

Matthew 28:19, 20.

Go ye therefore, and teach all nations, baptizing them in the name of the Father, and of the Son, and of the Holy Ghost:

Teaching them to observe all things whatsoever I have commanded you: and, lo, I am with you alway, even unto the end of the world. Amen.

Mark 16:17, 18.

And these signs shall follow them that believe; In my name shall they cast out devils; they shall speak with new tongues;

They shall take up serpents; and if they drink any deadly thing, it shall not hurt them; they shall lay hands on the sick, and they shall recover.

Christ's admonition to baptize in the name of the Father, Son and Holy Ghost was a call to the complete consecration of the Will (Father), the Love-Wisdom (Christ) and the Activity (Holy Spirit) principles. The first two principles, when united, complete the transmutation of the lower or carnal man into the higher or celestial nature. One who has received this baptism of the Father, Son and Holy Spirit shows forth the fruits of those that believe; that is, he becomes a first-hand knower and manifests the powers of the Initiate. Such an one speaks words that are filled with spirit and life because they are infused with the force of a love that is alive and a purity and holiness that no venom or poison can penetrate. His auric emanations are such as to break down the crystallizations that cause disease and thus open the way for perfect health. Such are the powers of the Christian Initiate, the fruits of a true spiritual baptism.

Luke 24:36-43.

And as they thus spake, Jesus himself stood in the midst of them, and saith unto them, Peace be unto you.

But they were terrified and affrighted, and supposed that they had seen a spirit.

And he said unto them, Why are ye troubled? and why do thoughts arise in your hearts,

Behold my hands and my feet, that it is I myself: handle me, and see; for a spirit hath not flesh and bones, as ye see me have.

And when he had thus spoken, he shewed them his hands and his feet.

And while they yet believed not for joy, and wondered, he said unto them, Have ye here any meat?

And they gave him a piece of a broiled fish, and of an honeycomb.

And he took it, and did eat before them.

Christ ate broiled fish and honeycomb in their presence. Then He opened their eyes that they might understand the Scriptures. It was not physical food with which He was concerned, but the mysteries pertaining to His mission and the furtherance of the great work. Each appearance before the Ascension is a deeper revelation and a promise of the bestowal of greater spiritual powers.

Luke 24:46-49.

And said unto them, Thus it is written, and thus it behoved Christ to suffer, and to rise from the dead the third day:

And that repentance and remission of sins should be preached in his name among all nations, beginning at Jerusalem.

And ye are witnesses of these things.

And, behold, I send the promise of my Father upon you: but tarry ye in the city of Jerusalem, until ye be endued with power from on high.

John 20:24-28.

But Thomas, one of the twelve, called Didymus, was not with them when Jesus came.

The other disciples therefore said unto him. We have seen the Lord. But he said unto them, Except I shall see in his hands the print of the nails, and put my finger into the print of the nails, and thrust my hand into his side, I will not believe.

And after eight days again his disciples were within, and Thomas with them: then came Jesus, the doors being shut, and stood in the midst, and said, Peace be unto you.

Then saith he to Thomas, Reach hither thy finger, and behold my hands; and reach hither thy hand, and thrust it into my side: and be not faithless, but believing.

And Thomas answered and said unto him, my Lord and my God.

John tells of the appearance of the Christ to eleven of the Disciples. Eleven is a master number, the number of polarity. The other Gospel writers record Christ's appearance to ten of the Disciples. Only those who had attained to the polarity represented by eleven were in that upper room of high spiritual consciousness and were found worthy to commune with and receive the deeper work of the Risen Christ.

After the doubts of Thomas had been allayed he commenced his glorious career as an eminent apostle of healing, and preached the truths of the new Christianity. No longer was there any doubt. Skepticism was replaced by that faith that removes mountains, and Thomas the doubter became Thomas the true believer. Only John records the story of the transformation of Thomas. Among the final works are the conquest of doubt and the ascendence of faith as the dominating principles of a life dedicated in love.

During the forty days or the traditional interval between the Resurrection and the Ascension, Christ was engaged in many works connected with all the life waves evolving upon this earth. This also included work with the various race and group spirits who guide their progression. These beings are all stragglers of the archangelic host of which the Christ is the highest Initiate. They are, by their sacrificial services, retrieving their lost estate. Their task will be finished when the love and unity radiated by the Christ shall have obliterated the boundary lines of race and nation. Christ's coming, therefore, was not for man only but for the Angels and Archangels; that is, for the fallen Angels or Lucifers and for the backward members of His own archangelic life wave.

Meeting With The Two From Emmaus

Luke 24:13-18.

And, behold, two of them went that same day to a village called Emmaus, which was from Jerusalem about threescore furlongs.

And they talked together of all these things which had happened.

And it came to pass, that, while they communed together and reasoned, Jesus himself drew near, and went with them.

But their eyes were holden that they should not know him.

And he said unto them, What manner of communications are these that ye have one to another, as ye walk, and are sad?

And the one of them, whose name was Cleopas, answering said unto him, Art thou only a stranger in Jerusalem, and hast not known the things which are come to pass there in these days?

Luke 24:28-31.

And they drew nigh unto the village, whither they went: and he made as though he would have gone further.

But they constrained him, saying, Abide with us, for it is toward evening, and the day is far spent. And he went in to tarry with them.

And it came to pass, as he sat at meat with them, he took bread, and blessed it, and brake, and gave to them.

And their eyes were opened, and they knew him; and he vanished out of their sight.

When the risen Christ vanished from the sight of the two in Emmaus, both of whom were filled with a holy joy and reverence, they returned to Jerusalem and the upper room where they had met with Him before His departure, bearing the glad tidings of the Resurrection, saying: "The Lord is risen indeed."

Only in the Gospels of Mark and Luke is recorded the tenderly intimate story of the walk with the two Disciples on that first Easter Day.

In the ceremonial of the Last Supper the Christ had shown them how to impregnate a physical object (bread) with spiritual power so that it could become a repository for healing forces and afterwards be used to heal. This He did again as He blessed the bread and gave it to them, and by this same act they recognized Him.

The Eleven were gathered in that sacred place, the upper room where the beloved ceremonial of the Last Supper had taken place.

Mark 16:14-15.

Afterward he appeared unto the eleven as they sat at meat, and upbraided them with their unbelief and hardness of heart, because they believed not them which had seen him after he was risen.

And he said unto them, Go ye into all the world, and preach the gospel to every creature.

In each Gospel Christ's appearance to the Eleven is emphasized by a promise of their future attainment.

The Disciples went to the Mount (high spiritual consciousness) to confer with their returned Master. The transformation in the lives of these eleven men begins with the Resurrection Day. They had bathed in the glory of His Transfiguration; the breath of His immortality had touched them. No longer did their interest center in a physical throne set up in Jerusalem. They now visioned the light which encircles that celestial throne in the fair land of the New Jerusalem. Once glimpsed, they never lost sight of its resplendent glory—which outshone the light of funeral pyres and gleamed about the cross of martyrdom.

The Initiatory Work of Peter and John

We have stated that Peter is the head of the work in the Christian Mystery Temple; this, however, has special reference to the initiatory work done in the western world (in Europe particularly) and during the Piscean Age which is now drawing to its close. When the Disciples apportioned the known world amongst themselves as fields for missionary service, Rome and the European Empire fell to Peter. He was the apostle to the West. Hence, Church history still retains fragmentary references to the peculiar role which this great Disciple plays in western Christendom, in that Peter is considered to be the founder of the Church at Rome and apostolic succession is traced from him in all orthodox communions. Legend has it that Peter holds the "keys" to the "gates of Heaven," and that after death each soul as it enters those gates must undergo the scrutiny and examination of this foremost Disciple of the Lord Christ.

Such statements are but half truths based upon the esoteric fact, as we have stated, that the European Mysteries of Christ were placed under his direction "for the Age." The Bible offers numerous keys to the Initiations of Peter.

Luke 5:1-11.

And it came to pass, that as the people pressed upon him to hear the word of God, he stood by the lake of Gennesaret,

And saw two ships standing by the lake; but the fishermen were gone out of them, and were washing their nets.

And he entered into one of the ships, which was Simon's, and prayed him that he would thrust out a little from the land. An he sat down, and taught the people out of the ship.

And when he had left speaking, he said unto Simon, Launch out into the deep, and let down your nets for a draught.

And Simon answering said unto him, Master, we have toiled all the night and have taken nothing; nevertheless at thy word I will let down the net.

And when they had this done, they enclosed a great multitude of fishes: and their net brake.

And they beckoned unto their partners who were in the other ship, that they should come and help them. And they came, and filled both ships, so that they began to sink.

When Simon Peter saw it, he fell down at Jesus' knees, saying, Depart from me; for I am a sinful man, O Lord.

For he was astonished, and all that were with him, at the draught of fishes which they had taken.

And so was also James, and John, the sons of Zebedee, who were partners with Simon. And Jesus said unto Simon, Fear not; from henceforth thou shalt catch men."

And when they had brought their ships to land, they forsook all, and followed him.

During the current Piscean Age the majority of people have been able to receive only an external concept of Christ's life and mission. The New Age demands a truer understanding of His work and of the Book of Books. Exoteric Christianity has not been able to deliver us from chaos and confusion. The human race is no longer content to worship merely an external Christ. In order to become Christ-like we must develop the Christ within. This is the work of the New Age and the inner process involved was revealed to the few by the Christ. This inner work and teaching are concealed within the various works and events of His life.

It is for this reason that much of His work with the Disciples is recorded as having been done in boats and on the water. The incident recorded in the foregoing passage is concerned with a definite process belonging to the inner preparatory work of true discipleship. The repeated reference in the New Testament to fish relates to the process of Initiation. It was after this incident recorded in Luke that the Twelve were chosen.

Christ Jesus taught the multitudes from the anchored ship, but Peter, James and John were admonished to launch out into the deep and let down their nets for a draught. However, though they succeeded in bringing up the fish, *their nets broke and the boat began to sink;* a familiar experience in early discipleship. Immediately following this experience they left the world and all its interests for a complete dedication to the work of *true fishermen.*

The Gospel of John, the most deeply occult of the four, closes with a similar incident in the lives of these same Disciples; it differs only in that it transpires on a still higher plane. It occurs after the Resurrection and just preceding the Ascension. The Disciples had then passed through the three-years' Ministry and were being prepared for their own Christing, which took place on the Day of Pentecost. On that occasion there were assembled only those who were ready for the deeper work—Peter, James, John, Thomas, Nathanael, and two others, possibly Philip and James.

John 21:1, 3-13.

After these things Jesus showed himself again to the disciples at the sea of Tiberias.

Simon Peter saith unto them, I go a-fishing. They say unto him, We also go with thee. They went forth and entered into a ship immediately; and that night they caught nothing.

But when the morning was now come, Jesus stood on the shore: but the disciples knew not that it was Jesus.

Then Jesus saith unto them, Children have ye any meat? They answered him, No.

And he said unto them, Cast the net on the right side of the ship, and ye shall find. They cast therefore, and now they were not able to draw it for the multitude of fishes.

Therefore that disciple whom Jesus loved saith unto Peter, It is the Lord. Now when Simon Peter heard that it was the Lord, he girt his fisher's coat unto him (for he was naked) and did cast himself into the sea.

And the other disciples came in a little ship; (for they were not far from land, but as it were two hundred cubits) dragging the net with fishes.

As soon as they were come to land, they saw a fire of coals there, and fish laid thereon, and bread.

Jesus saith unto them, Bring of the fish which ye have now caught.

Simon Peter went up and drew the net to land full of great fishes, an hundred and fifty and three; and for all there were so many, yet was not the net broken.

Jesus saith unto them, Come and dine. And none of the disciples durst ask him, Who art thou? Knowing that it was the Lord.

Jesus then cometh, and taketh bread, and giveth them, and fish likewise.

Casting nets on the right side refers to the manner of lifting the life spirit force by the right or positive way to form the union or the mystic wedding of the two currents (nets) in head and heart. Such a development gives the transformed mind of which Paul speaks and also the Sacred Heart of Jesus. This perfect union is the ideal of esoteric Christianity and its truth will be understood and taught in the churches of the New Age.

Fish, as previously stated, refer to the deeper esoteric truths gained through Initiation. The number 153 is but another form for nine, the number of humanity's present evolution, and here symbolizes the eventual attainment of all mankind.

Simon Peter drew the net to land, and the nets were not broken. Peter was thus ready to fulfill the words of his Teacher; he had become the rock (high Initiate) upon which the church was established. In the present Pisces-Virgo Age Initiation through chastity, the inner teaching, is understood and demonstrated by a very few only. Under Aquarius-Leo these truths will be publicly disseminated, *and lived* by many.

Peter was able to gird about him the fisher's coat and to go out to meet the Master. It was after that incident that the Master consecrated Peter for his future ministry. The other Disciples came in a little ship; but they brought the nets laden with fish. The Christ had kindled a fire (the process of transmutation was completed), and on that fire He prepared broiled fish and honey which He and the Disciples ate together. Esoterically this event marks the steps of unfoldment within the disciple himself. Honey, a sacred food, was regularly served in pre-Christian Mystery Temples when celebrating events having to do with spiritual attainment, and it was used also by the ancient Egyptians as an antidote for the bite of the serpent. In Babylonia sacred bodies were embalmed in honey.

The Cherubim no longer bar the Gates of Eden for these Disciples. Arrayed in their new garments which are veritable bodies of light, they are ready to follow the Christ whithersoever He leads.

Clement of Alexandria, in his renowned Orphic hymn, thus glorifies the sublime Christ spirit as the "most Holy Fish":

Fisher of mortal men,
All that the saved are,
Ever the most Holy Fish.

From the wild ocean
Of the world's sea of sin,
By thy sweet life Thou enticest away.

Matt. 17:24-27.

And when they were come to Capernaum, they that received tribute money came to Peter, and said, Doth not your master pay tribute?

He saith, Yes. And when he was come into the house Jesus prevented him, saying, What thinkest thou, Simon? Of whom do the kings of the earth take custom or tribute, of their own children or of strangers?

Peter saith unto him, Of strangers. Jesus saith unto him, Then are the children free.

Notwithstanding, lest we should offend them, go thou to the sea, and cast an hook, and take up the fish that first cometh up, and when thou hast opened his mouth, thou shalt find a piece of money; that take and give unto them for me and thee.

This profound teaching of Christ continues the inner work pertaining to the Initiations of Peter, which in turn becomes a key for all disciples of all time who would pass the sublime Rites belonging to the Christian Mysteries.

"Strangers" refers to the spiritually unawakened;" "sons who are free" to the Initiate who, through the attainment of the Christed consciousness, has freed himself from all bondage to past Karma, represented by the collection of coins as head-tax.

The Master states that while the kings of the earth (material law) collect this tax from strangers, the sons are free.

The sea, to which Christ instructs Peter to go, is the unrestricted area of the soul world opened to the Initiate. He possesses the ability now to serve upon all planes unrestricted by the barriers of time or space.

The coin which Peter is admonished to extract from the fish's mouth symbolizes the powers and attributes of the Initiate: healing the sick, raising the "dead," traveling in foreign countries, etc. The ability to perform such is itself the signature of the Christ on the soul. Hence, His words to Peter relative to the coin: "Take it and give it for me and thee."

John 21:14-17.

This is now the third time that Jesus shewed himself to His disciples after that he was risen from the dead.

So when they had dined, Jesus saith to Simon Peter, Simon, son of Jonas, lovest thou me more than these?

He saith unto him, Yea, Lord; thou knowest that I love thee. He saith unto him, Feed my lambs.

He saith to him again the second time, Simon, son of Jonas, lovest thou me? He saith unto him, Yea Lord; thou knowest that I love thee. He saith unto him, Feed my sheep.

He saith unto him the third time, Simon, son of Jonas, lovest thou me? Peter was grieved because he said unto him the third time, Lovest thou me?

And he said unto him, Lord, thou knowest all things; thou knowest that I love thee. Jesus saith unto him, Feed my sheep.

The work above recorded is included in the final chapter of the Gospels, that of John. The transmutation with which it deals is not for the original Twelve only. They were the pioneers who came to show that it is possible for all men to become Christed and to manifest the works of the Master's powers upon the earth.

The three interrogations put to Peter by his Teacher are ciphers concealing a summary of the three steps leading to mastership.

Christ Jesus did not repeat these words three times merely for the sake of emphasis or reiteration. There is added significance in this repetition. The numbers 3, 7, 9, 10 and 12 are the most important of all numbers for study and meditation if we would find the key to Bible mystery and Bible meaning. Three is the fundamental number upon which the great religions have been founded.

There are three steps of attainment leading to emancipation, or to that goal where man shall know the truth that makes him free. This truth is beautifully expressed in the following words: "From the cosmic point of view, the three steps leading up to the cross are the three Hierarchies of heaven which are at present most actively engaged in furthering the evolution of the four kingdoms of nature. These are the Lords of Individuality, the Lords of Form, and the Lords of Mind; respectively Libra, Scorpio, and Sagittarius." Masonically considered, they represent youth, manhood and old age, or Entered Apprentice, Fellowcraft and Master Mason; while from the mystical standpoint they symbolize the three steps of student, probationer, and disciple.

"When the student takes the first step, the Master casts a look upon him; when he stands upon the second step at the time of his admission to probationership and takes the solemn obligation to serve humanity by the sacrifice of the lower self to the higher, his aura is blended with that of the Teacher; at the point of discipleship he takes the third step when he treads upon the first rose. At this stage there must be no turning aside; if he stops by the way to pluck a flower, he will find that its fragrance is but a snare (lure), for under its petals is coiled a serpent. From this point he must brave the sharp thorns on the stem which winds around the Cross."

Christ Jesus in the quoted conversation with Peter issues a call (1) to the student to enter upon the Path of Attainment through the way of pure living; (2) to the probationer to dedicate himself wholly upon the altar of service; (3) to the disciple to live so purely, serve so worthily, and love with a love so holy that he may come to realize and to demonstrate the inner meaning of the mystic prayer: "At night while our bodies are resting in sleep may we be found *consciously* working in the vineyard of Christ, for as spirits we need no rest."

Matthew 17:24-27.

And when they were come to Capernaum, they that received tribute money came to Peter, and said, Doth not your master pay tribute?

He saith, Yes. And when he was come into the house, Jesus prevented him, saying, What thinkest thou, Simon? of whom do the kings of the earth take custom or tribute? of their own children, or of strangers?

Peter saith unto him, Of strangers. Jesus saith unto him, Then are the children free.

Notwithstanding, lest we should offend them, go thou to the sea, and cast an hook, and take up the first fish that cometh up; and when thou hast opened his mouth, thou shalt find a piece of money: that take, and give unto them for me and thee.

This profound teaching of Christ continues the inner work pertaining to the Initiations of Peter, which, in turn, become a key for all disciples of all time who would pass the sublime Rites belonging to the Christian Mysteries.

"Strangers" refers to the spiritually unawakened; "sons who are free" to the Initiate who, through attainment of the Christed consciousness, has freed himself from all bondage to past karma, as symbolized by the collection of coins as head-tax.

The Master states that while the kings of the earth (material law) collects this tax from strangers, the sons are free.

The sea to which Christ instructs Peter to go is the unrestricted area of the soul world open to the Initiate. He possesses the ability to serve upon all planes without being restricted by the barriers of time and space.

The "coin" which Peter is admonished to extract from the mouth of the fish symbolizes the powers and attributes of the Initiate—healing the sick, raising the "dead," travelling in foreign lands, etc. The ability to so perform is the Christ signature on an individual's soul. This is revealed in His words to Peter relative to the coin: "Take it and give it for *me* and for *thee*."

John 21:20-25.

Then Peter, turning about, seeth the disciple whom Jesus loved following; which also leaned on his breast at supper, and said, Lord, which is he that betrayeth thee?

Peter seeing him sayeth to Jesus, Lord, and what shall this man do?

Jesus saith unto him, If I will that he tarry till I come, what is that to thee? follow thou me.

Then went this saying abroad among the brethren, that that disciple should not die: yet Jesus said not unto him, He shall not die; but, If I will that he tarry till I come, what is that to thee?

This is the disciple which testifieth of these things, and wrote these things: and we know that his testimony is true.

And there are also many other things which Jesus did, the which, if they should be written every one, I suppose that even the world itself could not contain the books that should be written. Amen.

John and Peter are generally conceded to be the most advanced of our Lord's Disciples, so they are the two in whom the chief authority was vested. The nature of their authority, however, is far other than it appears upon the surface. Also, it extends over a vast period of time, for the spiritual domain of these two Master Disciples is nothing less than the Aryan civilization from the time of the Archangelic Advent in Palestine two thousand years ago until the Second Coming promised for the Capricornian era of the New Galilee—provided, of course, man has made the earth ready for Him by that time.

To Peter was given supreme direction over spiritual evolution, briefly designated as "the Church." To John, the highest Initiate of them all, was delegated the more difficult task of supervising the material progress of the Aryan civilization—

namely, the State. In Volume II of this Bible series is a study of the origins of Masonry, its beginning being traced to the Holy Land and to St. John as its founder.

All initiatory work ultimately leads to the overcoming of death, the last enemy. Only John of all the male Disciples made this demonstration, so to him was given the highest, and the most difficult, task in the Master's vineyard. This exalted Initiate passes at will from heaven to earth, laboring always where the darkest cloud of materialism precipitates its storm of suffering and ignorance. He endeavors at all times to inspire world leaders with the Christed Light and to infuse them with the Christed Powers.

A New Age humanity must know a spiritualized statecraft centered in the precepts of the Sermon on the Mount, and a scientific religion demonstrating the words and deeds of the Christ instead of merely *preaching* them.

It is Peter who "feeds the sheep" of the Church path. It is John who, in accordance with the Master's words, must "tarry till I come," ever working for the building of a spiritualized State.

Initiation centered in awakened soul power must be the *rock* on which the Church is founded, not the soulless ceremonialism of today..

Initiation centered in awakened soul power must be the *corner stone* of the New State, not the exoteric (Masonic) pageantry that prevails today.

In the new Christed Age to which the Master returns there must be a glorified race made up of individuals in whom the Christ Within has become manifest, and a civilization in which the forces of Church and State unite to reach a common spiritual goal.

Peter and John labor continuously to these ends. . And they will continue to do so until their sublime purposes are accomplished and man is ready to pass into a higher plane of spiritual development known as the *Religion of the Father*.

The Blessed Virgin understood these great mysteries as the divine union of head (State) to heart (Church) that she accomplished through high illumination during her Easter Vigil. Her present work is to prepare the remaining Disciples (five upon the Temple Path under Peter and five on the Path of Statecraft (under John) that they may know the divine blending which was consummated at the glory time of Pentecost.

The Rite of the Ascension

Christ's final appearance and work were with the innermost group, the chosen Disciples. Matthew writes: *They went away into Galilee into a mountain.* Mystically this refers to a withdrawal from the body and a conscious functioning in the higher realms. Only those who could follow Him there witnessed the glory of the Ascension.

"And He lifted up His hands and blessed them, and while He blessed them, He stood apart from them." Literally, He stood apart from them in all the radiance of His glorious spiritual body, and was carried into heaven. He returned unto His own home world, the World of Christ Consciousness.

In all religions the formula of Initiation has been revealed in the lives of their Teachers or Saviours. Each one teaches by this mystic ceremonial that there is no death and that Eternal Life is the heritage of one who believes (through spiritual illumination).

The Babylonians celebrated a two-day festival in honor of Adonis (the Syrian Tammuz). The first day was one of grief and lamentation; the second day one of joy for the resurrection of life triumphant over death. On the first day, the image of Adonis lay dying in the arms of his mother, Aphrodite. On the second day the image was taken to the seashore and the wounds washed by women amid woeful lamentation; then the resurrection was enacted and his worshippers proclaimed him alive amid glad rejoicings. Dionysus was torn to pieces by Titans. His mother put the body together again and he arose from the dead and ascended into heaven. The same story is told of Isis and Osiris.

All Initiations have taught the triumph of life over death, of spirit over matter. Every pre-Christian initiatory temple and teacher heralded the coming of the World Teacher and prepared the way for the deeper Christian mysteries. The Bible throughout bears the impress of these various schools and their mystic ceremonials.

Each world Teacher brought a phase of Truth best suited to the particular need of his people and time. Each of these

Teachers enacted in his own life the initiatory ceremonial from the Annunciation to the Ascension, foreshadowing the steps which the neophyte himself must pass through in order to gain liberation from the cross of the body and attain the power to ascend into higher spiritual realms. Members of the inner groups have always understood these things, while the outer or exoteric devotees have been content to worship form. They have looked to an image bound to a cross and observed in ceremonial the various trials leading to the Resurrection and Ascension. The Christ, the world Saviour, passed through this same Initiatory ceremonial, but He did definitely more; He passed through these steps as the Way-Shower for man in order that He might become the earth's Regent, its indwelling Planetary Spirit, and in a closer and more intimate way the Saviour and Redeemer of the entire earth.

"I have now finished the work which Thou gavest Me to do," declared the Christ to the Disciples before the Ascension. By this He meant that He had taken full charge of the earth and its functions, together with all the earth's inhabitants. Thus Christ is literally in us and we in Him, as also we are united in a most beautifully intimate and tender sense in the life of the spirit. This fact applies not only to so-called Christians, but to the entire earth and all its evolving life waves.

"Lo. I am with you always, even to the end of the world." The mystic Christian understands that Golgotha was not the end, but only the beginning of the great sacrifice of the Christ, who at each Autumn Equinox begins His annual descent, working during the three autumn months with both the superhuman and the subhuman beings that inhabit the finer envelopes of the earth. At the Winter Solstice He enters the heart or center of the planet. He is born amid the Angels' songs of peace and goodwill that all mankind may have life and have it more abundantly. During the three succeeding months He works directly with man and all physical earth manifestations. He is resurrected at the Spring Equinox, the Easter season, when He leaves the dense earth body and for the succeeding three months works again with the finer forms of life existing in the spiritual spheres surrounding the earth.

Such is the annual pilgrimage of the Christ for the benefit of all humanity. Thus He groans and travails, awaiting the day of His final liberation. And so, though He rises, yet He is with us;

though He ascends in glory to the very throne of the Father at the Summer Solstice His life and light and all-encompassing love remain within the earth as the prime cause of our evolutionary progress, both physical and spiritual. All evolution moves on a higher spiral since the coming of the Christ as Planetary Regent. The most beautiful of His words to man are those uttered at the Ascension: *"Lo, I am with you always, even to the end of the world."*

The forty days between the Resurrection and the Ascension were spent in teaching inner or deeper spiritual truths to the Disciples, and in appearing before the Sanhedrin. Christ told the Disciples that the work would not bear fruit for a long time. But they could not understand His meaning, and did not fully comprehend the reason for His coming until the great illumination at Pentecost.

In the Transfiguration the Christ endeavored to teach His foremost Disciples to follow Him into the World of Life Spirit, but they failed Him. In the Last Supper and the Triumphal Entry He taught them how to blend the principles of Fire and Water, as a requisite for ascending into that high world. The Ascension demonstrates its attainment, and the Disciples followed Him there on the Day of Pentecost. All of the Master's esoteric work *after* the Transfiguration was concerned with the great blending in preparation for the first of the Great Christ Initiations. The cosmic illumination in the lives of other world Teachers follows the accomplishment of the Transfiguration immediately with the Crucifixion and Resurrection. The greatest works of the Christ occur between the Transfiguration, the Crucifixion, the Resurrection and Ascension.

The life of the Christ is the perfect pattern for man. We are all Christs in the making. Our ideal as mystic Christians is to follow Him until we, too, shall be able to ascend into the world of the Christ consciousness, the Buddhic plane, the World of Life Spirit, the particular home realm of the Lord and Saviour, the Christ.

ADDENDA

Associated Activities of Christ Jesus and the Mother Mary

The two most important characters of the Bible are Christ Jesus and Mary, the mother. Prominence is given throughout the Gospels to the many events in the Master's ministry in which the two were associated.

The Church lists fifteen mysteries pertaining to their joint lives. These are divided into three groups, each of which includes five events.

The Five Joyful Mysteries

1. *Annunciation*—Preparation for holy birth within.
2. *Visitation*—Feminine exalted in consciousness of hill country.
3. *Nativity*—Birth of the Christ within.
4. *Presentation in Temple*—Consecration through Initiation.
5. *Teaching in Temple*—The works of the Initiate.

The Five Sorrowful Mysteries

1. *Agony in the Garden*—Further union of Fire and Water principles.
2. *The Scourging*—Transformation through lifting of the spinal fire.
3. *Crowning with Thorns*—Awakening of currents in head.
4. *Carrying the Cross*—Process of freeing spirit from body.
5. *Crucifixion*—Liberation.

The Five Glorious Mysteries

1. *Resurrection*—The consciousness of immortality.
2. *Ascension*—Freedom in higher realms.
3. *Descent of Holy Ghost*—Man demonstrating the Christed power.
4. *Assumption of Mary*—Complete transformation of feminine pole.
5. *Coronation of Mary by Christ*—The reunion in heaven.

The uniting of the two poles of spirit establishes the kingdom of heaven within. This event is foreshadowed annually amid the stars as the Sun passes from Leo into Virgo. The Sun crowns the perfect mother with the gleaming white radiance of spirit; the Christ and the Mother Mary symbolize the masculine and feminine in all mankind. The mystery embodied therein points the true way of accomplishment for all humanity. The Joyful Mysteries deal with the early work of preparation and accomplishment; the Sorrowful Mysteries with the deeper work; and the Glorious Mysteries with the blending of the two. These Mysteries are destined to find perfect consummation in all humanity at the end of this the Earth Period.

The Path of Initiation

Important steps in the life of Christ Jesus and outlining the initiatory Path for man as portrayed in the four Gospels are:

Matthew

1. Birth; visit of the Magi.
2. Flight into Egypt; slaughter of innocents; return to Nazareth.
3. Baptism.
4. Temptation.
5. First disciples chosen; Sermon on the Mount; the Lord's prayer.
6. Healings and early miracles.
7. The Twelve chosen; later miracles; parables.
8. Transfiguration.
9. The Triumphal Entry.
10. Last Supper.
11. Gethsemane; betrayals; trials.
12. Crucifixion; Resurrection; Ascension.

Mark

1. Baptism.
2. Temptation.
3. Healing and early miracles.
4. The Twelve chosen; parables; the Twelve sent out.
5. Transfiguration.
6. Later healing and miracles.
7. The Triumphal Entry; cleansing the Temple.
8. The Last Supper.
9. Gethsemane; betrayals; trials.
10. Crucifixion; Resurrection; Ascension.

Luke

1. Annunciation.
2. Birth; shepherds; circumcision.
3. Teaching in the Temple.
4. Baptism.
5. Temptation.
6. Early healings and miracles.
7. Choosing the Twelve; beatitudes.
8. Transfiguration.
9. Later healings and miracles.
10. Triumphal Entry; cleansing the Temple.
11. The Last Supper.
12. Gethsemane; betrayals; trials.
13. Crucifixion; Resurrection; Ascension.

John

1. Transfiguration; cleansing the Temple.
2. Changing water into wine.
3. Nicodemus; the Samaritan woman.
4. Healings and miracles.
5. Resurrection of Lazarus.
6. The Triumphal Entry.
7. The Last Supper.
8. The Foot Washing.
9. The Last Discourse and prayer.
10. Gethsemane; betrayals; trials.
11. Crucifixion; Resurrection; Ascension.

Note on Ascension

Christ gave His last message upon earth from the mightily charged area of Mount Olivet. This message to the Chosen Ones referred to their high Initiation during Pentecost when the very powers of Christ would descend upon them. He said, *But ye shall receive power, after that the Holy Ghost is come upon you: and ye shall bear witness unto me both in Jerusalem, and in all Judea, and in Samaria, and unto the uttermost part of the earth.* As He ascended in a luminous white cloud of effulgent beauty His arms were extended in blessing over the entire earth—a blessing that radiated throughout the planet long after He was gone. The Ascension was attuned to the sublimest of harmonies. It is a festival of rejoicing participated in by Angels and Archangels.

During the exaltation of the Ascension Rite the blessed Mary was lifted in consciousness to the highest heavenly realm and there given the choice of following her Lord into the heights of glory or remaining upon earth to further His work as no other could so well as she. Her decision was instantaneous—not where she aspired to be, but where she could best serve. And so, amidst the triumphant chorusing of happy Angels, Mary assumed her place as foremost among the little band of Disciples and began to prepare them for the further wonders of Pentecost.

A

B

C

N

O

R

S

NEW AGE BIBLE INTERPRETATION

Old Testament

VOLUME I — The Hexateuch
Genesis, Moses, Joshua, Leviticus, Exodus

VOLUME II
David, Solomon, Samuel Kings & Chronicles
Books of Initiation, Ecclesiastes, Ruth,
Judges, Job, Masonry

VOLUME III
The promise in China, India, Egypt, Persia, Greece
The Preparation — The Prophets, the Exile,
the Restoration, the Book of Daniel

New Testament

VOLUME IV
Preparation for the coming of the Light of the World

VOLUME V
The Christ and His Mission

VOLUME VI
The work of the Apostles and of Paul
The Book of Revelation

VOLUME VII
Mystery of the Christos
Christmas and Easter Mysteries — the Way
and Mystery of Christ

OTHER BOOKS ON BIBLE INTERPRETATION

THE BLESSED VIRGIN MARY — HER LIFE AND MISSION

MYTHOLOGY AND THE BIBLE

MYSTIC MASONRY AND THE BIBLE

OCCULT ANATOMY AND THE BIBLE

TAROT AND THE BIBLE

SACRED SCIENCE OF NUMBERS

QUESTIONS AND ANSWERS ON THE BIBLE

SUPREME INITIATION OF THE BLESSED VIRGIN

OTHER BOOKS

STAR GATES

MAGIC GARDENS

THE COSMIC HARP

BEETHOVEN'S NINE SYMPHONIES

MYSTERIES OF THE HOLY GRAIL

ESOTERIC MUSIC OF RICHARD WAGNER

COLOR AND MUSIC IN THE NEW AGE

THE TWELVE LABORS OF HERCULES

MUSIC — THE KEYNOTE OF HUMAN EVOLUTION

HEALING AND REGENERATION THROUGH COLOR
AND THROUGH MUSIC

THE MOON IN OCCULT LORE

LENTEN PEARLS

NEW AGE BOOKS
by
Theodore Heline

THE DEAD SEA SCROLLS
AMERICA'S DESTINY
THE ARCHETYPE UNVEILED
CAPITAL PUNISHMENT
ROMEO AND JULIET
ST. FRANCIS AND THE WOLF OF GUBBIO
GANDHI

A current price list may be obtained
from

NEW AGE BIBLE & PHILOSOPHY CENTER
1139 Lincoln Boulevard
Santa Monica, California 90403

Telephone
(213) 395-4346